Auditing for Managers
The Ultimate Risk Management Tool

KH Spencer Pickett

Jennifer M Pickett

John Wiley & Sons, Ltd

Email (for orders and customer service enquiries): cs-books@wiley.co.uk
Visit our Home Page on www.wileyeurope.com or www.wiley.com

Other Wiley Editorial Offices

John Wiley & Sons Inc., 111 River Street, Hoboken, NJ 07030, USA

Jossey-Bass, 989 Market Street, San Francisco, CA 94103-1741, USA

Wiley-VCH Verlag GmbH, Boschstr. 12, D-69469 Weinheim, Germany

John Wiley & Sons Australia Ltd, 33 Park Road, Milton, Queensland 4064, Australia

John Wiley & Sons (Asia) Pte Ltd, 2 Clementi Loop #02–01, Jin Xing Distripark, Singapore 129809

John Wiley & Sons Canada Ltd, 22 Worcester Road, Etobicoke, Ontario, Canada M9W 1L1

Wiley also publishes its books in a variety of electronic formats. Some content that appears in print
may not be available in electronic books.

Library of Congress Cataloging in Publication Data

Pickett, K.H. Spencer.
  Auditing for managers:the ultimate risk management tool/by K.H. Spencer Pickett,
Jennifer M. Pickett.
    p.   cm.
  Includes bibliographical references and index.
  ISBN 0-470-09098-7 (pbk.:alk. paper)
  1. Auditing, Internal.   2. Risk management.   I. Pickett, Jennifer M.   II. Title.
  HF5668.25.P528 2005
  657′.458—dc22   2004021737

British Library Cataloguing in Publication Data

A catalogue record for this book is available from the British Library

ISBN: 0-470-09098-7

Typeset in 10/12pt Palatino by Integra Software Services Pvt. Ltd, Pondicherry, India
Printed and bound in Great Britain by Antony Rowe Ltd, Chippenham, Wiltshire
This book is printed on acid-free paper responsibly manufactured from sustainable forestry in
which at least two trees are planted for each one used for paper production.

This book is dedicated to our nephew,
Daniel Harrison

'Lift up your head and hold it up high'

Auditing For Managers
The Ultimate Risk Management Tool

The initial audit process is called 'A4M.99' and is based around 11 statements and 88 key values that underpin the *Auditing for Managers* resource.

Contents

Abbreviations

A/Cs	Accounts
AGM	Annual general meeting
CEO	Chief executive officer
COSO	Committee of Sponsoring Organizations
CP	Commissioning party
CV	Curriculum vitae
ERM	Enterprise risk management
HR	Human resources
ICEM	Internal control evaluation matrix
ICQ	Internal control questionnaire
IIA	Institute of Internal Auditors
IS	Information systems
IT	Information technology
KPI	Key performance indicators
MIA	Manager's initial audit
MII	Manager's initial investigation
NHS	National Health Service
Ofsted	Office for Standards in Education
PC	Personal computer
RM	Risk management
SIC	Statement on internal control
SMWG	Self-managed work group
TIA	Team's initial audit
VFM	Value for money

1 Why auditing?

Things must be as they may.

William Shakespeare, *Henry V*, Act II, Scene 1

> **A4M Statement A** *Auditing is an important aspect of managing an organization and all employees should have a good understanding of the audit concept and how it can help organizations become and remain successful. Our approach to initial auditing is based on 11 statements and 88 values and is known as Auditing for Managers (or for short, A4M.99).*

Introduction

> **A4M 1.1** *Auditing should be considered by all managers as a powerful tool for reviewing the adequacy of their governance, risk management and internal control arrangements.*

Figure 1.1 shows how the book is put together.

Chapter 1 deals with the audit concept, which has to be set within the wider context of an organization's governance arrangements, covered in **Chapter 2**. Risk drives everything that goes on in an organization and **Chapter 3** describes the concepts that underpin risk. We then describe the different approaches to audit work, including the contrasting focus on the past, present and future in **Chapter 4**. **Chapter 5** focuses on management initial audits, which are straightforward reviews commissioned by the manager, while team initial audits in **Chapter 6** involve work teams in assessing their own risks and controls. The

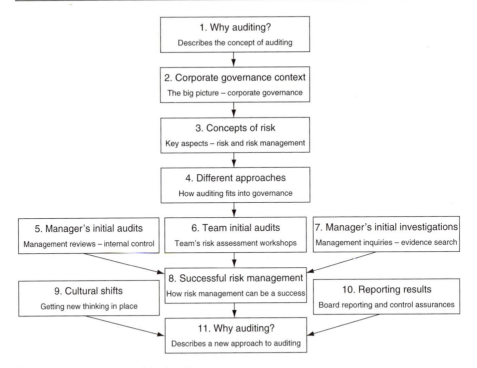

Figure 1.1   The shape of the book

final audit tool is addressed in **Chapter 7**, which relates to management initial investigations that may need to be carried out from time to time in response to specific concerns. **Chapter 8** goes on to suggest that a manager's audit effort is about promoting successful risk management. In this sense much is about creating a new, risk-smart culture at work, which is the subject of **Chapter 9**, while **Chapter 10** discusses how assurances may be provided to the board through formal reports. The final chapter of the book, **Chapter 11**, seeks to consolidate the audit concept and attempts to answer the question: 'Why auditing?'

Chapter 1 describes the basic audit concept and the different specialist audit aspects therein.

Audit skills

Most people working for an organization have little or no interest in auditing. The concept of auditing is seen as something relating to verifying the accounts or checking on workers and making sure that assets exist and are protected by contingency plans. So auditing may be associated with periodic reviews made by external checkers – something to be suffered in silence. One thing for sure is that auditing is regarded as nothing at all to do with managing. It is something that is 'done' to managers. Meanwhile, the members of the in-house audit team spend most of their time explaining their role and trying to convince everyone they meet that their work is important.

On the other side of the coin, the various government and industry regulators have for many years been dispatching an assortment of codes and guidance throughout the private sector, central and local government, the health sector and other not-for-profit organizations. The regulators' jargon tends to be written by accountants and typically consists of a mixture of advice and firm requirements regarding various topics such as risk, risk management, internal control, compliance arrangements, audit committees, nonexecutive directors, auditing provisions, financial reporting and other somewhat uninspiring issues. Not many business managers bother to delve into the mysterious world of audit, risk reporting and control, preferring to get on with their job and leave this sort of thing to the accountants and auditors.

In fact there is an abundance of key guidance that has not really been sold to nonspecialist employees. For example, the following documents provide a wealth of information on the governance, risk and control debate:

- Combined Code for companies listed on the London Stock Exchange;
- COSO Enterprise Risk Management;
- Sarbanes–Oxley reporting requirements;
- Institute of Internal Auditors professional standards;
- Institute of Risk Managers Risk Management Standard;
- Australian/New Zealand Risk Management Standard;
- British Government's Audit Committee Handbook (HM Treasury);
- Institute of Business Ethics guidance;
- Certified Fraud Examiners guidance.

The audit dilemma

The dilemma is simple: managers and employees generally *need* to be aware of the governance, risk and control agenda, but they tend to be far too busy to get involved in researching this debate. Moreover, most people would rather be doing the right things themselves than have teams of auditors checking up on them at regular intervals. This book aims to introduce the business manager to the debate and suggests an empowered approach to self-auditing, using a simple, toolbox-based style. The empowered approach is called 'auditing for managers' and is based on 11 statements and 88 key values that are set out throughout the main sections of the book. We have given the model a shortened name of 'A4M.99' (initial auditing). The hope is that these values will help managers and their staff get to grips with managing risk, self-audit, business assurances and controls. We have also developed an abundance of diagrams to help the reader through this simplified version of what might otherwise be a complex topic. In fact, we have provided diagrams and checklists rather than straight text wherever this has been possible.

A new way of thinking

Auditing for Managers is based on a new way of looking at business and accountability. This new thinking is found in many of the recent developments in commerce, public life and everyday events. An attempt has been made to capture some of this new thinking in the section of each chapter (called Newsflash – read all about it). Each chapter closes with a short narrative that tries to capture the main points from the book in an illustrative story or quote. Moreover, most sections end with a short statement of the key point at issue. The hope is to make a 'turn-off' topic so attractive that people actually want to get involved in auditing their systems as a good idea rather than a basic corporate requirement. It is an attempt to make the auditor's toolbox readily available to everyone who works for or is associated with an organization, regardless of the size or sector involved. As society changes to reflect both increased flexibility and regulation, the tendency is for organizations to lurch between apathy and paranoia. This represents both the challenges and the fun in working for or with different types of organizations.

The auditors

To get to grips with the A4M.99 initial audit process, we need to understand the formal audit process that exists in most larger organizations. Incorporated bodies, public-sector and not-for-profit organizations are required to have an appointed external auditor. Meanwhile, many larger organizations also have a team of internal auditors in place, either staffed by the organization or provided by an external firm. There is also a tendency for more complex organizations to employ other review teams that go by an assortment of different names, such as compliance teams, inspection teams, quality teams and so on. As well as outlining the audit concept, this chapter provides a brief account of the work of these different types of audit teams. The business manager needs to appreciate how the wider audit process fits together in order to benefit from employing audit tools in their own work.

In short

Unfortunately, many important messages on governance, risk management and internal control are often dressed up in coded jargon that means very little to busy managers and their front-line staff.

Why auditing?

> **A4M 1.2** *Each employee should understand their role and responsibilities in respect of the initial audit process. These roles will vary depending on the employee's position and duties within the organization.*

Auditing is a formal process for examining key issues with a view to establishing accountabilities and securing an improved position. The pressures on all types of organizations mean that there has never been a greater need for effective auditing. The requirement to perform, behave well and account properly for corporate resources has meant that things cannot simply be left to chance.

Before we examine the concepts further, we need to consider the concept of auditing. A search of synonyms reveals various suggestions for the term audit, such as:

inquiry	inquest
exploration	examination
inquisition	inspection
research	scrutiny
study	analysis
probe	account for
review	survey
report on	check out

The busy manager

None of these may appear attractive to a busy manager who has deadlines, various urgent problems and pressures to deliver the goods. Auditing is about taking a little time out to check things out before making a decision and pushing forward. It encourages a viewpoint and decisions that would be supported by what most stakeholders would consider to be adequate deliberation, based on reasonable information. A viewpoint or decision that does not meet this standard may leave the manager exposed. The secondary aspect of auditing is that it means a viewpoint or decision can be explained if necessary. This is important since all organizations are in a constant struggle to realign themselves in response to threats and challenges that alter almost on a daily basis.

A model of accountability

We need to use a few models to illustrate this idea of threats and challenges that mean managers cannot simply do their job in the same way they have done for years. That is to follow routine, put in the effort and hope for the best. The corporate climate has changed in such a way that this simple approach is not always enough. A formal audit process has been built into most businesses and Figure 1.2 demonstrates this change.

We can describe the four main aspects of Figure 1.2 in the following way:

1. **Board**. The board reports back to the stakeholders in line with the formal arrangements that are in place to ensure this happens. For private-sector companies this really means they report to the shareholders and the marketplace. For public-sector bodies, the accountabilities are to the public through

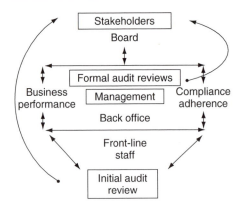

Figure 1.2   The accountability model

   ministers, local councillors, trustees, parliamentary committees or whatever
   format is in use.
2. **Management**. The manager runs the various front-line teams and back-office
   support people, and should have regard to ensuring good business performance
   and also compliance with laws, regulations and corporate policies.
3. **Formal audit reviews**. The audit review process tells the board and stakeholders whether what they are being told is happening is actually happening.
4. **Initial audit review**. The bottom box is most interesting. Here we are suggesting that there is a secondary level of audit; that is, the managers and work teams
   should carry out their own initial review and report on threats and challenges
   that have an impact on their ability to perform and conform. In this way the
   information received by the board (or management team) comes straight from
   the horse's mouth. The idea is that the formal audit process may well change its
   focus away from checking the performance reports and level of compliance,
   and more towards the way that management itself reviews these matters.

Summing up the book

Figure 1.2 entirely sums up this book. For readers who need a short-cut to auditing
for managers, then this figure is all that they need to make progress. The problem
for those who now wish to put down the book is that you will have not yet covered
how to carry out these initial audits. Accordingly, you are invited to read on.

Different levels of management

Directors tend to have a good appreciation of the audit process and more
senior managers know that corporate accountability is an important aspect of
running a business. The problem is that this message has not always got down
to grassroots level. Figure 1.3 illustrates the dilemma.

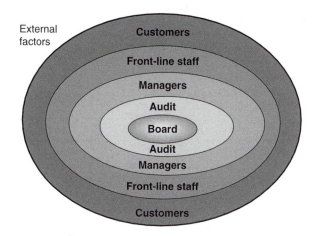

Figure 1.3 Corporate accountability

The review and accountability chain runs from the middle of the organization to report back to stakeholders, while it is the front-line people who tend to interact with those people who have the most impact on corporate success and failure; that is, the customers. Where threats and challenges are not being reviewed by front-line employees, there is much that can go wrong.

Reputation and performance

We need to explore further this idea of auditing and why it is so important. It is not just about working in a changing environment, where managers have to centralize and decentralize systematically to show that they are doing something drastic at least once a year. Figure 1.4 shows a more involved dynamic where the review and change process is aligned to the position of the organization.

Corporate processes form the centre point of Figure 1.4. The processes need to respond to external and internal risks to result in either a poor or well-respected reputation in the marketplace. This in turn is aligned to the corporate results, where there is either weak or strong performance over the year. The way the organization responds to risks is important. A weak performance and poor standing in the marketplace call for a focus on change strategies to close this gap. Risks are seen as forces that are stopping the organization scoring more goals than it is conceding. The question is:

• How can we change this unacceptable result?

The converse, where both performance and reputation are strong, encourages a focus on stability to maintain the hard-earned position. In this case, risk is seen more as what could spoil the game and we would ask:

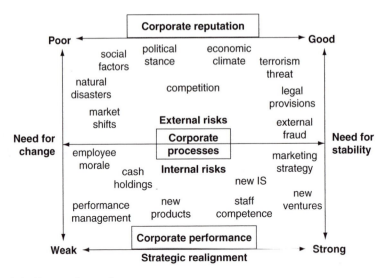

Figure 1.4   Reputation and processes

- How can we continue to be on the winning team?

Both questions are about the way corporate and business processes are responding to external and internal risks. The first organization with poor results is not in full control, while the good performer has been able to address these risks much more effectively. The audit process can help focus minds on reviewing risk and determining whether or not processes are up to the job.

A credibility gap

The auditors have an important job to do, as do line management and work teams. The auditors are well versed in assessing risk and controls, but tend to come from outside the core business. Conversely, the staff know the business but may not be skilled in assessing their risks and ensuring that controls are sound. Figure 1.5 shows the positioning of auditors and managers in this respect.

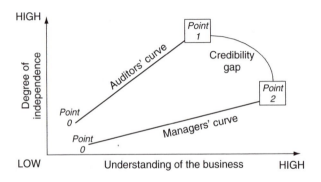

Figure 1.5   The credibility gap

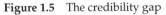

On both fronts, there is a credibility gap. The managers have total credibility in terms of understanding their business and the context and constraints that they work under. Meanwhile, the auditors pride themselves on their independence in examining aspects of a business and reporting without fear or favour. The gap lies in the fact that managers cannot be independent from their own work, while auditors cannot have an intimate understanding of the business under review. Hence, the standard solution is that auditors **audit**, while managers **manage**.

Self-assuring controls

Anther way of considering the situation is to ask what is needed to ensure that a business is able to self-assess its processes and people. Figure 1.6 seeks to address this question.

What we need is a self-audit process to be based on a clear understanding of the business in question. This is pretty much accepted, as managers and front-line people know what it is all about. Those that rely on reliable information about the business, that is the stakeholders, need to believe that the self-audit process is worthwhile and makes sense. The final aspect is that managers need to have the right tools to do the assessment. Stakeholder credibility may be derived from using our A4M.99 approach based on 11 key statements (A–K) and 88 key values. The tools and techniques are also found in the book. In this way, the focus may change to giving people a chance to check their own systems before the auditors come in. A4M.99 may also be referred to as **initial auditing**, to contrast it with internal auditing and external auditing.

In short

Whenever we need to know what's happening, it's normally best to ask those who are responsible – before asking outsiders.

Figure 1.6   Self-assuring controls

External auditing

> **A4M 1.3** *The results of the initial auditing process should be made clear to the external auditor, so that any implications for the external audit process can be considered and taken on board wherever appropriate.*

Most organizations have to have external auditors. Figure 1.2 above has shown the need for the board, or management team, to report back to its stakeholders. One form of this report is a set of financial statements prepared by the directors and then published to shareholders and filed at Companies House, or for public-sector bodies made available to stakeholders. External auditors perform a specialized role that is carried out by accountants involving the examination of financial statements of an entity to enable an opinion to be formed of whether the accounts show a true and fair view. In summary, the organization's finance people prepare the accounts, the board signs them off, the external auditors review them and they are then made available to interested parties. The idea is quite simple and this process has evolved over many years as the ownership of corporate bodies has become separated from those that actually oversee and run the business.

The external audit role

External auditors are appointed by shareholders, on recommendation from the board, and will tend to carry out the following tasks in their efforts to review the financial accounts and underpinning accounting systems:

- Planning the audit covering timing, scope, reporting lines, access to books.
- Examination of financial transactions in an objective, independent and professional manner.
- Quality control to ensure that the audit is complete and accurate.
- Reporting.

Professionalism

Meanwhile, the external auditor will operate to professional auditing standards that cover areas such as:

- Independence and objectivity.
- Professional competence and compliance with auditing standards and code of ethics.
- Management of the audit in line with risk-based audit plans.

- Audit work that involves the study and evaluation of records and information.
- Reporting standards and set formats for the published external audit report.

Audit committees

Larger organizations are starting to establish audit committees, and in many cases such as in quoted companies this forum is required as part of the listing rules. The monitoring role of the audit committee is helped by the need to ensure that at least one audit committee member has a degree of financial expertise. The audit committee will oversee the work of the external auditor, among other things, and will, in terms of the external auditing process, do the following:

- Evaluate bids from firms of external auditors and make suitable recommendations.
- Monitor the external auditor's work.
- Check the reality behind the claim to be independent.

Audit independence

In terms of independence there are many provisions that have entered the statute books to try to stop past problems where auditors had an obvious conflict of interest that affected the veracity of their work. There are restrictions on what other nonaudit services may be offered by an external auditor, such as those relating to:

- systems design or line functions;
- bookkeeping;
- recruiting managers;
- internal audit;
- tax planning.

The external auditor can perform some basic tax work and can provide services approved by the audit committee, such as assurance work and staff training and awareness seminars. There is no need to rotate the company's auditors at present, but the appointed firm is required to change reporting partner every five years. In the past a promise of a 'company position' for the external auditor also got in the way of perceived independence, so now there is a cooling-off period of some two years for hiring former external audit staff by the client company.

External audit process

The external audit process will be designed to suit the type of client in question, but as mentioned earlier, there are many standards that ensure the work is up to scratch and reviewed properly. The external audit process may appear as follows:

1. Entrance conference to discuss the audit and approach with the director of finance and other staff. Some consideration may be given to the accounting policies adopted by the organization.
2. Field work, which involves systems testing and site visits, focusing on the financial systems. External auditors will test samples of financial transactions to determine whether what should be happening is actually happening as it affects the final accounts.
3. Presentation of a findings memo on what came up during the reviews.
4. Exit conference to convey final opinions.
5. Formal reports and the management response.

Across the pond

Both in the UK and the US there are growing calls for a tighter, more dependable external audit process to ensure that the auditors ask tough questions and examine contentious issues carefully. The aggressive accounting policies used by companies such as Enron and WorldCom have led to an expectations gap, with auditors being asked about their role in stopping such scandals happening. In fact major shock waves occurred on the demise of Arthur Andersen, once the largest US firm of accountants, who were accused of shredding documents and obstructing justice. While the external auditor cannot look at everything, the general public feels they should uncover significant abuse.

The US approach to good governance was formulated in the Sarbanes–Oxley Act, which arose from the ashes of Enron, WorldCom and other similar, if not so spectacular, cases. The now famous Section 404 of this Act says that listed companies should issue formal published reports on their systems of internal control over financial reporting and that the external auditor will have to attest to this report.

In short

A trusted external audit process that involves the rigorous review of the board's financial statements is one of the cornerstones of investor confidence and therefore underpins economic prosperity. If this does not work, everything else falls down.

Internal auditing

> **A4M 1.4**   *The internal audit team's assurance and consulting roles should include efforts to review and support the initial audit process.*

Internal auditors are employed by many larger organizations, again across all sectors, to provide a specialized audit service. The internal auditor will tend to perform both an assurance and a consulting role concerning:

- **Corporate governance** – if we go back to Figure 1.2, we can see that that this means the arrangements for establishing a board and accounting to shareholders/stakeholders, to ensure that performance and compliance issues are addressed.
- **Risk management** – this is the way that risks that affect the organization's ability to succeed are identified and addressed.
- **Internal controls** – these are mechanisms that deal with specific risks.

In this way the internal auditor will give an assurance to the board as to whether the arrangements that ensure the above matters are properly dealt with are sound. Internal audit may also provide a consulting service to help improve these arrangements.

Defining internal audit

Internal audit is defined by the Institute of Internal Auditors (IIA) as follows:

> Internal auditing is an independent, objective assurance and consulting activity designed to add value and improve an organization's operations. It helps an organization accomplish its objectives by bringing a systematic, disciplined approach to evaluate and improve the effectiveness of risk management, control and governance processes.

Professional standards

Like the external auditor, the internal auditor works to firm professional standards that represent the characteristics of a professional audit set-up, called attribute standards. Other standards describe how the audit role is performed and are called performance standards. There are also standards that cover specific types of audit work such as fraud investigations. The IIA's attribute standards cover:

- 1000 – Purpose, Authority and Responsibility.
- 1100 – Independence and Objectivity.
- 1200 – Proficiency and Due Professional Care.
- 1300 – Quality Assurance and Improvement Programme.

The performance standards cover:

- 2000 – Managing the Internal Audit Activity.
- 2100 – Nature of Work.

- 2200 – Engagement Planning.
- 2300 – Performing the Engagement.
- 2400 – Communicating Results.
- 2500 – Monitoring Progress.
- 2600 – Management's Acceptance of Risks.

The IIA's Code of Ethics is based on principles relating to internal audit and rules of conduct for the auditors themselves that are broken down into four main areas:

- Integrity.
- Credibility.
- Objectivity.
- Competency.

Scope of audit work

The internal auditor will be concerned about the way an organization ensures the following:

- Reliability and integrity of financial and operational information.
- Effectiveness and efficiency of operations.
- Safeguarding of assets.
- Compliance with laws, regulations and contracts.

Adding value

Organizations need to add value to succeed and survive. For commercial organizations, value add is described by some as the total sales less the cost of bought-in materials and services. The result is wealth that is created and partly returned to shareholders. The public sector is more about delivering stated services and meeting key performance targets. Meanwhile, the internal auditors are also required to add value to an organization through their assurance and consulting services as part of their professional remit.

The internal audit process

The work of the internal auditors can have a great effect on an organization. They will formulate a strategy that results in an annual audit plan that will go to the audit committee for approval. The annual audit plan will be based on the corporate risk profile, which most organizations are starting to develop, to ensure that the auditors target the right areas as they deliver the audit plan. Meanwhile, the chief internal auditor will ensure that the audit team is equipped to perform in a competent manner and will give managers good notice before commencing an audit in a particular part of the business. Assurance audit work is performed to set terms of reference, which will be discussed with the business manager before the audit is started and will focus on the adequacy of risk management and internal control, while consulting services tend to be performed on request from a particular manager and the terms of reference will be developed by that manager. Whatever the format, there is always scope for a manager to be involved in discussing the terms of reference for an audit. Assurance work will get reported up to a more senior manager, and even go to the appropriate executive director. Summaries of the work and formal audit opinions on the state of internal control will go to the board and audit committee.

Types of audit work

Much of the internal auditor's field work will be performed at the operation being reviewed and most of the time will be spent evaluating systems of risk management and control and looking for evidence to support an audit opinion. Most audit teams employ specialist information systems auditors to complement their general audit staff. Moreover, some audit teams get involved in controls compliance reviews and fraud investigations where necessary. Fraud work differs from normal audit work in that it will involve some degree of confidentiality and higher standards of evidence in looking at the problem and identifying possible suspects.

In short

Internal audit is now firmly on the governance agenda, although the blended approach may mean that a consulting role is used to complement the main independent assurance role.

Compliance auditing

> **A✦M 1.5** *The initial audit process should involve the assessment of compliance with controls, whenever controls are being reviewed in the context of defined risks.*

There are quite a few of what can loosely be described as internal review teams, employed by organizations across all business sectors. The most popular of these are compliance units that have the role of examining the extent to which aspects of legal, regulatory or procedural requirements are being properly adhered to within an organization.

The compliance concept

All organizations have to comply with an abundance of laws, regulations and internal policies and procedures. As such, there will need to be in place a compliance system to ensure that things are done properly and that the organization is not exposed to unnecessary risks. For significant noncompliance, an external investigation may be launched by an assortment of different bodies, ranging in the UK from the Financial Services Authority to the police, the Department for Trade and Industry and the Health and Safety Executive, among others.

An integrated model

Because auditing for managers is about getting appropriate internal controls in place and reviewed on a continuing basis, we have to think about the compliance framework that complements the formal audit process. Compliance means that once controls have been set up there is a way of promoting the use of good controls across the organization. For example, if a building society has to inform all customers, both actual and potential, that the company adheres to the mortgage code of practice where appropriate to an enquiry, there needs to be a system in place to ensure that all contact with customers makes this clear. Moreover, there need to be further arrangements that ensure the customer is in fact dealt with as envisaged by the code.

A good corporate compliance framework will include many aspects found in the 10 key points below:

1. A culture where compliance is seen as important right from the top downwards.
2. Clear responsibilities defined across the organization in terms of compliance issues and who checks what.
3. Clear procedures that are employed across the organization, and are understood and reinforced.
4. Arrangements for changing procedures or introducing new ones that include training, awareness seminars and good communication. This should be linked to a formal and dynamic process for being aware of new developments, such as new regulations or legal provisions that swing into action on a stated date.
5. Formal complaints procedure for identifying weaknesses in the procedures or actual instances where they are not being used properly.

6. Disciplinary procedures aligned to the importance of compliance, whereby high standards are maintained and any exceptions are treated with some caution.
7. Efforts to seek to improve and streamline procedures so that they make sense and work and are seen as worthwhile by all employees and associates of the organization.
8. Formal reporting lines to keep stakeholders informed about the compliance system and any known problems and any investigations that have occurred or are ongoing.
9. Compliance built into the way people work.
10. A designated person in charge of compliance.

A designated person

The final point on our checklist is quite important. If this is done well, this person can consider the other nine points and ensure they are properly addressed. Once the compliance environment is established, then a small team may be employed to reinforce these nine processes and keep the pressure on. Meanwhile, the team may visit parts of the business, examine the veracity of compliance and look for aspects that could be improved or are obviously at fault. The compensation culture is a growing trend, which means that each organization is responsible for what it does or fails to do in the way it works. Moreover, there is now much talk of new laws on 'corporate killing', where directors may be held responsible for any fatal flaws in the way procedures are working.

In short

Compliance is a positive concept that is more than anything about the type of culture that is in place in an organization. If people want to do the right thing, have the means and support, there is a much better chance that any standards that are set at the top find their way right down to the most junior people who work for or are associated with the organization.

Fundamental components

> **A⁴M 1.6** *The initial auditing process aims to involve all employees in managing those risks that affect their business objectives so as to increase the chance that these objectives may be achieved.*

Now that we have provided a basic summary of the different types of auditors who together form the audit process, we can turn to the fundamental components of this process. In our world, auditing is defined as:

> A process for establishing the real position about the matter under review, with a view to addressing those issues that fall within the set terms of reference. Many audits focus on risks to achieving business objectives and the way these risks are managed. Investigative audits may also address the way that responsibilities have been discharged.

Audit work tends to be focused in three main areas that feed into the formal assurance reporting process, as illustrated in Figure 1.7.

Figure 1.7 is based on the view that the board needs to be able to report back to the stakeholders on three key issues:

1. The organization's financial and business performance over the period in question, normally the previous financial year.
2. The extent to which the organization is able to comply with formal disclosure requirements from the relevant regulatory authority.
3. Whether there has been or is any fraud or abuse, including extensive non-compliance that affects the reputation or assets of the organization.

Meanwhile, the audit process that underpins this reporting requirement consists of:

- External audit, who will review the financial systems and whether any material disclosed by the board is inconsistent with their knowledge of the business.

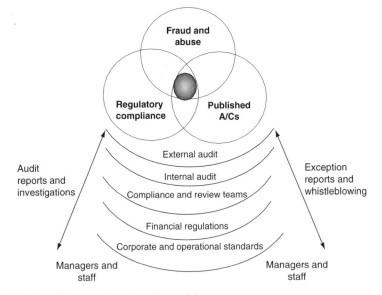

Figure 1.7   The old control and audit model

- Internal audit, who will review the systems of governance, risk management and internal control and determine whether these are adequate and properly in place.
- Compliance and review teams, who will determine whether the compliance arrangements are robust and that there are no obvious areas where noncompliance places the organization at significant risk.
- Corporate and operational procedures, which set out standards and guidance for the way systems are used, the way business is conducted and the way documentation and reports are managed.
- Another important component is the whistleblowing system, which is designed to highlight any breaches of the above audit process, which needs to be brought out in the open but may otherwise be concealed.
- The whistleblowing reports in conjunction with the formal audit reports will feed into a corporate reporting system that addresses the three areas that we have already mentioned; that is, financial accounting, regulatory compliance and fraud and abuse.

Figure 1.7 is a rather old interpretation of the audit process and although still found in many organizations, it can be improved. There is a new model used in this book that can be found in the final chapter (Figure 11.4), based on the initial auditing concept that we have started to discuss. Essentially we have asked:

- What is auditing all about?
- What is it seeking to achieve?
- Which are the best tools to apply?

In trying to get employees involved in the audit process, there is much work to do. The theory is simple but the reality is much more complex.

In short

The audit process is based on the use of specialist audit teams to provide assurances on the state of governance, finances, risk management and internal control. A much better interpretation of the audit process includes the people who really matter in making sure governance, finances, risk management and internal control are actually working in practice.

Common mistakes

A4M 1.7   *There should be a senior person in charge of coordinating and leading the initial audit process. This person should have a good understanding of initial auditing, performance management, business planning, project management, risk and controls as well as core management competencies.*

Figure 1.8   Division of responsibilities

Scenario one

People in an organization will work hard to achieve their targets, while the managers support and monitor their staff as they pull their efforts together. Meanwhile, the auditors, financial controller, compliance and other review teams check that controls are in place and people are behaving in accordance with set standards.

Scenario two

The A4M.99 process turns much of this on its head by suggesting that the scenario should change to the following:

People in an organization will work hard to achieve their targets, while the managers support and help them review their work as they pull their efforts together. Meanwhile, the auditors, financial controller, compliance and other review teams check that this initial audit process is being applied in the best way possible to ensure that controls are in place and people are behaving in accordance with set standards.

Is it that simple?

There is much that could go wrong in moving from scenario one to scenario two:

- **No one is in charge of making the transition work**. Where there is no one pushing and driving the changes, there will be little progress made.
- **Power politics**. Where initial auditing is about shifting responsibility to lower-paid staff, meaning managers shirk their responsibilities, then the process has not worked.
- **Airbrush**. Where problems are airbrushed out of the big picture by being relegated to the audit process, then there will be a failure to achieve good results.

- **Inconsistent messages**. Where different people have different interpretations of the initial audit process, then it will become blurred and confusing.
- **Duplicating others**. Where the initial audit process means that the work of the internal and external auditors is more or less duplicated, then this becomes a waste of time.
- **Irrelevant box ticking**. Where the audit outputs are based on filling in a series of forms, then there will be little value from the initiative.
- **Path of least resistance**. Where the audit process becomes associated with doing as little work as possible to complete the reviews, then the result will be poor.
- **Cumbersome**. Where initial audit work becomes bogged down by detailed analysis, which means that people are distracted from the front line, the process may fail.
- **No real ownership or feeling of involvement**. Where no one is prepared to stick their hand up and be counted in taking care of specific issues, then the initial audit process may not work.
- **No trust in the organization**. Where managers do not trust their staff and vice versa, there is no real platform from which the initial audit process may be launched.

Helpful models for overcoming problems

In view of the problems mentioned above, there are several tools that can help promote initial auditing in a healthy and dynamic manner. Figure 1.9 illustrates the different starting places so that a suitable approach to getting A4M.99 into an organization may be developed.

A4M.99 is about getting people to take responsibilities for their performance, systems and ways of working towards their goals. It is about getting them to understand their objectives and the risks involved in achieving them, as well as thinking through ways of dealing with the fallout from these risks – that is, it is about good internal controls. It moves an organization from an 'enforcement'

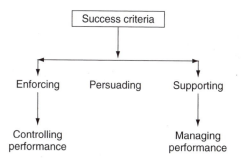

Figure 1.9   Getting initial auditing started

Figure 1.10   Pressures on managers

style of internal control to a 'supporting' style of managing risk and therefore performance, with persuasion being the middle ground for getting from one to the other. A4M.99 must be applied with full recognition of the pressures that face managers as they sit in the middle of a powerful set of forces, as shown in Figure 1.10.

- **KPIs**. The typical manager is forced into a corner by the set of key performance indicators (KPIs) that have to be reported back to their seniors. While the executives have their expectations of their managers, there are compliance issues that must also be borne in mind every time a decision needs to be made.
- **Customers and stakeholders**. Customers and other stakeholders are found on the other side of the model and their needs and demands must be addressed as a priority. There are also problems that confront a busy manager on a day-to-day basis and there is often scope to gain an advantage by seizing a particular opportunity that in one sense creates further pressures.
- **Staff and resources**. The final factor is the staff and resources that are under the care of the manager through which performance is delivered.

The key to the model is to bring the main factors that the manager has to contend with onto the radar of the staff and work teams and let them help in managing these issues. This is one of the cornerstones of A4M.99; that is, getting everyone involved in thinking about risks and resulting issues so that we can build ways forward in moving through problems and achieving good results.

In short

Auditing for managers can bring great benefits but needs to be driven, and driven well, if it is to work – and if it is to get round the many things that can go wrong.

Check your progress

> **A4M 1.8** *The initial audit process is based on the empowerment concept, which gives responsibility to management and staff to consider risks that have an impact on their objectives and review their controls and overall risk management strategy.*

One tool that can be applied to track your progress is to test the extent to which you have assimilated the key points raised in this chapter. The multi-choice questions below will check your progress and the answer guide in Appendix D is based on what is most appropriate in the context of this book. Please record your answers in the table at Appendix D. You may also record the time spent on each test and enter this information in the 'Mins' column of Appendix D.

Name ....

Start time .... **Finish time** .... **Total minutes** ....

Multi-choice quiz

1. Insert the missing phrase.
So auditing is essentially associated with periodic ...., something to be suffered in silence.

a. requests for assistance.
b. complaints made by customers.
c. reviews made by external checkers.
d. checks made by lawyers.

2. Select the most appropriate sentence.
a. The regulators' jargon tends to be written by business managers and typically consists of a mixture of advice and firm requirements regarding various topics such as risk, risk management, internal control, compliance arrangements, audit committees, nonexecutive directors, auditing provisions, financial reporting and other somewhat uninspiring issues.
b. The regulators' jargon tends to be written by accountants and typically consists of a mixture of advice and firm requirements regarding various topics such as risk, risk management, internal control, compliance arrangements, audit committees, nonexecutive directors, auditing provisions, financial reporting and other somewhat uninspiring issues.

c. The regulators' jargon tends to be written by professionals and typically consists of a mixture of advice and firm requirements regarding various topics such as risk, risk management, marketing strategies, product pricing, disciplinary rules and other somewhat uninspiring issues.

d. The regulators' jargon tends to be written by accountants and typically consists of formal legislation regarding various topics such as risk, risk management, internal control, compliance arrangements, audit committees, nonexecutive directors, auditing provisions, financial reporting and other somewhat uninspiring issues.

3. Insert the missing words.
The empowered approach is called 'auditing for managers' and is based on .... that are set out throughout the main sections of the book.

a. 10 statements and 88 key values.
b. 11 statements and 66 key values.
c. 9 statements and 88 key values.
d. 11 statements and 88 key values.

4. Insert the missing words.
As society changes to reflect both increased flexibility and regulation, the tendency is for organizations to lurch between ....

a. apathy and paranoia.
b. apathy and boredom.
c. panic and paranoia.
d. right and wrong.

5. Select the most appropriate sentence.
a. Auditing is an informal process for examining key issues with a view to establishing accountabilities and securing an improved position.
b. Auditing is a formal process for examining key people with a view to establishing accountabilities and securing an improved position.
c. Auditing is a formal process for examining key issues with a view to establishing accountabilities and securing a result.
d. Auditing is a formal process for examining key issues with a view to establishing accountabilities and securing an improved position.

6. Insert the missing words.
The .... process tells the board and stakeholders whether what they are being told is happening is actually happening.

a. annual review.
b. performance review.
c. audit review.
d. audit planning.

7. Select the most appropriate term for the 'gap'.
The gap lies in the fact that managers cannot be independent from their own work, while auditors cannot have an intimate understanding of the business under review.

a. performance gap.
b. credibility gap.
c. profit gap.
d. annual gap.

8. Insert the missing words.
External auditors perform a specialized role that is carried out by accountants involving the examination of financial statements of an entity to enable an opinion to be formed of whether the accounts show a ....

a. true and accurate view.
b. true and fair view.
c. balanced and fair view.
d. fairly true view.

9. Select the most appropriate sentence.
a. External auditing is an independent, objective assurance and consulting activity designed to add value and improve an organization's operations.
b. Internal auditing is an independent, objective consulting activity designed to add value and improve an organization's operations.
c. Internal auditing is an independent, objective assurance and consulting activity designed to add value and improve an organization's finances.
d. Internal auditing is an independent, objective assurance and consulting activity designed to add value and improve an organization's operations.

10. Insert the missing word/s.
Compliance is a positive concept, which is more than anything about the type of .... that is in place in an organization.

a. culture.
b. system of control.
c. rule book.
d. funding.

Newsflash – read all about it

There is so much behind the move towards effective governance and risk management in all walks of life, and a small selection of relevant examples is provided to illustrate this new way of thinking.

Top 10 new dimensions

Old thinking	New dimensions	A suitable example
Most professions operate quite well on a self-regulating basis.	Self-regulation must be used with care, and a watchful eye kept on rogue practitioners.	A doctor who gave hundreds of children mind-numbing drugs after misdiagnosing them with epilepsy was allowed to work on despite years of warnings.[1]
Auditing is about checking that things that should be there are in fact present and correct.	Auditing is now more about assessing whether risks that affect the achievement of objectives are being managed properly and if not, how controls may be improved to increase the chance of success.	Notable trends in internal and external auditing over the years.
We ensure that rigorous inspections are carried out at regular intervals.	An inspection is only useful if it gets to the bottom of problems and encourages real improvement.	A struggling school drafted in eight top teachers and banished problem pupils ahead of an Ofsted inspection, so as to create the best possible impression for the inspectors.[2]
The Home Office is responsible for ensuring that immigration rules are firmly in place.	Special care should be taken when there is great scope for embarrassing scandals.	The Home Office is facing embarrassment after dismissing a US citizen it employed, breaching its own immigration rules.[3]
It's a fair cop.	Artificially high targets can lead to inappropriate behaviour.	One motorist who was issued with a parking ticket did not remember the yellow lines that were clearly marked around her car. It was only when she drove off that she realized that the lines had been painted around her car and a parking ticket issued.[4]
A bowl of cereal each morning keeps you healthy.	Risk perceptions change as we gain a greater insight into the realities and do not just rely on manufacturers' claims.	Britain's bestselling breakfast cereals are feeding a childhood obesity epidemic with high levels of fat, sugar and salt, it is claimed today.[5]

The external audit ensures that the financial statements are sound and in so doing protects the shareholders and helps inform the marketplace.

The external audit process can be very fragile and needs to be kept under constant review through for example clear regulations on what services auditors can and cannot provide.

It works like this. Doing the audit gets their foot in the door. So they underbid and offer cut-price audits, which means less adequate work and corners cut. They then use the audit as a market stall to offer all sorts of other services from tax advice to management selection. That's what makes the money. Only a minor share of the profits from the Big Four comes from audit. It is merely a loss leader. Keeping up the profit flow and sale of other services is a clear incentive to soft pedal criticism and avoid conflict.[6]

It's as easy as slicing avocados.

For every slip, there may be someone who has to pay up.

A chef who cut his finger with a kitchen knife is suing a hotel for £25 000, claiming that nobody taught him the correct way to slice avocados.[7]

The best way to learn is to experience a major problem then rebuild the corporate name.

At times it is quite baffling to see a corporate name get immersed in problems time and time again.

Things seem to be going from bad to worse at infrastructure services group Jarvis, the biggest share price fall among second-liners today . . . following allegations that it certified work on sections of rail track on West Coast mainline when in fact, it had not done so . . . it was also berated following two derailments on the London Underground over the weekend, lambasted for its involvement in the Potters Bar crash and recently withdrew from several Network Rail contracts because of the damage such work was doing to its reputation.[8]

(Continued)

Old thinking	New dimensions	A suitable example
There's nothing quite like messing about on the river.	People taking part in sailing and watersports should be properly equipped to deal with the inherent dangers.	The Royal National Lifeboat Institution has reported that it is being stretched by the increase in watersport novices who have little training in the equipment they use or water safety.[9]

The key messages

The last section of each chapter contains a short story or quote that should provide an interesting format for illustrating some of the book's key messages.

Who do we work for?

Customers are everywhere, not just on the outside. When I started work in a large business it took me some time to realize that most of my customers were in fact inside the organization – other colleagues, other departments. If I took their requirements and their wishes seriously I would be of much more use to them and the organization.[10]

Notes

1. *Daily Mail*, Tuesday, October 21 2003, page 33.
2. *Daily Mail*, Saturday, March 20 2004, page 15.
3. *The Times*, Tuesday, March 23 2004, page 13.
4. *Daily Mail*, Thursday, March 25 2004, page 29.
5. *Daily Mail*, Thursday, April 1 2004, page 21.
6. *Daily Mail*, Monday, January 12 2004, page 56, Austin Mitchell, Labour MP.
7. *The Times*, Wednesday, January 7 2004, News, page 13.
8. *Evening Standard*, Thursday, 23 October 2003, page 42.
9. *Daily Mail*, Thursday, March 25 2004, page 39.
10. Charles Handy, *21 Ideas for Managers: Practical Wisdom for Managing Your Company and Yourself*, Jossey-Bass, San Francisco, 2000, page 153.

2 The wider governance context

Be just and fear not.

William Shakespeare, *Henry VIII*, Act III, Scene 2

A4M Statement B   *The A4M.99 approach involves deciding on the best arrangements to adopt having regard to the nature and impact of risks to the corporate governance process.*

Introduction

A4M 2.9   *A policy on the use of initial auditing should be approved by the board and this should be based around promoting the three related concepts of corporate performance, standards of integrity and relevant public disclosures.*

Figure 1.1 in Chapter 1 shows how the book is put together. Chapter 2 describes the overall corporate governance context, which sets the frame for all audit work. There is a big picture on the *Auditing for Managers* agenda and that is how it relates to wider corporate governance issues. We have spoken about risk as the driver for audit reviews, which managers should be carrying out on an ongoing basis. But the biggest risk to any organization relates to the way it is governed.

We have so far avoided making reference to detailed guidance, but there is one important document on the horizon called the COSO ERM. COSO stands for the Committee of Sponsoring Organizations, which was originally formed in 1985, consisting of five major financial professional associations in the United States. COSO ERM relates to its enterprise risk management framework, which was issued as a draft in 2003. All further references in this book to **COSO ERM** relate to the COSO ERM framework at July 2004. Further information on COSO and its publications can be viewed on its website, www.coso.org. The COSO ERM suggests that:

> Each manager's responsibility should entail both authority and accountability. Each manager should be accountable to the next higher level for his or her portion of ERM, with the CEO ultimately accountable to the board.[1]

The accountability chain

This chain of accountability is so important to any organization and as such, all organizations need to explain how they ensure high standards of:

- Performance.
- Integrity.
- Published disclosures.

In this chapter we deal with what we call the accountability dilemma. We also describe the concept of corporate governance and the most important ethical platform that it rests on. Risk management and internal control are touched on while, like all chapters in the book, we have standard sections on common mistakes, checking your progress, newsflashes, closing with key messages. Note that risk management is such an important development that it has its own chapter.

In short

Audit, review and risk management are great ideas but there is a big picture in all of this, which relates to the wider ideals of governance and accountability.

The accountability dilemma

> **A4M 2.10** *The initial audit process should be linked to the concept of corporate accountability and the need to ensure that all major business decisions are made in a transparent and ethical manner.*

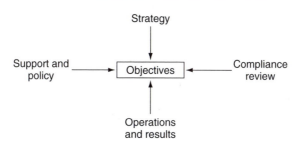

Figure 2.1   Achieving objectives

Before we discuss corporate governance and risk management, we need to mention accountability. Good accountability must be in place in a business before we can talk about successful risk management. Most people in an organization are responsible for achieving their set objectives, a situation which is simplified in Figure 2.1.

The overall strategy outlines the frame for set objectives. In fact, specific objectives should be derived from a wider strategy that is designed to move an organization from A to B. Policies and supporting guidance are there as a reference frame, within which the objectives are achieved. Compliance on the right-hand side of our model means that the pursuit of objectives must have regard to the need to stay within certain legal and regulatory requirements. For example, a personnel section may recruit staff but must ensure that all relevant employment legislation is properly adhered to. The final part of the objective's model is about the way the operation is established to achieve the agreed objectives and deliver the right results.

Responsibility and accountability

Responsibility is the authority given to act within a defined field of operation, while accountability is to render an account of how responsibilities have been discharged, and how problems have been sorted out. Responsibility gives someone the power and authority to make something happen and use defined resources in this respect. Moreover, it is about accepting the consequences of problems that have affected the area that someone is in charge of and could have been avoided or minimised. It also involves informing people about the issues and fully explaining what actions were taken.

Accountability and values

Again, things are not always straightforward. The accountability debate has to recognize the values that people have at work, which affect the way they prioritize matters. Figure 2.2 seeks to explore this issue.

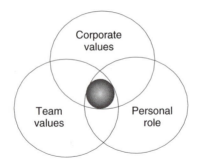

Figure 2.2   Values at work

The corporate body will have its stated values, perhaps about things like treating colleagues with respect and how people are accountable for their actions. Each work team will have its own value system regarding how colleagues relate to each other and how it supports workmates when they are under pressure. Moreover, each person will have their own set of values that guides and directs them. Corporate values may say do your work but remain civil at all times. Teams may have got into the habit of working hard but using profanities all the time. The individual team worker may have a value system that forbids swearing or, conversely, sees it as great fun. We would hope to achieve a good balance between these three perspectives so that a suitable middle ground is secured.

Blame – an emotive concept

There is an old saying, 'No one is to blame but everyone is accountable.'

Accountability is about accepting that we are responsible to someone else for our actions, while blame is about being stuck in the past. Many top people argue that they are responsible for overall policies, but not the ground-level operations and what happens on a day-to-day basis. We are all responsible for delivering things and therefore accountable for the results. We are also responsible for the actions of others who are in our charge, and the more people are rewarded for their role in an organization the more they must accept responsibility for what goes on, on their watch.

Blame is an emotional concept that can interfere with good accountability. It is associated with:

- Emotional feelings of fault finding, anger and fear of punishment.
- Judgements and people acting as judges of the righteousness of others.
- A culture where people tend to deny that there are problems for fear of being blamed.
- Scared people who feel the need to be careful and who do not take risks associated with, say, innovation and experimentation.

- A viewpoint that suggests whenever there is a failure, there is also a need to apportion blame and sacrifice someone.
- Empowerment used to locate blame as far down the organization as possible.

Most accept that we have a duty and responsibility to carry out tasks allocated to us in a given time to the best of our ability. But some say we need to have blame to ensure that roles and responsibilities are clearly defined. If we are able to take every part of the organization and work out exactly where to apportion blame where something does not work well, this reinforces clear accountabilities, but it can also create a negative blame culture.

Where something goes wrong it is generally much better to work out if there is a training need or evaluate where procedures failed. Intentional flouting of rules is different, as is gross neglect in the performance of one's duties. The question to ask is: did the person cause the problem or fail to take steps to avoid it? The difficulty lies in the fact that many problems can have a complex series of causes. A value-based approach is founded on getting teams to own their processes and targets so that they can plan their work and take responsibility for the results. This is where auditing for managers fits in, where staff may assess the processes applied by teams in an organization. Blame is discussed again later in the book.

In short

Empowering people to assess their own systems is about encouraging them to want to be accountable for what they do by giving them the tools to do a good job – since a learning organization is based on a constant search for good, workable solutions to everyday problems.

Corporate governance

> **A⁴M 2.11**   *The initial audit process should acknowledge and take on board regulatory compliance and the expectations of key corporate stakeholders.*

The private sector

We have mentioned the way boards are appointed by and are responsible to their shareholders in Chapter 1. The board of directors must publish an annual company report, hold corporate responsibility for ensuring there is integrity in the accounting arrangements and ensure that there are sound business and financial controls in place across the organization. Amongst other things, corporate governance is about:

- The role of the board.
- The board structure.
- Director selection and remuneration (including bonuses and pensions).
- Board meetings.
- The role of nonexecutive directors.
- Self-evaluation of the board.
- The way the CEO's and other senior officers' performance is judged and rewarded.
- Succession planning for key figures.
- Shareholders and how their interests are protected.
- External auditors and their role in verifying the financial accounts.
- Risk management, internal control and arrangements for securing assurances on these matters.

In addition, we now expect clear leadership in corporate governance in line with published guidelines for the sector in question. There is a lot going on in the private sector, with great strides being made by many leading companies in their efforts to report back to the market about the way they are managing their affairs. A leading bank talks about its system of risk management in its annual report, which discusses:

- Credit, liquidity, market, regularity, enterprise risk.
- The fact that a statement on internal control is reviewed by the board and audit committee by directors for each business line.
- That there are quarterly reports on risk and control assessment by each business line, which are aggregated into risk management reports at group level.
- That risk is seen to run across the enterprise and is derived from failed internal processes, people and systems or external events.

A large retail company says that its systems of internal control are designed to provide reasonable but not absolute assurance against material misstatement and loss. It goes on to describe how:

- The board covers strategic risk at every meeting.
- Accountability for managing operational risk is assigned to line management in line with the risk appetite set by the board.
- Procedures are present for establishing significant risk and control failures to senior management and the board on a daily, weekly and periodic basis.
- The board has a key risk register and considers action taken to mitigate risks.

The public sector

The public sector model is pretty similar, although management boards account back to the public instead of shareholders. In one local authority the following matters are mentioned in the published annual report:

- The risk management strategy and the way it is approved.
- The way risk management is embedded into services by risk champions.
- The way strategy is set.
- Project planning and implementation.
- Decision-making mechanisms.

In a housing association, a code of governance is followed that contains the spirit of the combined code for listed companies. Its annual report mentions that the board has received the directors' internal assurance report and has conducted its annual review of the effectiveness of the system of internal control and has taken account of any changes needed to maintain the effectiveness of the risk management and control process. There is an ongoing process for identifying, evaluating and managing significant risks faced by the association.

A National Health Service (NHS) Trust's annual report states that the assurance framework is still being finalized to provide the necessary evidence of an effective system of internal control. Actions so far include:

- Self-assessment exercise against core controls assurance standards (governance, financial management and risk management).
- System in place to monitor as part of risk identification and management processes and compliance with key controls assurance standards.
- Risk awareness training for all staff.
- Local clinical risk assessment.
- A comprehensive risk register.
- Plans to integrate clinical and nonclinical risk management with the creation of a risk strategy committee chaired by the nonexecutive director.

Elsewhere, a central government agency describes the following aspects of its governance arrangements:

- Balanced scorecard approach to planning and reporting performance based on:
  - customer service;
  - innovation and development;
  - efficiency and finance;
  - quality and security;
  - achieving through people.

- Strengthening internal control and risk management.
- Improved management information systems.
- Implementation of an efficiency programme.
- The risk management group will help review, report on and respond to significant risks to key business objectives and outcomes.

Not-for-profit sector

One charity has developed a three-year risk management plan and states that:

- Risk management systems mean that directors are named as responsible for managing specific risks (that is, taking and monitoring action).
- Trustees have overall responsibility for internal controls.
- Risk falls into three categories: external environment, the brand and the internal infrastructure.

Another charity has a council of trustees that is responsible for satisfying itself that systems are in place to monitor, manage and mitigate exposure to major risks, while the corporate management team assesses the risk as identified in its risk register through the normal business planning process.

Governance, risk and control

We have so far mentioned governance, risk and control in the same breath, and it is as well to set out how these three concepts relate to each other with the help of Figure 2.3.

In Figure 2.3 the corporate governance arrangements are about the managers of an entity behaving well and delivering the goods under the strategic oversight of a balanced board of directors who appreciate the following:

- The context of the governance arrangements is set by the control framework that needs to be in place to ensure what we call a sound control environment. That is, people know what is expected of them and are equipped and motivated to perform.

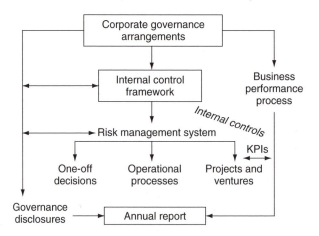

Figure 2.3   Governance, risk and control

- Having got clear objectives, the management and staff can devise a system for managing risk that includes an assortment of internal controls.
- Risk management and control are about dealing with one-off strategic decisions, such as whether to market goods in a new but volatile developing country; or it could be managing risk in a new project that is essential to corporate success.
- The final aspect of risk management relates to the ongoing operations and the way they are handling threats and opportunities that affect the business.
- All of this needs to form part of disclosures in the annual report, which together illustrate the risk appetite that the organization has adopted.

It is then up to the investors and stakeholders to work out whether they are happy with this level of risk and whether it fits their own personal risk profile as they decide whether to continue their association with the organization. For the public sector the risk appetite is more about whether the level of risk fits the manifesto set by the political machinery and expectations of customers and the general public. There is much to be said about risk appetite and this is dealt with later in the book.

In short

An organization's governance arrangements are important in that they help determine the level of risk that it has assumed on behalf of its stakeholders, and if this risk appetite fits with the expectations of key stakeholders then all is well. This is why formal disclosure provisions are so important in informing outsiders about the state of affairs in an entity.

The ethical platform

> **A4M 2.12**   *The initial audit process should be applied in a way that enhances the ethical values of the organization and promotes a culture based on mutual trust and good communication.*

An ideal world?

Initial auditing or what we have called A4M.99 is really about trust. Directors trust their managers, who in turn trust their people to behave well and deliver. In this equation, the front-line staff trust their bosses and so it goes around. In this ideal world we would all be honest, all the time, and armed with the necessary tools and clear goals and lots of personal drive, there would be no need for auditors at all. The closer we get to a trusting organization, the more chance there is for A◀M.*99* to become the pivotal force for assuring stakeholders that, as far as is possible, all is well and will probably be so for the foreseeable future.

Government has adopted a code of standards in public life that is based on the following main attributes:

- selflessness;
- integrity;
- objectivity;
- accountability;
- openness;
- honesty;
- leadership.

In this way, all decisions and actions should be based around an open and honest culture and all major problems are fully reported and tackled. This generally means improving the systems of risk management and internal control.

The three factors

It all boils down to how each person sees things, as shown in Figure 2.4 – how the three factors influence the moral codes of individuals.

The framework is set by society and the moral codes that are in place and known about. In essence it can come down to a choice between doing right and wrong. There are many organizations where people know about dishonest and suspect behaviour at work and choose to get involved or simply turn a blind eye to what is going on. The way senior management behaves and the stated corporate values are also key factors that influence an individual's perception of right and wrong. If there are any flaws in these influencing factors, then little

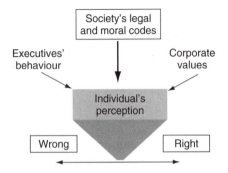

Figure 2.4 Individual moral codes

real progress will be made. CEOs and executives are now having to justify their pay and bonuses as the spotlight falls on detailed transparency. The impact of the way people at the top behave is seen clearly in cases such as Enron – where it is said that a fish rots from the head downwards.

Two dimensions of ethics

The ethical equation is set through two levels of perception. One relates to a position where the individual prioritizes self-interest above all. That is what suits and enhances the person's own position. The contrasting dimension relates to a perception that legitimacy is the more important concept – that is, doing what is always correct and proper in the eyes of society. There are times when these two dimensions pull in opposite directions, where, say, one is tempted to take credit for another person's idea to progress one's career.

Corporate ethics is less about compliance and more about people's attitudes and behaviours. Where there are low levels of trust, management needs to recognize the current position and the need for change, and to motivate people to plan these changes.

In short

People can be trusted if they have earned this trust and more than anything it depends on an organization having values in place that mean something. It tends to be trusting organizations who are able to develop initial auditing and have it work in practice.

The risk management concept: roles and responsibilities

> **A4M 2.13** *The initial audit process should help support the wider risk management process and reinforce respective roles and responsibilities throughout the organization.*

Risk across the organization

Risk management is a separate chapter of the book. Here we are merely concerned with an overview, and in particular respective roles and responsibilities across an organization. Risk is described by most people in terms of the uncertainty that something could have an impact on your ability to achieve your objectives, in terms of stopping you from getting there or stopping you from taking

Figure 2.5 Breaking down the organization

advantage of short-cuts or opportunities. When it is identified, risk can be measured in terms of the potential to affect your business and this is called its impact. The extent to which the risk could actually materialize is referred to as its probability.

Highly significant risks that are likely to occur will inevitably cause much concern to organizations. Risks that affect corporate reputation must be addressed, since if a brand name comes unstuck it could spell problems in the short term and even disaster in the longer term. If a public-sector service loses credibility, again there are major repercussions and, more recently, heads have started to roll.

Figure 2.5 represents a well-known model that starts our overview of risk management.

In many organizations we have a basic mission or 'aims' right at the top and then the process of determining the best strategic choice to achieve these aims. As well as the basic corporate support services that are established, top management will also create a series of programmes to deliver the strategic objectives. This will result in various projects and operations that end up as the heart of the organization. It is against this background that the risk management process should be developed; that is, risks to strategic analysis, risks to programme management and risks to basic operations and specific projects that are set up and implemented. Moreover, the driver behind good risk management is to allocate responsibility for managing risks to those best placed to control them.

Ask the experts

Internal auditors tend to have a great deal of expertise in the concept and tools of risk management and their professional body, the Institute of Internal Auditors, carried out what it calls a flash survey in 2004 to try discover why people rate risk management as important to their organization. Some suggestions as to why risk management was important came out from the survey results and include the following:

- keep up with developments;
- compliance;
- good practice;
- regulatory requirement;
- part of strategic planning;
- financial reporting;
- everyday concerns;
- affect everything;
- improve communications;
- fulfil responsibilities;
- good governance;
- assurances obtained;
- implications of weak controls;
- understand auditors;
- primary responsibility;
- help design controls;
- important for risky activities;
- help control costs.

Features of risk management

There are many reasons why organizations seek to mitigate risk, although there are many types of risk that are hard to eliminate altogether. It has been said that risk management goes to the heart of a problem and we can cut through red tape in designing and redesigning good internal controls. Figure 2.6 draws out the key features of risk management.

Figure 2.6 starts with what an organization is trying to achieve – that is, its objectives – and then sets a context for this task. It may be that managers and staff teams are expected to work together to consider operational risk, or that a facilitator is available to support this task. The risk policy may suggest that managers, or a specialist person, should review the extent of risk facing certain areas of an organization. Whatever the case, once the context has been established, significant risks that get in the way of success need to be identified.

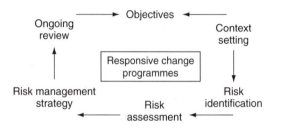

Figure 2.6 Features of risk management

Once this list of risks is compiled, each one will need to be assessed so that those that demand the manager's attention can be isolated through a process of prioritisation. Armed with this knowledge, strategies may be devised for managing those risks that simply cannot be left alone, or dealt with through normal operational procedures. The cycle loops back and pivots around the change programme that is in place in most organizations. This is a simple concept, but one that will take up much space in later chapters of the book.

Some argue that there is no such thing as perfection in risk management and there will always be some scope for concern left over, even after the most careful attention has been paid to the issues that result from defined risks. This residual risk may be simply ungovernable or result from, say, more controllable issues such as poor training, lack of funds, poor staff motivation, poor integrity, senior management not committed to objectives, or impoverished management.

In short

Risks are everywhere and where they have an impact on your business they need to be dealt with. One way of ensuring this happens is to carry out an audit of the extent of risks out there and check the status of countermeasures that are currently in place.

Internal controls

A4M 2.14 *Wherever possible, the initial audit process should result in a consideration of the state of internal controls and whether there is a need to update or otherwise amend any set corporate or operational procedures.*

We have mentioned corporate governance, risk management and internal control as the principal drivers for the A4M.99 process. That is, managers need to audit their arrangements in respect of these three areas and make sure they are sound and make sense. We have explained what governance is all about and have just finished a discussion of risk management. Now we need briefly to summarize where internal controls fit in.

Internal control frameworks

There are two really important frameworks for assessing internal control, COSO and CoCo. COSO was set up by the Committee of Sponsoring Organizations some years ago, while CoCo was designed by the Canadian Accountants as

Figure 2.7   The COSO model

their Criteria of Control. COSO is in Figure 2.7 and this suggests that control is about having the following five key components in place:

1. A sound control environment where people understand internal control and have the drive and ethical direction to want to make sure that controls work well in the organization.
2. Risk assessment, where people are equipped with the skills and tools to identify risks to the achievement of their business objectives and work out which ones need to be addressed.
3. Control activities, where people appreciate the range of measures that are available to address risks identified and prioritized during the risk assessment process.
4. Monitoring, where there are measures in place to ensure the control model is properly established and risk management (risk assessment and control activities) is actually happening in an acceptable manner.
5. Information and communications that run throughout the control framework to ensure everyone is singing the same tune and reports are delivered for internal use and to ensure stakeholders are kept informed.

CoCo (Figure 2.8) is a separate model that sees control as a dynamic process containing the following key elements:

1. A clear purpose or goal that harmonizes activities and resources around a common aim.
2. A commitment from staff and associates to achieve the goals, in that people are prepared to release their energies and pull in the same direction.
3. The capability to achieve in terms of skills, resources, competence and tools to make sure goals and energies can be applied in the right way to achieving success. It is here that the activities are performed – that is, with a purpose, full commitment and the right skills and budgets.

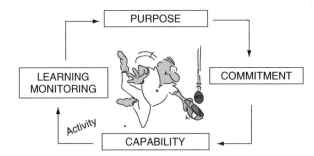

Figure 2.8   The CoCo model

4. The final part of the model relates to the learning dynamic, where we can assess the extent of success and ensure steps are taken to seek improvement and learn from our experiences how to do more or avoid problems in future.

An organization is in control if it has a control model in place that works. It is in control if its board has information that enables it to judge the extent to which the business is delivering. And it is in control if there is a reliable way of scanning the horizon for real or potential risk so that the management may reposition the business to maximize value and minimize loss in the face of these risks. Meanwhile, the audit process is about taking time out to conduct a little research to assess whether these things are happening.

Control by whom and to whom?

Control models ask that certain things happen and this may be in a way that empowers people to take ownership of this activity, or in a way that forces people to stay on a defined route. In one sense, control may be achieved through four different control cultures:

- **Type one**: Supporting and empowering people to get their business under control.
- **Type two**: Persuading people to do the right thing through example and explanation.
- **Type three**: Directing that certain things are done through the use of rules, guidance, discipline and supervision.
- **Type four**: Or a bit of all three depending on the type of organization, product, market, size and the way risk is managed.

A4M.99 works best in **type one** organizations, but can also be applied in the other types of control culture. Much also depends on the environment and business procedures tend to stabilize after change strategies have kicked in, as most people like periods of calm. If this stability stops an organization adapting to change, then controls can become less efficient and there needs to be some degree of firm intervention. The initial audit process will take on board these factors, as we can get people to think about adaptability when reviewing their internal controls.

The control environment

Like all things, the control culture responds to the pressures that confront business where there may be more customers generating more work, meaning that less time is spent servicing existing customers' needs, which may lead to less job satisfaction. Where this drop in quality leads to lost customers we will have created more risk of losing existing customers, simply through efforts that attract new customers. This residual risk may not be properly appreciated as the causal chain is not clearly understood. Growth strategies are generally a good thing, but they need to be properly resourced on the basis that we need to spend money to make money – rather than simply cutting back on staff while at the same time trying to attract new customers.

Statements on internal control

The risk management process underpins the system of internal control, as controls are measures such as corporate standards and operational procedures designed to address risk. An internal control reporting system needs to be part of business processes and it will tell the board about the state of controls in the organization. We can turn again to the COSO ERM for inspiration:

> Control activities are policies and procedures, which are the actions of people to implement the policies to help ensure that management's risk responses are carried out.[2]

The call for corporate bodies to issue statements on internal control is happening in the UK through the Combined Code and in the US through Sarbanes-Oxley S404, and for that matter in most other developed and developing countries. The board is responsible for preparing this statement on internal control and some argue that it has to go through a set process to get there, including:

1. Compiling an inventory of internal controls, against a control framework such as COSO or CoCo.
2. Documenting controls and action to deal with weak areas.
3. Testing controls to ensure they are working as intended.
4. Bringing this activity together into a statement on internal control.

Mechanistic versus organic controls

This needs to be done within the organization and is not just a matter of buying a piece of control reporting software and installing it. There needs to be careful research and a way of pulling everything and everyone together in a dynamic manner. In our view, this is what A◄M.99 is all about. It certainly is not about reporting that we have always done things like this and this is the justification for the current state of play. It is more about being proactive and not waiting for mistakes to happen, but reviewing our controls so that we can anticipate problems and even minimize them.

Controls are not that which is required by the regulators, or information technology development people or auditors. Controls are that which the business needs to satisfy all stakeholders and deliver a quality product. This push–pull factor is quite significant, whether controls are there because of strict requirements or because people at the sharp end build them to make their life easier and help them succeed. This contrasting perspective is drawn in Figure 2.9.

Some controls are there because they always have been there, while others develop from emerging needs; that is, they are mechanistic or organic. It depends on the culture and level of stability that is present, although together these controls enter the overall risk management strategy. Moreover, **preventive controls** are built into a system to help prevent risks from materializing, while **detective controls** are designed to warn when risks do materialize. **Corrective controls** are more about reacting to the fall-out from real risks and putting things right in the event of a material problem. One other interesting category of control relates to a type of control culture that is focused on managing risk and making sure the right things happen, rather than responding to things going wrong. These are known as **directive controls**. An example may help illustrate these differences.

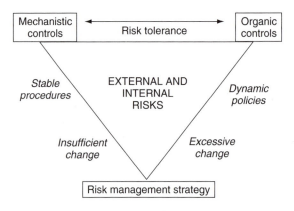

Figure 2.9   Mechanistic versus organic controls

Example – risk of fire

1. **Preventive controls** – no smoking policies, checks by staff for fire hazards, locks and other access controls, maintenance of electrical and gas equipment.
2. **Directive controls** – fire safety training and awareness, policies and procedures, zero tolerance.
3. **Detective controls** – fire alarms, smoke detectors, exception reports.
4. **Corrective controls** – fire brigade, fire extinguishers and contingency plans.

Much depends on the risk appetite. During the UK's fire crew strike of November 2002, it was clear that people took greater care with fire safety issues since there could have been delays in help arriving in the event of a fire.

Procedures

A powerful control response to many types of risks that affect a business operation is good procedures. In many cases of failure, neglect, error, fraud and misreporting, the result of the post-mortem comes down to a failing of procedures. Establishing good procedures entails the following process:

1. Set clear objectives for the procedures – what are they for? See if it is possible to measure the extent to which each procedure is able to meet its aims.
2. Determine the scope – what does the procedure cover? Make this specific so that there are not too many blurred areas.
3. Talk to the people affected by the procedure – what will work? Make sure it addresses all key risks and is worth the cost, and is accepted by the people who operate it.
4. Draft and test it, again with the people who most matter.
5. Communicate any changes to all concerned.
6. Hold workshops to train people where they have to operate the new procedure so that they understand how it works and that it should be applied consistently.
7. Hold meetings to discuss whether the procedure is working or not and if in doubt, simplify where possible.
8. Secure feedback on the success of the procedure from customers and others and make sure people buy into the new procedure and understand how it helps the business.
9. Maintain the procedure and ensure it is improved wherever possible to maximize value add.
10. Review procedures regularly.

In short

Controls, if they are designed well and make sense, can lead to control – and this is a comfort to all even if perfection is never possible. Such a positive response to risk is

Figure 2.10   Energizing people

what most people would expect from those responsible for a successful business, in other words from all employees and associates.

Common mistakes

> **A4M 2.15**   *The initial audit process should ensure that any controls required to manage known risks are reviewed by those persons most responsible for the area affected by these risks.*

Scenario one

Corporate governance codes are pretty onerous and require a great deal of paperwork to ensure that the requirements are met and the board can sign the disclosure reports that are put in front of them each year.

Scenario two

The A4M.99 process turns much of this on its head by suggesting that the scenario should change to the following:

Corporate governance codes are based on good business practice and a sustainable future. The idea is to shift cultures so that the board is able to oversee the way these principles are applied right across the business, before it reports on progress to stakeholders.

Is it that simple?

There is much that could go wrong in moving from scenario one to scenario two:

- **Governance codes seen as representing a rigid set of rules that have to be applied to satisfy the regulators**. Where a mechanical approach is applied there will be little scope to develop strong business benefits.

- **Annual disclosures copied from formats and wording used by other enterprises in the same industry**. Where a 'boilerplate' approach is applied to published disclosures, there is less scope to develop a meaningful dialogue with people who use the annual reports.
- **Narrow interpretation of internal control**. Where a limited view of internal control is applied, based around the accounting and financial reporting system, it becomes difficult to bring the control concept home to all employees.
- **Governance issues given to the finance director**. Where the finance people drive the governance and risk management initiatives, it will be more difficult to implement anything like enterprise-wide risk management.
- **Risk management built on, not built in**. Where risk tools are applied in a way that is removed from the real day-to-day business, it will be hard to secure real benefits from embedded risk management.
- **Internal control seen as belonging to the auditors**. Where internal control is seen as an audit issue, employees will have trouble developing an interest in this topic.
- **No real link between risk management and internal control**. Where risk management does not feed into the internal control agenda, an opportunity to develop an integrated risk and control reporting system is lost.
- **No real control framework in use**. Where there is no high-level framework such as COSO in use, it is very hard to attach the risk and control activities to a firm platform.
- **No thought given to the ethical platform**. Where there is no consideration of corporate ethical standards, there is less scope to use a value-based approach, where principles not rules are seen as important.
- **Insufficient thought given to accountability arrangements**. Where there are poor accountability structures in place, the concept of risk ownership becomes very hard to put into practice.

Helpful models for overcoming problems

The governance arrangements may fall outside the real way an organization functions. There are ways of ensuring that governance, risk management and controls work well in an organization so that they fit with the corporate reality. For example, risk management workshops need to be seen as part of everyday life, since an assessment is pretty well out of date after it has been carried out and documented. The main problem is that while the directors have a good idea of their disclosure requirements, the key messages do not go much further than senior management. The real heart of the business has little or no interest in meeting the expectations of stakeholders. Figure 2.11 explains this further.

The audit and accountability framework sits right at the top of the entity and concentrates the minds of board members and top executives. The problem is the **fog** that is found below this framework, where front-line people, the back office and associates do not hear the same messages but simply get on with their work. Much is about improving communications and ensuring that

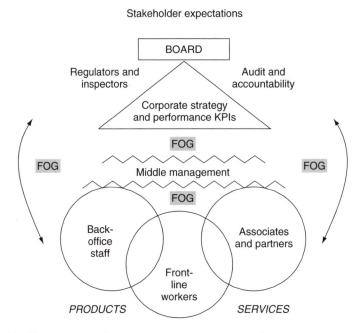

Figure 2.11   Foggy expectations

everyone is part of the governance process. Good communications is no mean feat and requires dedicated efforts to explain, illustrate and persuade people to take their review of internal controls seriously – and to understand where this fits into the wider governance picture.

In short

Top executives tend to know a lot about their responsibility to develop good governance arrangements, including systems for managing and reporting on risk and controls. But this knowledge does not always reach the real heart of the organization and inspire those closest to the internal controls that executives rely on.

Check your progress

> **A✦M 2.16**   *All employees should receive suitable training in initial auditing to ensure they are able to meet those aspects that relate to their area of responsibility.*

One tool that can be applied to track your progress is to test the extent to which you have assimilated the key points raised in this chapter. The multi-choice questions below will check your progress and the answer guide in Appendix D is based on what is most appropriate in the context of this book. Please record your answers in the table at Appendix D. You may also record the time spent on each test and enter this information in the 'Mins' column of Appendix D.

Name ....

Start time .... **Finish time** .... **Total minutes** ....

Multi-choice quiz

1. Insert the missing phrase.
This chain of accountability is so important to any organization and, as such, all organizations need to explain how they ensure high standards of ....

a. performance, compliance and published disclosures.
b. performance, integrity and published disclosures.
c. performance, integrity and internal disclosures.
d. compliance, integrity and published disclosures.

2. Insert the missing words in the right order.
.... is the authority given to act with a defined field of operation, while .... is to render an account of how responsibilities have been discharged and how problems have been sorted out.

a. accountability and responsibility.
b. responsibility and accounting.
c. seniority and accountability.
d. responsibility and accountability.

3. Select the most appropriate sentence.
a. No one is to blame but everyone is accountable.
b. Everyone is to blame and everyone is accountable.
c. No one is accountable but everyone may be blamed.
d. No one is to blame and no one is accountable.

4. Insert the missing words.
It is then up to the .... to work out whether they are happy with this level of risk and whether it fits their own personal risk profile as they decide whether to continue their association with the organization.

a. investors and stakeholders.
b. investors and shareholders.

c. bankers and stakeholders.
d. bankers and the government.

5. Insert the missing word.
Initial auditing or what we have called A4M.99 is really about ....

a. money.
b. beliefs.
c. control.
d. trust.

6. Select the most appropriate sentence.
a. Senior managers tend to have a great deal of expertise in the concept and tools of risk management.
b. Internal auditors tend to have a great deal of expertise in the concept and tools of risk management.
c. Internal auditors tend to have a great deal of expertise in the concept and tools of risky management.
d. Internal auditors tend not to have a great deal of expertise in the concept and tools of risk management.

7. Insert the missing phrase.
It has been said that .... goes to the heart of defined problems and we can cut through red tape in designing and redesigning good internal controls.

a. auditors.
b. strong management.
c. risk management.
d. compliance checking.

8. Insert the missing words.
There are two really important frameworks for assessing internal control, ...

a. COSO and CoCo.
b. COSO and CoPo.
c. COPO and CoCo.
d. COSO and CoSy.

9. Select the most appropriate sentence.
a. The corporate planning process underpins the system of internal control.
b. The risk management process underpins the system of internal control.
c. The financial management process underpins the system of internal control.
d. The staff management process underpins the system of internal control.

10. Insert the missing words in the right order.

Moreover, ... **controls** are built into a system to help prevent risks from materializing, while .... **controls** are designed to warn when risks do materialize. .... **controls** are more about reacting to the fall-out from real risks and putting things right in the event of a material problem.

a. detective, preventive and corrective.
b. corrective, detective and preventive.
c. preventive, corrective and detective.
d. preventive, detective and corrective.

Newsflash – read all about it

There is so much behind the move towards effective governance and risk management in all walks of life, and a small selection of relevant examples is provided to illustrate this new way of thinking.

10 new dimensions

Old thinking	New dimensions	A suitable example
A focus on growth and market share can only lead to a wealthier economy.	Excessive market domination can lead to a stagnant market.	The European Union has criticized Microsoft for the abuse of its near monopoly, ordering it to change its business practices and pay a substantial fine.[3]
Executives work hard and should reap the rewards.	The mutual greed of fat cats is no longer acceptable.	While mutuals boast that they put the customer first, an investigation revealed that member-owned building societies are shunning guidelines on pay and contracts and giving themselves packages such as two years' pay if they are told to go.[4]
We must protect the nation at all costs.	Sensible spending means careful budget management in all public services.	Spending on defence has rocketed out of control, with £3bn overspends in 2003.[5]
Corporate scandals are a thing of the past.	The risk will always be there. The only positive is nowadays, we are more vigilant in watching for it to materialize.	Italy's Parmalat scandal looked ever more like a Hollywood mafia movie today as one of the main suspects in the alleged fraud issued a dark message to journalists covering the investigation. 'I wish you and your families a slow and painful death,' the former finance director told the media.[6]

(Continued)

Old thinking	New dimensions	A suitable example
We need to chase the money since more profits mean a better society.	Regulations exist because chasing money without thinking about anything else is simply not good enough.	'It's about saying, thinking, breathing: "Yes, we can have the profits and do the right thing at the same time." You know, you would think it is so bloody easy but it seems to be almost impossible,' says Dame Anita Roddick, founder of The Body Shop.[7]
I understand that this is a well-regulated industry.	Written rules and regulations do not always reach the front line.	An investigation into London's nanny agencies found that many recruit girls without carrying out proper checks into their background. All agencies contacted were prepared to take on a candidate who provided false references and a fake CV. Meanwhile, an Ofsted report found that six in ten nurseries were not up to standard.[8]
A clearly stated code of ethics is a fundamental requirement in these times where pressures on big business have never been greater.	A clearly defined code of ethics is only the start. What is more important is that competent people from the top downwards behave in a way that gives real meaning to the words 'business ethics' and 'personal integrity'.	The executives left at Shell's headquarters have been far too busy hunting the missing barrels of oil to have time to browse through the company's website. But a visit to it underlines just how big a gap there can be between the platitudes that companies peddle and reality. 'Our core values of honesty, integrity and respect for people define who we are and how we work,' declares Shell. 'These values have been embodied in our business principles since 1997.' Shell's former chairman does not appear to have been aware of these business principles. He and his head of exploration have both left the company as details emerge of a long-running campaign of deception which has shocked the City.[9]
Nonexecutive directors should possess a suitable level of financial expertise in order to discharge their obligations properly.	Nonexecutive directors should possess a suitable level of financial expertise, and access to external experts, in order to discharge their obligations properly.	NEDs at Standard Life have sought advice from independent experts on the state of the mutual's finances. Worries have been mounting after it emerged that it has been locked in high-level talks with the Financial Services Authority over its solvency.[10]

When risk assessing a promotion, the only thing that could go wrong is that people will not bother to take up the offers in question.	When risk assessing a promotion, think through all eventualities, because people get upset when any offers made are not fulfilled.	Cosmetics giant Avon is facing a public relations disaster after a skincare range promotion which offered customers free mobile phones backfired...the firm severely underestimated demand for the pay-as-you-go phones. Insiders claim that Avon told Orange to prepare 60 000 handsets but demand rose to an astonishing 750 000.[11]
Companies know how to organize their affairs and should be allowed to get on with it.	Governance codes are there to ensure no return to the major corporate scandals of the past decade.	The chairman (who was also CEO) of the trade finance group Versailles has been found guilty of involvement in fraudulent operation at an offshoot company, Versailles Traders Limited, where reported sales were dramatically higher than reality.[12]

The key messages

The last section of each chapter contains a short story or quote that should provide an interesting format for illustrating some of the book's key messages.

What is responsibility?

A lot of leaders have catchy slogans on their desks; many believe in them. A two-word sign on my desk genuinely summarizes my whole philosophy: I'M RESPONSIBLE. During my time at City Hall I did my best to make those words a signature theme for every employee, starting with myself. Throughout my career, I've maintained that accountability – the idea that the people who work for me are answerable to those we work for – is the cornerstone. And this principle starts with me.[13]

Notes

1. Committee of Sponsoring Organizations, Enterprise Risk Management, draft framework at July 2004, page 94 (www.coso.org).
2. Committee of Sponsoring Organizations, Enterprise Risk Management, draft framework at July 2004, page 60 (www.coso.org).
3. *The Guardian*, Thursday, March 25, 2004, Business, page 18.
4. *Mail on Sunday*, Sunday, March 14, 2004, Personal Finance, page 15.
5. *Daily Mail*, Friday, January 23, 2004, page 37.
6. *Evening Standard*, Monday, January 5, 2004, Business, page 32.

7. *Evening Standard*, Monday, January 5, 2004, page 35.
8. *Evening Standard*, Thursday, April 3, 2003, page 19.
9. *The Times*, Friday, April 23, 2004, Comment, page 24, Penny Wheatcroft.
10. *Daily Mail*, Tuesday, January 13, 2004, page 67.
11. *The Mail on Sunday*, Sunday, April 25, 2004, page 15.
12. *The Times*, Thursday, May 27, 2004, Business News, page 62.
13. Rudolph W. Giuliani with Ken Kurson, *Leadership*, Time Warner, New York, 2003, page 69.

3 Basic risk concepts

My endeavours have ever come too short of my desires.
William Shakespeare, *Henry VIII*, Act III, Scene 2

A4M Statement C *The A4M.99 process will normally involve documenting risks and controls on a register, in line with a policy on risk tolerance, which records relevant information to support action points that result from the initial audit.*

Introduction

A4M 3.17 *All key risks should be associated with a diagrammatic representation of the organization that illustrates and highlights aspects of the business that need attention – prioritized in conjunction with a risk appetite that enables management to make decisions that optimize business performance and accountabilities.*

Figure 1.1 in Chapter 1 shows how the book is put together. Chapter 3 describes some of the basic concepts that underpin the new risk agenda. We have discussed the wider corporate governance perspective and where risk management fits into this picture. We have also outlined the audit approach that is needed to enable managers to review their position and account for their actions. Each main approach to initial auditing that fits with our A4M.99 viewpoint is detailed in later chapters.

In this chapter we have a further look at risk and how it is so important to the whole audit and accountability agenda. The risk cycle has already been mentioned and follows a 14-stage format that involves:

1. Establishing the business context, including risk policy and set tolerances.
2. Setting business objectives.
3. Determining accountabilities for risk management across the organization.
4. Identifying risks.
5. Assessing impact and materiality of risks that have been identified.
6. Considering those risks material to the delivery of objectives.
7. Evaluating existing risk management strategy in terms of its ability to address significant risks.
8. Reviewing residual risk after all controls have been enacted for acceptability.
9. Checking the level of compliance with the key controls.
10. Taking a holistic view of the level of risk exposure in question – that is, how much scope there is for failing to achieve one's objectives.
11. Redesigning internal controls and evaluating control awareness where necessary.
12. Designing an action plan to implement any selected solutions, with dates, names, targets and review points.
13. Reporting on the above in terms of assurances on risk management and internal control.
14. Continuing actively to monitor the risk portfolio and reporting periodically.

It is hard to see how the above can be done without a process of review, consideration and research – that is, an audit by the relevant risk owners. The risk process and how it fits together are summarized with the help of a few models. Risk registers are important and this document often arises as an output from the initial audit process. As well as the usual sections on 'read all about it' and 'checking your progress', we have a go at tackling '**the big issue**' – that is, risk appetites. Risk appetites is one of those subjects that sounds simple in theory but in reality is open-ended to the extent that it has no definite conclusion. That said, much progress can be made in considering the underlying issues that spring up when looking at the big issue.

In short

Many feel that the risk register is the pivotal item for managing risk and accounting for an organization's position. In fact, the pivotal aspect of risk management is the setting of risk appetite – all else flows from this.

The risk model

> **A4M 3.18** *The initial audit process should consider the risk cycle and the operational risk management review process in use.*

Most people now accept that risk runs right across an organization. The old viewpoint of specialist silos such as insurance, projects, finance and health and

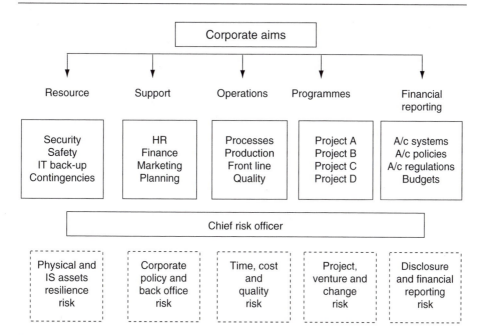

Figure 3.1 Enterprise-wide risk management

safety fits into a wider picture of risk that encompasses all aspects of risk management. Figure 3.1 seeks to captures this sweeping view of enterprise-wide risk management.

It is clear that there are pockets in all organizations where the risk and control dimensions are being dealt with in a way that best suits the type of work in question. The security people view risk as a physical thing revolving around unauthorized access to buildings, people, systems and assets, whereas the financial accounting staff may be concerned with risks to the need to present the financial statement in an accurate and fair manner. The operations teams may be concerned about the risk to the production of quality outputs in a timely and efficient way. It goes on and on, with each section talking about risk in a way that suits them. This is why many organizations are employing chief risk officers to bring together these disparate parts of the organization around some kind of common framework. In Figure 3.1 this is expressed as physical assets, back-office support, operations and quality issues, change projects and published financial reporting.

So different people across the organization can talk about risk as it affects various themes that run through the organization. The IT manager will talk to the security officer about, say, a change project and the fact that a team of consultants will need access to the IT rooms. Meanwhile, the marketing people will talk to the accountants about the way the costs of a large design scheme are classified so that it hits the right accounting period.

Figure 3.2   Integrating risk

There are many ways of classifying risk and it is important that those risks that are identified at local levels can be aggregated upwards and noted, and those risks that cannot be addressed locally are relayed to the right part of the business management. The role of the chief risk officer is really quite difficult and requires someone with great skill and experience. For example, it may well involve coordinating the issues set out in Figure 3.2.

The focus is on categories of risk such as strategy, projects and those items in the bottom lefthand corner of Figure 3.2. Most good classification systems end with reputation risk as the culmination of all other material risks. Risk management also involves a consideration of:

- **The ethical framework** – and whether risk management is done in an open and honest way.
- **Planning systems** – and whether risks are properly taken on board when planning and also when implementing and reviewing plans.
- **Key performance indicators** (KPIs) – and whether risk tolerances are associated with KPIs so that when a target is missed, this indicates that a risk of failing to deliver on time, for instance, is thrown up for action. This may well be aligned to a formal performance framework such as the balanced scorecard.
- **Competence levels** – and whether people in the organization are equipped to understand and deal with the changing risk portfolio.
- **Disclosures** – and whether people understand how their activities fit into the published disclosures about the state of internal control.
- **Review systems** – and whether risk mitigation strategies are monitored and kept up to date.

Top 12 practicalities

The A4M.99 approach is about making internal controls work in the context of the integrated management of risk across the business. It is also about being accountable for this task. A lot comes back to risk and how it is dealt with, which is why we need to list 12 practical aspects in moving towards a structured approach:

1. **Develop a corporate risk profile**. This is about thinking through how the organization will deal with risk across the business lines and offices. Much can be gained from developing categories that fit the bill.
2. **Think about shareholder value**. Aim to get risk management in place to enhance management performance, and to help embed good governance and accountability. It is mainly about promoting stakeholder confidence by doing the right things and communicating well.
3. **Determine roles**. This covers everyone including the board, nonexecutive directors, the executive team, management, staff, work teams and internal and external audit teams.
4. **Develop a handbook**. Write a note about risk management and post it on the intranet with, say, a PowerPoint presentation to explain the basics.
5. **Establish an integrated risk management function**. This is someone to turn to for advice and information. A good chief risk officer is a start, along with, say, a risk forum of senior managers to oversee the way the risk registers are coming together and the use of accepted best practice.
6. **Develop risk maps**. These run across the organization and show the sources and types of risk and where they fit into the organization.
7. **Practise integrated risk management**. This should be done by including everyone in a worthwhile and transparent way.
8. **Integrate risk into decision making**. The key to good risk management is that it affects the way decisions are made and we move away from reckless posturing and rubber stamping – it can become more a question of managing by example and shifting the cultural bias to better understand risk and how it affects our work.
9. **Use good tools**. This may include interviews, risk reviews, workshops, risk registers and contingency plans and perhaps some of the approaches from this book.
10. **Feed into business systems**. The risk activity will need to be part of business planning, implementation and review and set within the context of corporate policies, performance review and reward systems.
11. **Ensure continuous learning**. One way is to build risk management into employee performance appraisal schemes.
12. **Promote risk-smart staff**. This may be done by placing risk management understanding and use of appropriate tools into all employees' core competencies.

In short

Auditing for managers needs to be used by working around some kind of risk model that brings all parts of the organization together, not in terms of everyone doing the same thing, but more about developing a shared understanding of what others are also doing.

Risk identification

A4M 3.19 *The initial audit process should seek to identify risks to the business in a way that acknowledges the four Vs of values, value add, valuables and valuation.*

One of our greatest fears is that something will jump up out of the blue and bite us. It is a fear of the unknown. Risk entails a degree of uncertainty, and it is this uncertainty that means our response must be flexible and geared to the pressure to do something. Immaterial things deserve much less of our attention than that which could cause grief, if simply left. An important stage in risk management relates to identifying all those risks that could jump up and bite us. This is why auditing is so important – it is the act of looking for risk and issues that arise to ensure our controls are okay. Figure 3.3 starts the ball rolling.

As usual we start with the business objectives; that is, what we are trying to achieve at work. But this is gross, before it is tempered with constraining factors. So in achieving our goals we do not want to hurt anyone on the way, or put out misleading information, or hurt other parts of the business at the same

Figure 3.3 Global business risk

time. The sales team should not really be selling to people who can't pay the credit terms, or who have not been told about the drawbacks of the product in question. Someone who approaches an investment firm for a low-risk, life-time product to act as a pension should not be sold a high-risk piece of stock that may climb or crash depending on world markets.

There are things that have to be assimilated into the straight business objectives to ensure that success is sustainable and these include:

- Financial reporting standards so that the pursuit of performance (and performance pay) does not involve massaging the figures.
- An ethical base so that we act and are seen to be acting in a correct and proper manner.
- Compliance with procedure so that laws, regulations and standards are observed and obeyed.
- A strategic framework so that we act in accordance with the overall direction and pace set by the enterprise.

These things are so important and are what some people call 'control objectives'; that is, pure performance but with an eye on the wider duty of care and the need to be responsible employers.

The brand new four V model

One key aspect of A⬛M.99 relates to what we are going to call the **four V model**. The standard context for risk management and control design has been established by the TQC model; that is, time, quality and cost. Objectives are set and performance monitored having regard to the inherent conflicts in achieving something with regards to:

- The **time** it takes.
- The **quality** of outcomes.
- The amount it **costs**.

The point is that these three forces tend to pull in different directions. If staff are told to answer the phones quickly to meet set targets, then it is likely that they will try to get rid of the customer as quickly as possible – and this could mean a poor quality of service is received by the customer. If a project has to meet tight design standards that are added to as it progresses, then it will either take longer to deliver or cost more in that we will need to throw extra resources at it to meet the new requirements. So before we can talk about risk identification we need to establish what objectives are affected by the risk and the constraints to achieving these objectives.

The TQC model comes to our aid by asking us to prioritize which of the three factors reigns supreme in the event of any material tensions. However, the governance debate has broadened the horizon by saying that everything should be done in a proper manner and with a view to maintaining a good reputation. Doing things cheaply, quickly and to set specifications is no longer enough. The value factor comes into the frame where a company can be criticized for, say:

- Employing people in notorious sweatshops in developing countries.
- Poaching trained people from poorer countries that need them more.
- Laying people off without providing any support for them.
- Discouraging mothers from breastfeeding by saturating the market with powdered milk.
- Encouraging youngsters to eat junk food and high-sugar-content drinks.
- Paying executives huge sums of money for slimming down the workforce and enforcing pay cuts on employees.
- Monopolizing a market and eroding competition by aggressive short-term pricing strategies.
- Making excessive profits by exploiting dependent customers.
- Encouraging people to take out large loans that make them vulnerable to market forces and interest rate changes.
- Pressuring customers to take out extended warranties where there is no commercial benefit.
- Making associations between fashion and drinking alcohol or smoking.
- Advising householders to employ contractors for work that is not needed.
- Providing discounts to new customers that are subsidized by existing ones.
- Charging premium-rate phone lines for basic aftercare services.
- Exaggerating the risk to personal security in order to sell high-tech surveillance tools.

The list goes on and on and each strategy fits comfortably with the rather rigid time, quality, cost model. Our four V model tries to promote a new approach to this problem by providing a less rigid framework for objective setting and strategy formation, as illustrated in Figure 3.4.

Figure 3.4 is really quite simple. We build on the TQC model and base our audit review around:

- **Values** – the corporate standards that direct the conduct and performance of our people. It is really about saying what is important to us in terms of, say, being fair to our customers, respecting our employees, having a positive effect on society, caring about disgruntled customers, building partnerships with associates and suppliers and so on.
- **Valuables** is about our resource; that is, our people, buildings, information, knowledge, relationships, contacts, current assets, finances and so on. It is about protecting our resource from things like fraud, abuse, disasters, terrorist attacks, sabotage, waste and material losses. We manage the corporate resource on behalf of the owners and it is right to ensure it comes to no harm, and even

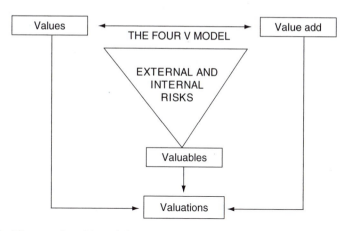

Figure 3.4   The new four V model

grows over time. If a disaster strikes then we must plan a considered response and employ suitable contingencies.

- **Value add** is what we do to generate wealth. This relates to production, operations, services and outcomes that we deliver as part of the business process. Value add is achieved by sharp processes, responsive production cycles, well-thought-through strategies and the application of our resource in a way that works best. A subset of this factor is found in the time, quality, cost model that was discussed earlier.
- **Valuation** – the final V relates to the way the business is presented to the public. It is about the published financial statements and annual reports that all organizations prepare and publish. Valuation should be accurate, fair and meet the needs of stakeholders who want to know that their investment (or their public services) are working in line with their expectations and that there is no hidden 'hole'.

In the middle of the four V model is reputation, affected by internal and external risk to the four Vs, as this is the most important thing that an organization has. People will not travel on trains that have a reputation for poor safety. People will not buy drugs that have been linked to serious side effects, while many people will not buy from a company that is associated with unethical behaviour. Meanwhile, the final part of the model contains all those risks that have an impact on one or more of the four Vs. As well as risks to the strict business objectives of achieving A, B or C, it is risks to the four Vs assimilated into our core objectives that must be fully responded to. Note that there may well be a fifth V in the form of **Validation**; that is, a process to review and report on whether the four Vs are in place and meet stakeholders' expectations. We set some store by the usefulness of this approach and will return to the four V model several more times in the book.

In short

If organizations see risk management as simply about what gets in the way of their success, then the bigger picture of providing something of worth that benefits society may well get lost along the way.

Risk assessment

> **A4M 3.20** *The initial audit process should include an attempt to score the impact of identified risk on the achievement of objectives, and the probability that key risks will materialize if not mitigated properly.*

Risk assessment is about setting business objectives within the wider context discussed earlier, and after having identified risks to the achievement of these objectives, prioritizing them in some way. Most people argue that such prioritization should consider the impact of the risk if it materialized, and then the likelihood that such an event would occur if not addressed. We have already discussed risk categorization as one useful way of getting a structure for the assessment stage. As an example, the National Health Service has in the past employed criteria for evaluating risk that include the following elements:

- Financial.
- VFM issues.
- Service delivery.
- Quality of service.
- Reversibility or otherwise of realization of risk.
- The quality of reversibility of evidence surrounding risk.
- Impact of risk on organization and stakeholders.
- Defensibility of the realization of risk.

Perceptions of risk

We need now to go on to mention that different people, and different groups, will have their own view on risk. Our risk assessments will involve people who have their own personal perspectives that they bring to the task. A manager who is going to retire in two years' time will have a different perspective from a newly appointed manager who is seen as a bright young thing. Corporate reputation has been described as the key aspect of risk impacts, but this may be different from team reputations and for that matter an individual's personal reputation.

Table 3.1 The young and older generations

Longstanding employees	Bright young things
Risk and control balance	
Solid, reliable	Flighty
Stick to the rules	Not always rule bound
Low energy	High energy
Long-term view	Short-term view
Ignore new management fads	Know all about new fads
Very experienced	Not very experienced
Fair rewards for good work	Super bonuses for extra effort
Risk averse?	Risk taker?

Table 3.1 has a go at reviewing personal perspectives of longstanding employees as compared to newly appointed bright young things.

So the team mix will affect the way risk is seen by employees. This personal risk assessment is explored further in Figure 3.5.

Some explanations:

- **Value** – what something means to someone. What do they want from their job? Is it social contact, a sense of fulfilment or just the money?
- **Current earnings** – is the person dependent on their job for survival or is it just beer money?
- **Prospects** – are they on a fast career path or stuck in the mud?
- **Work–life balance** – is work everything to them or is their job just a 9–5?
- **Chance of failure** – does their work entail lots of opportunity for failure and is failure accepted or despised?

The simple risk assessment process that most people know and love has to be taken with a pinch of salt. There are many complex factors that mean one person's view of risk and its importance does not always fit with someone else's perception. A stark example comes where an employee is approaching an age where early retirement is a real prospect, but only if they become dispensable or, even better, perform below standard. This person will have a different view of risk than someone who has been promised promotion if they can excel on the job. There are a few more models that might help us discuss the concept of risk assessment, such as Figure 3.6.

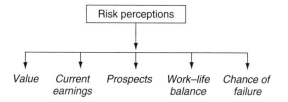

Figure 3.5 Risk perspectives

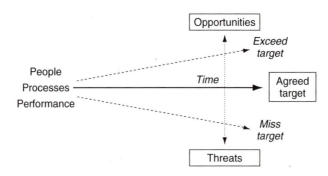

Figure 3.6   Upside and downside risk

Figure 3.6 is about what are called the 'upside' and 'downside' aspects of business risk. Many organizations concentrate on threats to achieving their goals. But there are others that try to get a balanced view and consider the risk of not grasping opportunities as well as drawing back from threats. So in terms of people, processes and resulting performance and efforts to reach their targets, there is a straight line from A to B – that is, meeting agreed targets. Threats lead to below-standard performance or results and these have to be tackled. But opportunities are also present in many business lines where targets can be exceeded if these are exploited – which in itself is a risk.

The parallel argument is that a fear of risk means we never try out new things, and it is the new things that move organizations forward and help them become more successful. Many successful businesses use threats as a springboard for developing new opportunities. The risk of a major fall in student intake for a college course may lead that college to develop online learning modules and use this threat to move into a new market opportunity, which in itself leads to further risks if not managed well.

We all stop at the traffic lights

Most organizations use a model based on traffic lights as in Figure 3.7, where risk may be assessed as green, amber or red. The red risks fall at the top right-hand corner of the model and those are prioritized for treatment as being high impact and likely to materialize. The idea is to manage those risks down so that they fall within an acceptable level.

In short

Getting people to rate business risks for impact and likelihood as an idea is fairly straightforward. When we drill down to what makes people tick, however, it becomes much more fraught with assumption, emotion and out-and-out oddities.

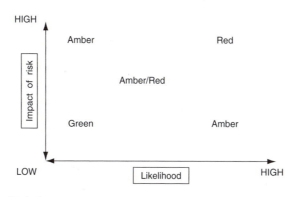

Figure 3.7 Traffic lights

Risk mitigation

A4M 3.21 *The initial audit process should include an attempt to assess the need for more or fewer controls in response to the assessment of key risks that affect the business objectives.*

We have said that risks need to be identified and assessed. Having done that, we will have a look at the significant ones and start thinking about our success in mitigating unacceptable levels of exposure for the business. We would have already mapped the organization in terms of roles, responsibilities and potentially high levels of inherent risk.

When we ask our managers and work teams to address operational risk in their areas, it will probably involve the construction of some form of risk register. That is a document that captures the analysis of risk and how it is being managed, as well as action plans to address any gaps in this strategy. A basic risk register is shown in Table 3.2.

Table 3.2 Basic risk register

Business objective:...									
1	2	3	4	5	6	7	8	9	10
REF	RISK	IMPACT %	SCORE	CONTROLS	OPINION	ACTION	RISK OWNER	REVIEW DATE	

The columns explained:

1. This is a reference number so that decisions can be traced back at a later date if necessary.
2. The risks that affect the set business objective are listed here.
3. The significance or impact of the risk is rated here in numerical terms.
4. The likelihood of the risk materializing if there were no controls in place is rated here in numerical terms.
5. The score in terms of the combined impact and likelihood.
6. The controls that are in place to guard against the top risks.
7. An opinion on whether the controls are adequate or not.
8. Action required to ensure controls work and make sense.
9. Risk owner or the lead person for the required action.
10. Review dates, performance criteria, assurance reports and other reporting arrangements.

A working example follows that involves a decision to buy a new car. The detail that would be recorded on a simplified risk register is shown in Table 3.3.

Table 3.3 Buying a new car

Objectives – right family car, right time, with the best pricing package available.

Stage	Risks	Controls	Tests	Opinion	Recs
Define need for new car	Old car does not need replacing	Clear criteria for replacing existing car	Car replacement period set but subject to emotional pressures (friend has a new car)	Irrational factors can blur good judgement	Stick to two-year replacement and try to avoid illogical pressures
Agree price range possible	Car too expensive – drains resources	Costing model used to determine what family can afford to pay for replacement car	Determination of maximum price done very carefully with written budgets made of all financial commitments	Good risk management arrangements	Keep updating the budgeting system
Agree make and model	Car too small, too large or not satisfactory to family members	Family conference to agree best car for price, capacity properly tested before purchase	Latest car is too small for children who have grown over the past year	Development of family and need for more capacity not always fully anticipated	Growth during the two-year replacement period needs to be programmed into car capacity decisions

Evaluate suitable source	Inconvenient, expensive or poor supplier selected	Rating system used for best supplier	One well-presented supplier always used	Lack of analysis of other suppliers restricts the choice of car available to the family	Research other local suppliers and expand number of car makes that feature in the option analysis
Evaluate suitable finance package	Excessive interest paid on loan	Finance properly researched for best deal on market	No mechanism in place for becoming aware of better finance deals	Cannot guarantee that best source of finance always achieved	Purchase financial journal that contains up-to-date details of all available finance options
Pay for and collect car	Car delivered late or in unacceptable condition	Car checked and test-driven before being taken away	Last but one car had a fault (poor suspension) that was not identified before car driven away	Insufficient attention given to car testing before car taken away	Test-drive actual car before taking it away
Use aftercare package	Aftercare not in line with expectations	Clear notes on what is available, e.g. warranties	One feature (free first 1000 miles oil change) not taken advantage of as it was not made clear to family	Concessions not always known about by family	List all concessions and make sure they are utilized wherever possible

Decisions, decisions, decisions

When we have judged which risks are significant and where existing controls have been taken into consideration, there is lots of scope to respond to the risk that remains. We can use an assortment of 'Ts' to gauge the range of responses that are available:

- **Terminate**. Where the risk is so great, or the costs of controlling the risk are not worth the effect, we may wish to think about terminating the activity in question.
- **Tolerate**. Where the level of risk after controls is pretty well acceptable, then the response will be to leave well alone – that is, tolerate the remaining risk.
- **Transfer**. Where the risk would be material if it occurred, but in the circumstances is unlikely to occur, we may transfer it elsewhere – say by insurance. If we contract out services we still retain the risk if things mess up, but we may well lose some risks relating to, say, staff sickness.

- **Treat**. This is about establishing internal controls to treat or deal with the risk. If there is a risk of impersonators calling an insurance company, we may need to establish security checks in the form of some careful questioning before accepting that it is actually the client on the phone.
- **Tell someone**. Where a risk has impacts on those outside the specific business, then there may be little or nothing that can be done about it. It may simply be a matter of informing someone. Where customers complain to a store manager that a cash machine outside a shop is faulty and does not provide receipts, it may not be the shop manager's responsibility, but it would help to convey this information to the bank on behalf of the shoppers.
- **Take advantage of**. We have said that we tolerate acceptable risks, but where there are so many controls that bolt down any fall-out from the risk, it may be that we can free up some of these controls. The risk of cash misappropriation is minimized where only a few staff are authorized to use the till – but where this means queues build up, it may be an idea to expand access to other shopfloor workers and think of other ways to ensure security of cash.
- **Talk about**. A risk that has not been marked significant and likely may be a hidden menace. It may be that people just do not know much about the issues in question. 'Talk about' is a strategy that applies where a potential risk has been sidelined but needs to be further explored before we can determine its full impact. The risk of employees logging wrong data about someone who has called to make a booking may not be seen as an issue, but it may be something that needs to be discussed further, say with the systems manager to see whether errors could readily happen. Having gone through the matter, the full implications may become clearer.
- **Test the water**. Linked to the point above, it may be possible to check something out rather than impose more controls to deal with a degree of uncertainty. If we believe that operatives are always polite when dealing with customers, then we may need to confirm that this is happening before saying that this system is watertight. If supervisors say that they check whether customers are happy with the service and invite comments, again we may need to test that this is happening before relying on this control.
- **Trend analysis**. Risks impose uncertainty about the future and we can identify and assess those risks that we understand, but it may be that we need to do some more research. For example, we may feel that our online services are quite good and can cope with peak demand between, say, 6 and 8 in the evening. The capacity planning process may be seen as a good control over ensuring customers are not kept waiting, but we may need to analyse the growth rates of online enquiries to assess whether this control needs enhancing.

Fixes and control improvements

Figure 3.8 takes us a stage further, since many organizations have already been able to compile basic risk registers.

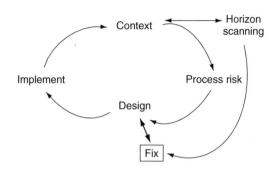

Figure 3.8 Fixing risk registers

The first point to note is the importance of the context within which risk management happens; that is, the structures, accountabilities, risk policies and general cultures in place, be they risk averse, reckless or well balanced. The 'process risk' stage of Figure 3.8 is the risk identification and assessment, which should be ongoing. This leads into the control design stage, which in turn goes into control implementation.

Two important issues jump out from this figure:

- **The importance of horizon scanning**. There is little point going around the organization and asking people if they have identified all their risks. What is more apt is for risk advisers to equip managers with the necessary tools to scan the horizon and set up an intelligence system for capturing anything here or in the future that can have an impact on the way business is currently being done. Risk is about uncertainty and uncertainty is at times about not knowing enough about something or not being in a position to become aware of something if and when it breaks. Horizon scanning means that parameters are established where sources of information, both internal and more often external, are scanned to see if signals come together in a way that triggers the parameters. It is a bit like a local shopkeeper keeping an eye on pricing practices and new gimmicks adopted by competitors. The more sophisticated the scanning technique, the more chance that it will bring forth material that creates a little more certainty where uncertainty rules.
- **The fix**. The second aspect of the model is about fixing things where they are wrong or underperform. One criticism of risk registers is that they do not always fit the reality of what is happening in the business. They are compiled as an annual exercise and result in reams of paperwork that is filed away. A few action points may pop out of the register, but they tend to fall outside the normal business priorities and are put to one side for a 'rainy day'. The 'fix' is important, as we need a further source of intelligence to tell us when controls are not working, or more importantly where a new and important risk has been left off the risk register. The risk management system must be put right if it falls out of step with real business practices. In fact, some consultants argue

Table 3.4 Assessing ideas

New idea	Risk mitigation	Costs	Practical issues	Timing	New risks	Score
			Importance (score 1–10)			
	1–10	1–10	1–10	1–10	1–10	5–50
1						
2						
3						

that the entire internal control system should be redesigned periodically to meet enhanced disclosure reporting requirements such as Sarbanes-Oxley and other regulations. Here the fix is more of an ongoing project to review, update and improve controls to earn that business edge and meet stakeholder expectations. This in turn means there is a constant series of implementations of what are normally new procedures. Having a workforce that is used to their working procedures being constantly updated is a valuable asset for any business, especially when the workers are coming up with good ideas for improved working practices.

Control change approval criteria

Control redesign sounds simple in concept but can be quite demanding. The problem is that control changes can have a knock-on effect and what is meant to bolt down the fall-out from specific risks can in turn create, different risks. For example, we might feel that the risk of misappropriation is great where a cashier can delete a transaction and mark it as an 'error' and start again. A good control is to get a supervisor to approve the deletion before the transaction is restarted. But this may bring in a further risk where the customer has to wait for this to happen and feels dissatisfied. If we need to approve deletions then a suitable routine will need to be developed to overcome the secondary problem.

One way forward is to impose a sense of discipline over all significant control changes by the use of set criteria that work for the organization. One example follows a fixed format where control changes have to go through an analysis before they can go live, as shown in Table 3.4.

In this way we can score the suggested changes (ideas 1, 2, 3 and so on) and come up with a way of prioritizing them and dealing with major new risks that pop up at the same time. This system can be applied to changes to systems, projects, new products, proposals and innovations.

Risk and controls

Our next model tries to coordinate the dual concepts of risk and control, as in Figure 3.9.

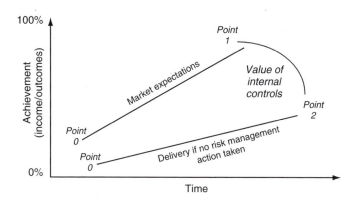

Figure 3.9   The value of controls

Over time a business will perform in a certain way and will need to install controls to tackle risks to its progress. If no controls are installed, then we would argue that risks that are contained by controls would be likely to arise. For example, if we do not carry out credit checks before advancing loans to clients, the risk of loan defaults increases in likelihood. The value of the credit checks as a control equates to the degree to which losses from defaults are reduced. An organization only has to perform in line with market expectations, or the public's expectations for public-sector bodies, and deliver to point 1 on Figure 3.9, while point 2 is set at a level to reflect the fact that controls do not exist, or are poor or are ignored. The value of these controls can then be estimated as achievements in terms of profits or outcomes between points 2 and 1.

Lots and lots of data

Risk registers and control evaluation exercises (i.e. audits) can result in masses of data that could end up a fire hazard if not kept in check. Figure 3.10 explains this further.

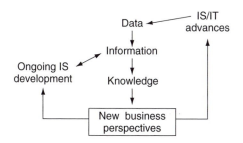

Figure 3.10   Turning data into value

The difficulty is to turn the raw data in information and then knowledge as a basis for better business decisions. Risk registers will tell managers whether the control focus is right or whether it needs adjusting. The other thing they can do if planned carefully is to help set a new business perspective, where a knowledge of where risk lies and how we can best respond to it empowers teams to take responsibility for what they can control and what they know presents a challenge. As information systems advance it is possible to start profiling the data to give clear profiles of where risk lies across an organization and reports that give insights into areas that can be further exploited and other parts of the business where we need to tighten up a little.

In short

Risk mitigation is important to stop nasty things jumping up and biting you on your legs. But a holistic perspective would suggest that controls that mitigate risk are only as good as efforts to identify and assess risk in the first place.

Risk appetites

> **A4M 3.22** *The extent to which defined risks to the achievement of business objectives have not been addressed by the action plans that result from the initial audit process should fall in line with the corporate framework for establishing various positions on risk tolerances.*

The theory

This is the '**big issue**'. Risk appetite is a simple concept, in that all good governance codes across the world, along with the COSO ERM guidance, say something along the lines that the organization (e.g. the board) should set the risk appetite and that this should guide people throughout the organization in the level of tolerance for risk in their work. The organization tells its stakeholders about this appetite and they can decide whether to invest, work with or accept the position, as it fits (or does not fit) with their own risk appetite. In general, the riskier an organization, the more returns one would expect from investing in such a entity. Younger and more affluent people may care to invest in risky products in the hope of higher returns, while older people and those who are less affluent may have the opposite view. Like is matched with like and all are happy. Meanwhile, employees have been told that the risk tolerances are set at ABC for period XYZ and again, all is well. This is why regulators, legislators and policymakers will all insist that an

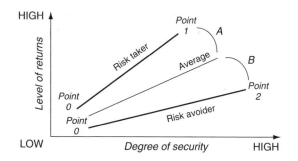

Figure 3.11   Respective positions on risk

organization should determine and disclose its risk appetite. If only it were that simple.

Models to the rescue

We have developed a few models to help us work though this risk minefield. Our first, Figure 3.11, is simply about consolidating the link between risk and return.

Anticipated returns from investing in one organization/product can be low or high and this can be contrasted with the degree to which the investment is secure; that is, subject to a low or higher level of uncertainty in performance and results. Risk takers are at point A where they seek more returns for less certainty that they will achieve the desired results. Risk avoiders are on the opposite side of the coin. So a risk-averse investor may place their funds in a high-interest bank account and earn a fairly small return each year, but with a high degree of certainty. A risk taker may buy a house and let it sit for a year in the hope that upward movements in house prices would mean a return greater than the bank interest and after taking out the costs of acquiring the property. Where house prices are climbing the risk is less severe, but where they are not moving well the risk is inherent in anticipating market trends.

We could argue that all investors and all organizations are located somewhere on the risk appetite spectrum. The point is that their interests should coincide and investors should be attracted to products that match their profile. Any mismatch means that there is a problem with the understanding, communication or integrity of one or both sides to the affair.

Driven by residual risk

Our next model is in Figure 3.12. This widens the discussion and brings in our four V model mentioned earlier in the chapter.

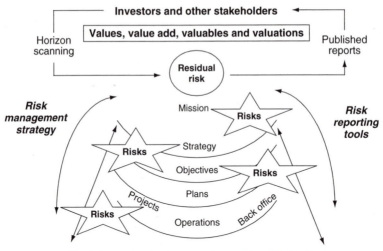

Figure 3.12 Focusing on residual risk

We have switched our perspective of an organization to suggest that residual risk – that is, risks that remain after we have put in all the controls we deem necessary – can be seen as the centre of an organization's concerns. Investors and stakeholders can take comfort in the value-based four Vs that form the understanding between them and the organization. The strategic positioning of the business is continuously responding to risk assessments that run up and down the enterprise and a risk management strategy draws together the controls that are needed to ensure good performance. This is essentially about the decisions, standards, IS (information systems), procedures and behaviour along the bottom of the model. Meanwhile, risk reporting tools ensure that information about risk is located in the residual risk box right at the top of the model. The organization reports on the residual risk in the context of the four Vs and is also scanning the horizon looking for anything out there that changes the risk profiles. The dialogue between the entity and its stakeholders revolves around changing risks to the four Vs and the level of residual risk that is reported on. The four V agenda will come more into focus in later models.

Perceptions and tolerances

So far we have tried to structure the risk appetite debate around the need to determine residual risk and tell our position to everyone, both inside and outside the organization, who needs to know about it. This still does not answer the question: what is our risk tolerance anyway? Some organizations try to dig down into this problem and say that they will allow 5% errors, or 10 complaints each quarter or less than 10% failures in new business projects. Some give a philosophical view and say that they will support people who have a go at new things but who stay within budget and who take great care in planning and reporting progress.

The problem is that one error, one complaint and one failed venture can erupt and cause untold damage. Gerald Ratner's off the cuff remark that one of his products was 'crap' wiped out a business almost overnight. An undercover reporter who finds one case of employee exploitation can lead to huge embarrassment for a business that trades on having a good, respected name. Allegations of financial services misselling and/or business practices that could lead to misreporting of annual profit before tax can mean that a full investigation is launched. Managers or civil servants who attend an expensive international conference to get real ideas can be seen as extravagant and wasteful, when staff are being laid off or public funds are under great pressure.

We have said that risks can jump up and bite you and it is those specific unidentified risks that hide in dark shadows that can cause most damage. Figure 3.13 develops our theme further.

Figure 3.13 suggests that we need to widen our thinking about risk in terms of how it hits our stakeholders. We can set different levels of risk between levels 1 to 5 (and 6), as Table 3.5 shows.

These levels escalate upwards as they get more and more serious until they reach a quite unusual level 6 risk, such as faced the accounting firm Arthur Andersen in the wake of the Enron and WorldCom affairs. The other dimension of the model relates to the impact on stakeholders and these are classified A–D. So a risk can be less or more severe but also needs to be related to the impact on specific groups of stakeholders. A tolerance of 55 errors allowed in each accounting period may have little effect on most stakeholders, but could

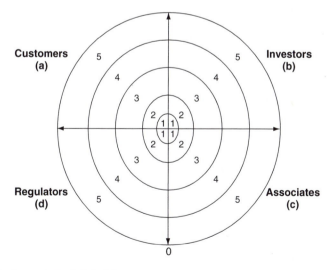

Figure 3.13 Impact on stakeholders

Table 3.5　Risk tolerances

Levels of risk	Tolerances Impact on stakeholders			
	A	B	C	D
1. Basic business context				
2. Occasional error and loss				
3. Risk-taking practices				
4. Complaints and concerns				
5. Media investigations				
6. Collapse, e.g. Barings Bank				

provide a level 4 risk to A groups; that is, customers. A misreporting fraud may cause a level 5 risk that affects regulators D and investors B, while a financial loss may affect associates C, who may lose business as the company pulls out of several joint ventures. If a member of staff assaults a customer this may seem to be a one-off level 2 matter and we may allow, say, five staff misconduct cases a year, but one case may result in a major press campaign if not tackled properly and result in a level 4 or 5 risk. It is clear that much comes back to attitudes rather than straight figures and it is these attitudes and understanding of stake-holders' needs that are most important to work on in discussing tolerances.

Putting it all together

We have suggested that risk appetite is not about setting a figure as such. It is more about perspectives and using frameworks to cover all angles. We have introduced the four Vs model as one way of classifying things. What we need to do now is put all our ideas together in a model of risk appetites, and we have one such three-dimensional model in Figure 3.14.

Each organization will have its own view on risk, ranging as follows:

- Just go out there and get 'em!
- We have very clear standards, so please follow them!
- If you've made all the checks, go ahead!
- Don't do a thing until I get back!
- Desperate times call for desperate measures!
- I'll let you know when you are not doing it right, don't worry!
- I'll pretend I did not see that!
- No gain without pain!
- Get back you fool, it's far too dangerous out there!

Corporate traditions will have developed over the years and society lurches between 'steady as she goes' and 'let's rock and roll', depending on whether

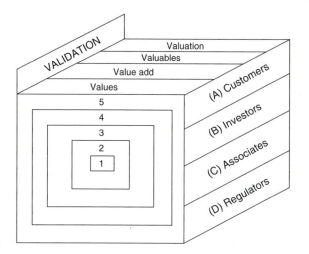

Figure 3.14   The risk appetite model

we are in times of recession or rapid growth. The integrated risk appetite framework in Figure 3.14 simply says that whatever the strategies, put them within a framework than ensures all bases are covered. For example:

- **Values A 1–5** is about the way we treat our customers and deal with risks that interfere with the need for high levels of honesty, ranging from basic operational problems (level 1) to complete collapse (level 6). Where a company has been overtrading and is not able to handle the demand for information online and over the phone, it will interfere with one of its values in responding to customers within 24 hours of an enquiry.
- **Valuations B 1–5** means risks that mean our published figures are wrong and that affect investors. These can again range from the insignificant level 1 to the much more serious level 5 or even 6 risk. If an oil company has been overestimating its reserves, then it will have to adjust and restate its published information, which will affect its overall valuation.
- **Value add C 1–5** We may have a poor operation in one part of the company and our employees, colleagues and associates may realize that they could be closed down if level 4 or 5 risks continue to affect the work and performance does not improve.
- **Valuables D 1–5** addresses those risks to the resilience of business capacity and resource base that may concern the regulator, either marginally (level 1) or urgently (level 5 and above). The Financial Services Authority will assess a bank's capital adequacy to determine the magnitude of risks and when to trigger discussions between it and the bank's management.

We need to think about our stakeholders and their stated and changing expectations and we need to consider the level of risk 1–5. We also need to ask whether it is a risk to our values (behaving badly), our value add (poor performance), our valuables (resources exposed to loss, waste and physical damage) or finally our valuations (reports and accounts that are misleading or downright wrong). We have superimposed over Figure 3.14 one further 'V', validation – how our framework of values is confirmed by people who have no vested interest in the matter and who are wholly professional.

Any gaps in the model may well pose a risk to our overall corporate reputation. Or, put another way, we can use the model as criteria for ensuring we have addressed all aspects of managing risk and ensuring residual risk does not jump up and bite us. Meanwhile, we can use the four V model to measure risk. Examples of factors associated with the four Vs are shown in Tables 3.6 and 3.7.

So risk appetite leads to different tolerances for different aspects of the business. In terms of value add we are looking for creative change and improvement at the local level, while the other Vs are held at corporate level to be non-negotiable. If a new project is being considered for fast-track development, we will need to ensure it fits with our values (e.g. does not harm the local community), our asset base is protected (e.g. it won't create huge losses) and that the work is fairly disclosed (e.g. it is reported as part of our strategic growth).

Table 3.6 Analysing the four Vs

Values (respect for)	Valuables (protect)	Valuation	Value add
Others	Our assets	Accurate records	Strict timelines
The law	Our people	Asset valuation	Lower costs
Integrity	Our systems	Financial systems	Efficient systems
Procedures	Our information	Final accounts	Quality standards
Customers' needs	Our knowledge	Financial regulations	Streamlined teams
Stakeholders	Insurance cover	Accounting policies	Good suppliers
Accuracy	Contingency plans	Statistical information	New projects
Behaviour	Damage limitation	KPIs	Budgetary control
Local community	Antifraud	Published disclosures	Customer focus

Table 3.7 Risk appetites per four Vs

V factor	Risk appetite	Focus	Controls	Driver
Values	Averse?	Emphasize corporate values	Insist on adherence	Corporate behaviour
Valuables	Neutral?	Protect major assets	Safeguards and contingency plans	Corporate standards
Valuation	Averse?	Promote good transparency	Comply with financial rules	Corporate policies
Value add	Risk taker?	Continuous improvement	Challenge and innovate	Local procedures

That means we should allow less scope for discretion on the first three Vs but much more on the final one, value add.

Risk appetite is difficult to formalize because it is very hard to get corporate intentions into all employees' personal perceptions. What one person sees as difficult, another may see as exciting. What one person sees as boring, another may see as relaxing. What one person may see as beneath them, another person may see as a chance to consolidate learnt skills. In terms of the wider view, risk appetite is about posing four basic questions:

1. Does investors' risk appetite fit with the organization's?
2. How does the organization's risk appetite relate to other companies in the business sector?
3. How do people within the organization prioritize things?
4. Does published information fit with the reality of the company from top to bottom?

The next stage is to use some kind of corporate framework such as our four V model that is able to address these and other related issues.

The CRSA Forum – viewpoints

The UK's Control Risk Self-Assessment Forum has spent some time discussing the concept of risk appetites and it recognizes the difficulties involved in addressing the challenges that arise from this debate. It was clear from the discussions that no one felt that risk appetite was properly understood and evaluated in their own organizations and, in fact, many were just beginning to consider the concept. The only conclusion that could be reached, apart from agreement that we have to consider risk appetite (many preferred the concept of risk tolerance), is that it is much easier said than done.

Some CRSA Forum members felt that risk appetite can be expressed in terms of impact and likelihood as high, medium and low, and any risk within the high–high category is above the tolerance threshold. This might be oversimplistic but is relatively simple and arguably it means that you assess appetite and risk in one go. Other members suggested that risk appetite can only be determined in relation to a particular decision where the risks can be weighed against the benefits. This would mean that risk appetite could not usefully be defined when evaluating risks in a broader, more abstract setting. Risk appetite could, however, be defined in relation to a particular business strategy.

In short

Risk appetite is it – the big issue – and it requires a bit of thinking about to get the right messages across to employees and out to stakeholders. Explaining how we see things and what makes us tick and what makes us scared is not easy. Although models help, they are only the start of a much bigger task.

Common mistakes

> **A4M 3.23** *The initial audit process should be documented in an efficient manner.*

Scenario one

People in an organization try to do a good job, but there are always things that interfere with work. When problems occur we all do our best, but this is often more to do with luck that anything else.

Scenario two

The A4M.*99* process turns much of this on its head by suggesting that the scenario should change to the following:

People in an organization try to do a good job, but there are always developments that interfere with work. A good understanding of risk concepts gives us a better chance to deal with uncertainty and rely less on luck and more on good analysis and forward planning.

Figure 3.15 Risky times

Is it that simple?

There is much that could go wrong in moving from scenario one to scenario two:

- **People in an organization do not feel that they have any control over their role at work**. The initial audit concept builds on a positive view of control. Where this is not in place at work, the audit process will be less dynamic.
- **Risk is in no way pulled together in an organization but is seen as a set of random occurrences**. Where there is no appreciation of risk and the need to reposition in response to changing risks, there will be a gap in the risk management process.
- **The person dealing with risk coordination has a very narrow perspective**. Where there is no real driver, with a holistic approach there is less scope to get enterprise risk management in place.
- **There is no systematic process for identifying risk used in the organization**. Where there is no sound method for identifying risks, there may be gaps in the validity of risk assessments and therefore internal controls.
- **There is no attempt to understand the effect that different cultures in the organization have on the way risk is perceived**. Where a one-size-fits-all approach is in use, it will be hard to fit the tools to the way different people work and relate to each other at work.
- **A policy is not in place that incorporates the risk of missing potential opportunities, which is seen as a risk in itself**. Where there is recognition of the risks of not doing enough and not taking the occasional chance, the self-audit process will become fairly negative.
- **The wide range of risk strategies implicit in the various 'Ts' is not properly recognized**. Where the range of potential responses to risk is not fully appreciated, the output from initial audits will be restricted.
- **The complex issues related to risk appetites are not discussed at all**. Where the complex matter of risk appetites is not fully addressed with an appropriate framework, the difficulties and scope for a better understanding of this issue will be missed.
- **There is no real belief in the dynamic link between risk and internal control**. Where the initial audit process focuses on risk and not longer-term control redesign, this will be a lost opportunity.
- **Risk registers are seen as something removed from the real business**. Where the compilation of risk registers is seen as an onerous and nonproductive task, there will be less scope for making this document a dynamic management tool.

Helpful models for overcoming problems

Note that all the figures in this chapter can be used to overcome the common mistakes, although there is one particular model that can be used to good effect, Figure 3.16.

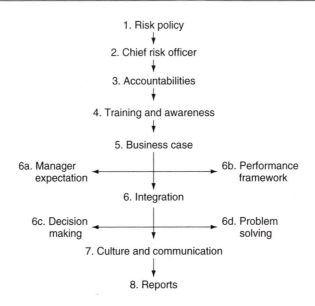

Figure 3.16   Risk flows

Some explanations of Figure 3.16:

1. Develop a board-level risk policy that sets out definitions, roles, board-level sponsorship and the need to ensure risks are managed in line with set risk appetites.
2. Appoint a chief risk officer to coordinate the risk agenda throughout the organization, with a focus on enterprise risk management and full integration.
3. Establish clear accountabilities so that risk ownership is as clear as possible.
4. Train people and ensure they are aware of the risk policy and how it affects their day-to-day work.
5. Ensure there is a clear business case for risk management and that people understand the benefits of the initiative.
6. Integrate risk management into the way business is conducted:
   6a. Make sure people are expected to get involved.
   6b. Link risk management into performance and assess how people are responding.
   6c. Ensure that all significant decisions are made only after risks are assessed.
   6d. Encourage people to use risk management in solving operational problems.
7. Get people talking about risk so that it is part of the team culture.
8. Establish reporting arrangements linked to business control assurance policies.

The final model, Figure 3.17, gives a four-level dynamic for looking at risk and control.

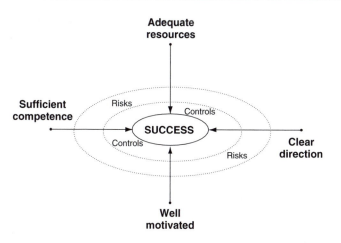

Figure 3.17   Risk, control and success

Here we link risks and controls to the success agenda and make sure we have:

- A clear direction and focus on the set objectives.
- Well-motivated staff who work towards the objective.
- Sufficient competence.
- Adequate resources.

These four factors make or break the way risks are managed.

In short

Risk management is based on risk concepts and if we do not get our people to appreciate these concepts, any progress becomes much more difficult.

Check your progress

> **A4M 3.24**   *The initial audit process should be designed to make people think about risk at work in much the same way as they think about and manage risk in their personal life.*

One tool that can be applied to track your progress is to test the extent to which you have assimilated the key points raised in this chapter. The multi-choice questions below will check your progress and the answer guide in Appendix D is based on what is most appropriate in the context of this book. Please record your answers in the table at Appendix D. You may also record the time spent on each test and enter this information in the 'Mins' column of Appendix D.

Name ....

Start time ....   **Finish time** ....   **Total minutes** ....

Multi-choice quiz

1. Select the most appropriate sentence.
a. Many feel that the risk register is the pivotal item for managing risk and accounting for an organization's position. In fact, the pivotal aspect of risk management is the setting of risk policies – all else flows from this.
b. Many feel that the risk register is the pivotal item for managing risk and accounting for an organization's position. In fact, the pivotal aspect of risk management is the setting of risk appetite – all else flows from this.
c. Many feel that the risk reviews is the pivotal item for managing risk and accounting for an organization's position. In fact, the pivotal aspect of risk management is the risk register – all else flows from this.
d. Many feel that the risk workshop is the pivotal item for managing risk and accounting for an organization's position. In fact, the pivotal aspect of risk management is the risk reviews – all else flows from this.

2. Insert the missing phrase.
Promote .... by placing risk management understanding and use of appropriate tools into all employees' core competencies.

a. risk-averse staff.
b. control-compliant staff.
c. risk-taking staff.
d. risk-smart staff.

3. Insert the missing word/s.
The four Vs model is based on values, valuables, value add and:

a. valued people.
b. valuation.
c. value of company.
d. value ethics.

4. Insert the missing word.
In the middle of the four V model is ...., as this is the most important thing that an organization has.

a. performance.
b. assets.

c. reputation.
d. people.

5. Select the most appropriate sentence.
a. Our risk assessments will involve people who will have their own personal perspectives that they bring to the task.
b. Our risk assessments will bring together people so that they will have a common perspective that they bring to the task.
c. Our risk assessments will not involve people who will have their own personal perspectives that they bring to the task.
d. Our risk assessments will involve people who will have their own personal perspectives that they keep confidential.

6. Insert the missing phrase.
Most organizations use a model based on .... where risk may be assessed as colours.

a. risk models.
b. decision grids.
c. danger spots.
d. traffic lights.

7. Insert the missing number.
We can use an assortment of .... Ts to gauge the range of responses that are available.

a. nine.
b. eight.
c. ten.
d. five.

8. Insert the missing phrase.
.... means parameters are established where sources of information, both internal and more often external, are scanned to see if signals come together in a way that triggers the parameters.

a. Strategic planning.
b. Decision making.
c. Horizon scanning.
d. Risk profiling.

9. Select the most appropriate sentence.
a. The problem is that risk changes can have a knock-on effect and what is meant to bolt down the fall-out from specific risks can in turn create different risks.

b. The problem is that control changes can have a knock-on effect and what is meant to bolt down the fall-out from specific risks can in turn create different risks.
c. The problem is that control changes can have a knock-on effect and what is meant to bolt down the fall-out from specific risks can in turn create more controls.
d. The problem is that control changes can have a knock-on effect and what is meant to bolt down the fall-out from specific risks can in turn create fewer risks.

10. Which is the odd one out?
Each organization will have its own view on risk, ranging from:

a. 'just go out there and get em!', 'we have very clear standards, so please follow them', 'if you've made all the checks go ahead'.
b. 'don't do a thing until I get back!', 'desperate times call for desperate measures!', 'I'll let you know when you are not doing it right, don't worry!'.
c. 'I'll pretend I did not see that!', 'no gain without pain!', 'get back you fool, it's far too dangerous out there'.
d. 'we need to work hard', 'get communications going', 'always do your best'.

Newsflash – read all about it

There is so much behind the move towards effective governance and risk management in all walks of life, and a small selection of relevant examples is provided to illustrate this new way of thinking.

10 new dimensions

Old thinking	New dimensions	A suitable example
Debt is not a problem, since if a company gets itself into trouble it can always restructure itself and get back on a even keel.	Once you get yourself into trouble, it's a devil of a job to dig your way out of the mire.	Telewest, the stricken cable company, will pay about £110 million to the advisors connected with its £3.8bn rescue – making it the most expensive restructuring fee in the UK ... Enron's bill for restructuring came to £550m while WorldCom's is ongoing at £120m.[1]

Risk management makes for better, well-run organizations and benefits everyone.

Risk management, when applied with common sense, makes for better, well-run organizations and benefits everyone.

For almost ten years, children in a Devon market town have enjoyed their traditional Pancake Day races. About 600 friends and family usually turn up to watch and the winners are given a big Easter egg .... Next week's event in Okehampton has fallen victim to the spiralling compensation culture ... the cost of insuring the event, in case someone gets injured has shot up from £75 last year to £280 ... and 25 marshals would be needed along the 80 yard route – which goes through a pedestrian area – to guarantee public safety ... as a result, the event is in danger of being cancelled.[2]

Buyers should take care when buying consumables by for example checking the best-before dates of foodstuff.

Legal loopholes mean you cannot always be sure about best before dates, and it's best to ask a few questions to be safe.

Chicken well past its use-by date is being re-packaged as 'fresh', says a report out today ... a legal loophole means food producers can decide the use-by date for their own products ... Meanwhile the Food Standards Agency said ... Any producer who extends the use-by date on chicken so that it is unfit when it reached the consumer would be liable for prosecution under the Food Safety Act.[3]

Risk resilience is essential in a world where terrorism is an ever-present threat and as a result, we have developed comprehensive contingency plans.

Contingency plans are an important aspect of risk management, but they are only as good as the testing arrangements that are applied.

'Given the right altitude and distance away from the spectators, they will easily mistake these models for the real ones.' Comment from Bickley model flying club, which has stepped in after organizers of a flypast failed to book the RAF for the 60th anniversary of D-Day.[4]

(Continued)

Old thinking	New dimensions	A suitable example
Risk management ensures we only back winners and not losers.	The drive towards effective risk management is based on the view that everything, even failures, can be used to move us forward.	Inevitably exploring strange ideas carries with it high risk; as Art Fry of 3M famously observed: 'You have to kiss a lot of frogs to find your prince.' So it's not enough to back every outsider in the race. The trick is to make multiple bets but at an early stage when new technologies or markets are taking shape. 'Probe and learn', 'fail fast and find out' and 'learning through fast failures' are the emerging recipes for handling discontinuous innovation.[5]
There is always a risk that some people will not enjoy a luxury cruise as much as others.	If a risk on a luxury cruise would hit the press if it materialized, it needs to be seen as a big risk.	A luxury cruise liner has become a floating prison for Britons hit by a virulent stomach bug. More than 450 have been struck down on P&O's £200 million flagship *Aurora* in the middle of the Mediterranean.[6]
Risk is loosely linked to rewards, in that we would expect to take bigger risks for better returns.	In business risk is fundamentally linked to rewards, and the stark reality of this link can be seen in trouble spots around the world.	The risk/reward relationship is familiar to anyone in business. And in a globalizing era businesses are inevitably drawn to previously inaccessible markets, where risk (and potential rewards) may be much higher. When it comes to precious raw materials such as oil and gas – increasingly in demand as former Third World countries seek to industrialize rapidly – and other valuable commodities, it is uncanny how often these materials are located in some of the most dangerous and unpredictable parts of the world. There may be great profits to be won, but can we get these profits home safely? The crucial first step is for boards to assess risk vigorously before committing to significant investment in high-risk areas.[7]

Once we have identified risks we can ensure they are dealt with in a way that best suits the business.	Once we have identified risks we can ensure they are dealt with in a way that best suits our stakeholders, which will therefore benefit the business.	Executives at a large insurance company knew they were misselling mortgage endowments during the late nineties, Financial Mail can reveal . . . yet despite these concerns, the risk to customers and the threat to its reputation, the company continued to sell them for at least two more years.[8]
Important systems that affect the whole of society must be carefully safeguarded against known risks.	Important systems that affect the whole of society are not always carefully safeguarded against known risks.	The astonishing ease with which fraudsters are corrupting the electoral system is exposed today. As abuse increases, especially by benefits cheats and illegal immigrants, a *Daily Mail* investigation has highlighted a culture of inefficiency and political correctness within local councils. It allowed us to register a fictitious student called Gus Troopbev – an anagram of Bogus Voter – on 31 electoral registers within just a few hours, and to obtain further bogus votes in the most marginal seats in Britain.[9]
We can only assess those risks where the consequences of our actions are reasonably foreseeable.	We need to try to assess all those risks that may make us vulnerable to any extent, even if it is not clear how far the consequences will reach.	In assessing damages to compensate a victim of unlawful race discrimination, the appropriate test to be applied was the establishment of a causal link between the act of discrimination and the injury alleged. It was unnecessary to superimpose the requirement that the injury be reasonably foreseeable.[10]

The key messages

The last section of each chapter contains a short story or quote that should provide an interesting format for illustrating some of the book's key messages.

Does risk management always pay off?

Inspector Clouseau (Peter Sellers) bends down to stroke a small dog yapping at his feet. Before doing this he asks the old man at reception, 'Does your doggy bite?', to which the old man solemnly shakes his head. So Sellers strokes the dog – only to have it sink its teeth into his hand. With a cry of pain, Sellers turns to the man and says, 'I thought you said your doggy didn't bite.' The old man puffs on his pipe a couple of times before declaring, 'That is not my dog.'[11]

Notes

1. *The Times*, Thursday, April 1, 2004, Business, page 1.
2. *Daily Mail*, Friday, February 20, 2004, page 9.
3. *Independent*, Saturday, March 27, 2004, page 4, B43.
4. *The Times*, Wednesday, May 19, 2004, T2, page 2.
5. John Bessant, Julian Birkenshaw and Rick Delbridge, 'Theories of Creator', *People Management*, 12 February 2004, pages 29–31.
6. *Daily Mail*, Saturday, November 1, 2003, page 1.
7. *Daily Telegraph*, Thursday, April 22, 2004, Business and Jobs, page A3, Stefan Stern, SAS veteran.
8. *Financial Mail*, Sunday, January 25, 2004, page 1.
9. *Daily Mail*, Saturday, February 7, 2004, page 7.
10. Court of Appeal, *Essa v Laing Ltd*, Judgment, January 21, 2004.
11. Mark Robertson, 'The Pink Panther Strikes Again', *Daily Mail*, Saturday, November 15, 2003, page 60.

4 Different audit approaches

We will answer all things faithfully.
William Shakespeare, *Merchant of Venice*, Act IV, Scene 1

A4M Statement D *The A4M.99 audit approach may involve a consideration of the past, present and the future, although its main focus should revolve around enhancing the prospects of the organization.*

Introduction

A4M 4.25 *The initial audit process should be formed around a clear mission and approach that best suits the issues that are being addressed by this management tool.*

Figure 1.1 in Chapter 1 shows how the book is put together. Chapter 4 covers the different approaches a manager can take to audit work. To make sure systems work well and controls do the job that they are intended to do, managers should consider carrying out audits of their existing arrangements. There is no set format for this task. It is just about getting a clear aim and employing the most appropriate tool. Some of these tools include:

- **Workshops**. This can be an extremely powerful tool where we get teams together to work through ways of making improvements, but it can be a time-consuming and cumbersome way of getting to the right results. For really high-risk areas such as new projects, new ventures or where a significant new risk appears to threaten parts of the business, it can be worthwhile.

- **Surveys**. Surveys can also be applied. Where we need to find out where people sit on a particular issue we can survey them. We can review levels of compliance, control awareness and other matters from large numbers of staff through the use of these surveys.
- **Interviews**. Interviewing people is another way of finding out about relevant issues and how they affect our systems. Where key concerns mean that specific decisions have to be made, an audit of the situation can be conducted by talking to people who know most about the matters in question.
- **Evidence evaluation**. It is possible to review the available evidence on the way controls are being applied to mitigate risk.

When carrying out an initial review, managers need to bear in mind the wide choice of approaches and tools that are available to help them work through the issues and develop good ways forward.

In short

The **A4M.99** *process has an underpinning perspective that is based on promoting integrity, accountability and ensuring that controls have a clear focus on risk.*

Different strokes

> **A4M 4.26** *The initial audit process should involve a consideration of risks to the business, risk management strategies and associated systems of internal controls. These matters should be discussed using terminology that suits the area in question, so long as the resulting disclosure reports and action plans are acceptable to senior management.*

We have seen that there are different tools available for different approaches to the initial audit task. The approach chosen should suit the organization and much depends on:

- Whether the organization is extrovert or introvert.
- The degree to which empowerment in encouraged across the organization.
- Past experiences of audits and review.
- Regulators' interests and the need to respond to specific concerns they may have.
- The type of culture in place and whether it is based around command/control or more flexible attitudes towards creative growth.

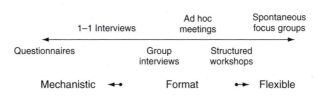

Figure 4.1   Degrees of interaction

Degrees of interaction

Figure 4.1 illustrates the different styles of initial auditing and the way these vary between a more mechanistic style on the left through to a more interactive one on the right.

On the extreme left of Figure 4.1 sits formal questionnaires, which is a one-way tool for eliciting views and basic information to help find out what is going on in parts of the organization. Questionnaires may also be used to gather one-way information across the organization on a common issue. At the other extreme we have focus groups that break out as and when required. Where there are flipcharts scattered around the offices, this suggests an atmosphere where spontaneous focus groups may flourish. If an issue breaks, we get some of the players together and work through the matter at hand and set viable ways forward. In between these extremes are various degrees of interaction.

Accountability versus trust

The initial audit process has to be set in reality if it is to work. Most managers in most organizations are routinely auditing their systems. It is just that there is no real standard or set of principles that can be used to promote, measure and provide guidance to support this effort. Figure 4.2 has a go at tackling the tensions between basing reviews on accountability frameworks and simply

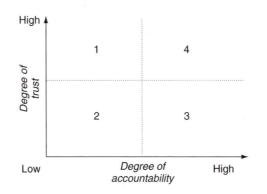

Figure 4.2   Trust and accountability

using a trusting approach, where we ask people to get involved in problem solving in addition to their regular duties. Moreover, we need to work out how far our systems are steeped in clear role definition and accountabilities and how far they are based on people just 'helping out'.

Some explanation of Figure 4.2 follows:

1. Where people are asked to perform and behave well but there are no formal accountabilities in place, this can lead to some confusion in the event of a significant problem occurring.
2. Where both managers and staff are not trusted and no form of accountability is established, there is a recipe for chaos.
3. Where managers are not trusted but strict accountabilities are imposed, this situation tends to result in an inspection regime where checking up on people and constant monitoring is the norm.
4. Where employees are trusted and there are clear lines of accountability, there is much more scope to empower people to deliver while avoiding any confusion where things need sorting out.

What type of audit are we doing?

One important consideration for the manager as a review is commenced is the general shape and form of the work. Figure 4.3 tries to explain this concept.

The review could focus on past events or seek to consider future prospects. Meanwhile, the work may be pretty independent and objective in the way matters at hand are assessed, or it could be a quick review that has no claim to independence but is more about moving forward. The four types of audits in Figure 4.4 are explained below:

- **Type 1**. These types of reviews are backwards looking and are entirely under the direction of those responsible for the area in question. This type of work will have some value but should avoid being seen as a 'whitewash'.

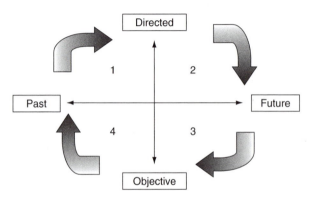

Figure 4.3   Focusing the audit

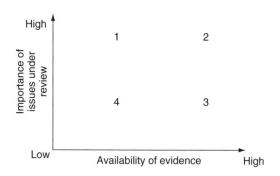

Figure 4.4   Evidential standards

- **Type 2**. Directed reviews that focus on the future are of more worth. They are more about setting strategy in the sense that people responsible for aspects of the business need to plan improvements wherever possible.
- **Type 3**. Future-focused reviews can be used to ask challenging questions. These reviews may be employed to endorse current strategies or help steer the business in a new direction.
- **Type 4**. Type 4 audits will appear more as investigations into what went wrong and why. That is an independent resource looking at what happened in the past. Like type 1 reviews, the value needs to be made clear and in general the work will tend to consider past problems and standards of conduct for those implicated by the findings.

The type of audit in question really needs to be determined at the outset, as this will have an impact on the approach, standards of evidence and whether it will result in sensitivities for the business and people concerned.

How far do we go?

It takes time and effort to look into things and uncover the reality. The question that Figure 4.4 seeks to answer is about the level of detail that a manager needs to delve into before it starts to become a waste of time.

The first reference frame that we use in Figure 4.4 is related to the importance of what we are considering. If it is a large change project that could have a fundamental impact on the organization, then the assessment of risk and controls may go into some level of detail. The other frame is the availability of evidence. Turning again to the large project, it may be that previous attempts have failed and we need to examine past data to get a view on best ways forward. The importance/evidence categories are explained as:

1. Important issues where there is not much information to look at may have to be dealt with through making assumptions. Future-oriented work may have this attribute.
2. Where significant issues are considered and there is a great deal of evidence to review, we may have to move into a formal project.

3. Where there is an abundance of evidence but the matters in hand are not overly material, it may be a question of selecting a small sample of evidence to appraise and analyse.
4. The bottom left corner relates to areas where it will probably not be worthwhile to carry out a review at all.

A holistic approach to initial audit work

We have considered some of the factors that we need to take into account when performing audit-type work. A dynamic way of looking at the prospect is set out in Figure 4.5.

All review work has stakeholders. It may be people who are directly affected by the work, say mortgage endowment policyholders who feel that they have been missold policies and have complained. Stakeholders may have a wider definition in meaning all those who are affected by the way the organization performs and behaves. There is a need to ensure that stakeholders' expectations that an organization conducts its affairs properly, and reviews and addresses any problems that get in the way of this ideal, should form a backdrop to the manager's audit work.

The aim of the review, who accounts for what, how the work is to be carried out and what is actually achieved form the 4As in Figure 4.5. The focus on past, present and future has already been mentioned and these alternatives sit inside the model. The initial audit culture is aligned with the need to report the results of such work, while this activity feeds into the wider remit of risk management and control. All initial audit work should have a view on how risks are identified, assessed and managed and how internal controls are suitably formulated to assist this task. Good governance is about good organizations that are able to isolate and deal with anything that presents a threat to their

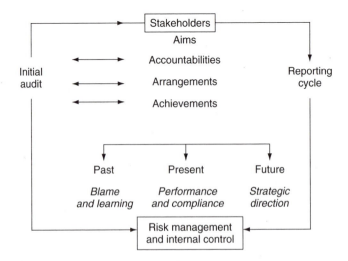

Figure 4.5   The 4As for stakeholders

continuing good name. Good governance also provides an avenue to further improve and promote an organization's continuing good name.

Formal or informal audits?

As we have seen, there are many options for the audit task and there are many choices to be made in terms of which techniques to use and how to apply them. One way of dealing with this scenario is to set out different levels of initial auditing. Table 4.1 provides four such levels. Level 1 is the full-blown formal audit set up by the manager to review a high-level risk, while level 4 is an ongoing consideration of inherent risk as part of the overall business process, with the other levels falling somewhere in between.

Table 4.1   Levels 1–4 audits

Consideration	Level 1 audits	Level 2 audits	Level 3 audits	Level 4 audits
1. CONTEXT	Formal	Semi-formal	Semi-informal	Informal
2. LEAD	Appointed investigator	Appointed reviewer	Workshop facilitator	Manager
3. TERMS OF REFERENCE	Investigate issues	Review issues and systems	Review risk management	Continuous review and improvement
4. APPOACH	Research past events	Review of current arrangements and compliance	Team assesses their objectives, risks and controls	Ensure decisions and plans address key risks
5. EVIDENCE	Compelling	Satisfactory	Adequate	Useful
6. TOOLS	Detailed analysis and document search, formal interviews	Procedures review, compliance tests, interviews	Facilitated discussions, voting, brainstorming, problem solving	Appreciation of risk, controls, compliance and assurance embedded into the business
7. TIMING	On request from sponsor	Regular occurrence and in response to specific problems	Whenever risk register needs updating	Ongoing as part of the business processes
8. USES	Irregularities and performance problems	Control compliance	Team-based risk assessment	Continuous risk management
9. REPORTS	Confidential report to sponsor on the implications of findings	Formal assurances to board and audit committee	Internal report and periodic assurances on system of internal control	Ongoing assurances on system of internal control
10. BENEFITS	Review sensitive problems to ensure an appropriate response	Formal review of the way staff are managing risk and employing key controls	Team ownership and agreement of current risk management strategies	Change in culture to ensure risk is addressed throughout the organization

In short

The manager may employ a variety of tools, approaches and models when reviewing aspects of the business. This variety of choice enriches the audit agenda and assists in both flexibility and value.

The past

A4M 4.27   *The initial audit process may be applied to reviewing past events with a view to assessing whether lessons may be learnt so as to promote a healthier and more successful organization. Meanwhile, any unacceptable past actions should be dealt with using the agreed corporate procedures.*

Each organization will have a set of corporate traditions that form part of its history. Heroes, villains and just plain characters that have spent time at the offices and sites over the years all go to make up the stories, both real and exaggerated. There will also be a tradition in the way events of the past are viewed: whether the past is seen as past, or whether there are ongoing attempts to analyse failings, behaviour and actions that belong to days gone by. This said, there are times when we really do need to go back a bit and discover what happened. Formal complaints, allegations of breach of procedure or improper conduct and even reports that contracts have not been organized properly all call for some kind of action from the manager in charge. Figure 4.6 outlines the questions that need to be addressed when we are reviewing past events.

It is important that the lessons learnt aspect of the inquiry is built into the terms of reference. It may be that managers need to be on guard for one-off

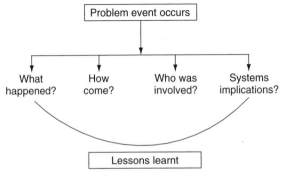

Impact on corporate history and traditions

Figure 4.6   Key questions

occurrences that cause problems. It may be that controls have failed to swing into action and this has led to a major failing. It may also be that someone, or for that matter a whole group of people, has behaved badly in chasing business or in dealing with colleagues or customers. Changes that result from these lessons should be about dealing with aspects of an organization's history and traditions that no longer stand up to close scrutiny. Aggressive sales tactics or creative accounting or unique tax haven schemes may have been the norm in the past, but today may be outlawed or just not seen as the done thing.

In short

All investigations of past events should be grounded in the need to promote a better future.

The present

> **A4M 4.28** *The initial audit process may be applied to reviewing current arrangements with a view to assessing whether any changes are required to promote a healthier and more successful organization. Meanwhile, any unacceptable actions should be dealt with using the agreed corporate procedures.*

This type of review offers much scope for corporate development. Inquiries into the past may be needed to sweep an area clean, but reviews of current arrangements are about what is happening right now. There are two approaches to current reviews, the first of which is set out in Figure 4.7.

Here we are concerned with the way objectives are achieved through the set performance framework, where standards are established and progress is monitored through key performance indicators (KPIs). Compliance with this

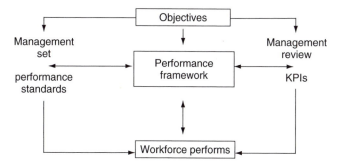

Figure 4.7   Performance and review

system is the basis for most review work in terms of getting the entire performance process to work well.

A better approach to managing people is found in Figure 4.8, where we introduce the POAC format. That is a new focus on pride, ownership, accountability and capability.

Here the review will move away from the old version of performance management and consider:

- **Pride**. Do people have pride in their work and an honest belief in what they are doing with and for the entity?
- **Ownership**. Do people feel part of the entity and empowered to get involved and make decisions at local level?
- **Accountability**. Have people got a clear and accepted idea of what they are accountable for and how they account for their responsibilities?
- **Capability**. Are people fully equipped and geared up to deliver the set objectives with enthusiasm and a clear sense of purpose?

The POAC factors can be superimposed over the regular performance framework with a further addition. That is an additional process of identifying risks and then designing controls to tackle these risks with support from management. The rigid KPI format is replaced by a more dynamic risk management process, and monitoring by line management is replaced by support for the adopted risk management process from the same line management. The KPIs are therefore derived from the risk management process rather than the standard rules imposed from top management. An audit process that considers this new framework in Figure 4.8, rather than the first, old-fashioned version in Figure 4.7, will have a real effect on the way people work and how they are able to get involved in their duties.

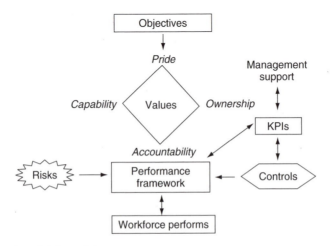

Figure 4.8   The POAC model

In short

New ways of thinking mean that a management review of a business line may shift from its previous focus on performance to be complemented by an additional focus on risk management and improvement.

The future

> **A4M 4.29**   *The initial audit process may be applied to considering future proposals with a view to assessing whether any action is required to promote a healthier and more successful organization.*

Most organizations are involved in change programmes, and most have quite a few information and general business development projects on the go at any one time. Before launching into a new venture, A4M.99 suggests that any new risks that are likely to emerge from a new venture or change programme should be reviewed and suitable controls developed to ensure there is a good chance of success. To make sure that A4M.99 is applied properly, there needs to be a sound context for it in place. Figure 4.9 sets out a dated framework for assessing future business developments.

Everything starts with the corporate mission and this needs to be in place and understood by all before we can make progress. This mission is matched

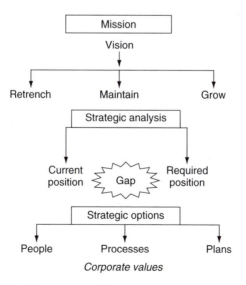

Figure 4.9   Old-fashioned strategic analysis

with a vision of what the business could look like if the right strategy were in place. All organizations must decide whether to **maintain, retrench** or for that matter **grow** their business – or develop a mix of all three for different business lines. The strategic analysis will help determine the gap that needs to be addressed. The rest of the work is about getting the right people, processes and basic plans in place, all set within the view that whatever is done is done in the right way; that is, in line with the corporate values. We can build the initial audit process into strategy formation to arrive at a more modern framework for assessing future business in Figure 4.10.

Figure 4.10 incorporates risk assessment (i.e. the audit) within the strategy formation and internal factors such as the various specialist teams and their attitudes towards KPIs, complaints, budgets and projects. External factors such as the economy, customers, partners, the media and investors will also be taken on board. At all stages, risks and the way they are addressed and controlled will form the basis for all the underlying initial audit activity, as highlighted in our model.

In short

Audit work by the manager is well spent when directed towards future ventures and a consideration of risks and controls can mean that we can claim a better chance of success.

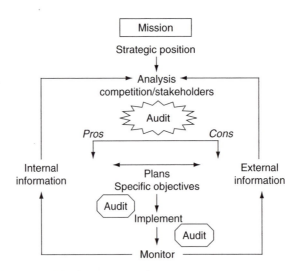

Figure 4.10   A new model of strategic analysis

Making choices

> **A4M 4.30** *When using the initial audit process to assess the extent to which existing and potential risks are being managed, consideration should be given to the need to ensure that the most appropriate initial audit approach is applied.*

The COSO ERM says that:

> Senior managers usually assign responsibility for specific ERM procedures to managers in specific functions or departments. Accordingly, these managers usually play a hands-on role in devising and executing particular risk procedures that address unit objectives, such as techniques for event identification and risk assessment, and in determining responses such as developing authorization procedures for purchasing raw materials or accepting new customers. They also make recommendations on related control activities, monitor their application and meet with upper-level managers to report on the control activities' functioning.[1]

There are many ways that audit tools can help ensure strategic decisions are soundly based. Moreover, because the audit approach is based on an ethical platform, there is always regard to the risk to various compliance and reporting obligations as well as the more traditional reference to operational efficiency. So we are also concerned with values such as being responsive, respectable, effective, safe and entirely accountable. There is one model that can help consolidate this viewpoint and assesses the impact of three Es, As, Ps and Vs on a business as follows:

- 3Es – economy, efficiency and effectiveness.
- 3As – assessment, acceptability and accountability.
- 3Ps – position, people and performance.
- 3Vs – vision, values and verification.

There are several issues relating to the use of A4M.99 for advancing the business in the right direction and audit tools can be applied in any given situation. When determining the best approach to use, consideration should be given to various factors, including:

- The role of the commissioning party (CP). Each level 1 and 2 audit (see Table 4.1) should be authorized by a commissioning party. That is a specific manager who asks that the work be done, authorizes resources and sets reporting lines. It should be clear at the outset whether the CP can make executive decisions.

- The adopted audit approach should be used for a defined purpose and this should form part of the plan for the work.
- Responsibility for actioning any decisions that arise from audit work should rest with the most appropriate manager in line with normal business practice.
- There is a need to make clear decisions based on outcomes from audits, including any findings, advice and recommendations.
- A focus group should be convened to discuss the subject at hand, drawing from experiences and their position in the organization. In this way we can gather views, feelings and attitudes. This forum with, say, six to ten people can be used to generate further questions, where a good facilitator can explain purpose and process, put people at ease and help promote positive interaction.

A really useful way of looking at risk and how it affects an operation is set out in Figure 4.11.

Some explanation of Figure 4.11 is required:

A. In pursuit of the mission the business managers need to establish an appropriate operation.
B. Risks will naturally arise at both strategic and operational levels and these will vary in impact and whether they are likely to materialize or not.
C. Controls are needed to mitigate aspects of those risks that have an unacceptable impact on the business.
D. What is left is residual risk and, hopefully, this will have a limited impact on the business.
E. The impact of the residual risk will affect the outcomes and the ability to deliver the mission to a lesser or greater extent.
F. The residual risk is okay and can be tolerated if it fits within the corporate risk appetite and is accepted by the key stakeholders.

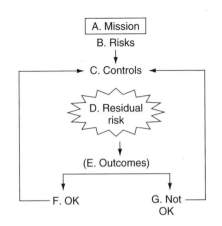

Figure 4.11   Focusing on residual risk

G. Residual risk may be outside the scope of the tolerance and so cause an imbalance, in that the entity is not performing in line with its own internal policies or is not able to broadcast its actual risk exposure as it would not be accepted by its investors and stakeholders.

In short

It takes time to work through the way controls address issues, challenges and threats and the only surefire way to perform a systematic and reliable assessment is to conduct a structured review that makes sense and is geared to the risk and control dimensions.

Common mistakes

> **A4M 4.31**   *The initial audit process may be used to secure reliable evidence regarding the manner in which decisions about corporate resources are being made in response to known risks.*

Scenario one

Managers have a duty of care in accounting for past performance, current procedures and future strategies. This duty extends to accounting to investigators for problems that happened on their watch, current working practices and future plans.

Figure 4.12   Helping busy managers

Scenario two

The A4M.99 process turns much of this on its head by suggesting that the scenario should change to the following:

Managers have a duty of care in accounting for past performance, current procedures and future strategies. This duty extends to carrying out reviews of problems that happened on their watch, reviewing current working practices and formulating sound future plans.

Is it that simple?

There is much that could go wrong in moving from scenario one to scenario two:

- **Managers not empowered to perform their own audits**. Where there is no provision for empowering managers, then the initial audit concept becomes more like a good idea than a real business tool.
- **Managers not equipped to perform their own audits**. Where managers have not been supported and trained in the approach and techniques, the scale of engagement will be much reduced.
- **Audits seen as involving blame-based investigations of past events**. Where the audit concept is perceived as blame-driven investigations, the real benefits from auditing will not be achieved and people will be put off.
- **Concentration on mechanistic approaches such as questionnaires**. Where the audit approach is immersed in surveys and questionnaires, a mechanical format will develop and real issues may get left behind.
- **Ignoring the three aspects of performance, compliance and assurance**. Where the audit concept is not integrated with the performance management systems, compliance mechanisms and the giving of assurances, it will sit outside the heart of good risk management.
- **Excessive rules so that there is no flexibility to the audit product**. Where the format and methods for performing initial audits are too rigid, there will be less chance to focus on local circumstances and suit the tool to the context.
- **Failure to appreciate the stakeholder role in the initial audit process**. Where the audit work is not seen as having any value to stakeholders, it will be narrow and inward looking.
- **Confusion over levels 1, 2, 3 and 4 audits**. Where there is no clear guidance on different levels of audits, the entire concept may become blurred and fragmented.
- **No real appreciation of the POAC model** (Figure 4.8). Where there is no consideration of the importance of pride, ownership, accountability and capability, the audit work may become vague and less valuable.
- **No real attempt to integrate the audit task into the business process** (Figure 4.10). Where the audit work is mainly seen as an additional burden, it will be hard to draw links into current business priorities.

Helpful models for overcoming problems

There are several models that are helpful in overcoming some of the problems mentioned above. We start with Figure 4.13.

Figure 4.13 demonstrates the effect of enforcing controls over people. This is in contrast to the A◀M.99 approach, where we get managers and their work teams to design their own controls. Our cycle suggests that the mistrust and negativity implicit where controls are forced onto people enhances the need to check and inspect that they are actually being employed properly. This in turn creates resistance and leads to the need to impose more and further controls to enforce compliance. This model contrasts with Figure 4.14, which is closer to the A◀M.99 principles.

In Figure 4.14 controls are based around a good understanding of risk management and audit reviews, which are an essential part of the risk management

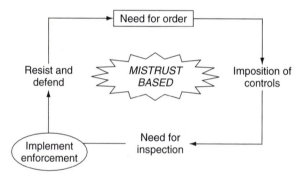

Figure 4.13   Trust and controls (Part One)

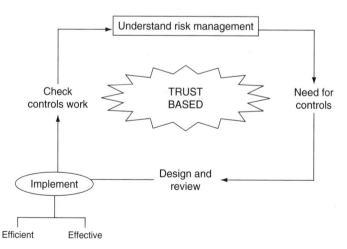

Figure 4.14   Trust and controls (Part Two)

process. This is used by workers to identify key risks and the need for controls so that they can be discussed and designed. Once people are engaged in control design and understand the need to use their controls and comply, we can hope for a trust-based culture. This is not to say that what is produced should not be open to regular checks, it is just that the initial audit provides a starting place for all other, more formal audit work.

A further step is to move on from a trust-based format to a more realistic accountability-based one. Figure 4.15 shows how we may try to get to this even more demanding level.

Here, instead of saying to staff 'Go ahead and design whatever controls you like', we are saying that there are corporate standards that everyone has to honour, but over and above this there may be further steps the local team members may want to apply to help them succeed. So enforcement moves to trust and then on to accountability as a further goal. Figure 4.15 suggests that the implementation of controls is about ensuring those controls are efficient, effective but also agreed with the people at the sharp end. In this model people at work want to check for compliance, even where there may be outsiders who may want to make a further check, just to be on the safe side.

Figure 4.16 addresses the concept of change management as it affects control design and argues that there are four main stages of balancing change and stability:

1. Here change is resisted and most people are looking for stability. This happens in slow and stagnant organizations, but could also affect those that have been going through rapid changes and need some time off to consolidate and reflect.
2. Type 2 set-ups need no further mention as they are not that significant.

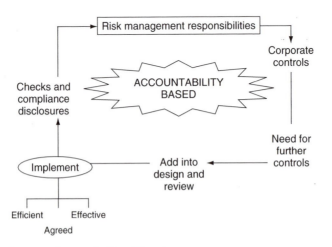

Figure 4.15   Trust and controls (Part Three)

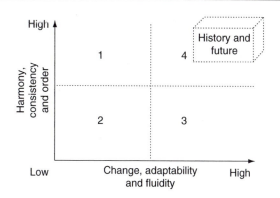

Figure 4.16 Building on corporate history

3. Type 3 goes to the other extreme by encouraging change as the norm. These entities will be trying to meet brand new challenges or moving out of periods of poor performance.
4. The final scenario is quite interesting. Here the organization holds on to the traditions and overall direction, but at the same time is flexible and alters to take on new ideas and projects. It rather parallels Figure 3.13 where there are certain important values that are retained as being part of the organization, while local aspects alter and flex to reflect local circumstances and demands.

Risk assessment and control design need to be set within the context of the organization and the type of change strategy that is in place. So rapid change organizations need to work on controls that can quickly fix brand new risks as they appear over the horizon, while those that are slowing down for a bit need to work on rethinking tried and trusted controls to make sure they can deal with known quantities as well as possible. The final Figure is 4.17.

Here the manager becomes the coach and translates the corporate vision into something that makes sense to front-line people and lets them get on with the

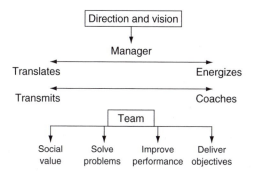

Figure 4.17 The manager as coach

task; that is, dealing with delivery through good performance and problem solving, while maintaining positive social systems to make this happen.

In short

Devolving the audit task to managers is no mean feat. It takes time and trouble to get around the many problems that are associated with rethinking accountabilities, trust frames and different ways of fitting audit work into the strategic direction of the business.

Check your progress

> **A4M 4.32** *Management should employ the initial audit process wherever there is a need to review any issues that fall within their area of responsibility. The results of such reviews should be considered in determining whether there is a need to conduct a more detailed review by external specialists.*

One tool that can be applied to track your progress is to test the extent to which you have assimilated the key points raised in this chapter. The multi-choice questions below will check your progress and the answer guide in Appendix D is based on what is most appropriate in the context of this book. Please record your answers in the table at Appendix D. You may also record the time spent on each test and enter this information in the 'Mins' column of Appendix D.

Name ....

Start time .... **Finish time** .... **Total minutes** ....

Multi-choice quiz

1. Insert the missing phrase.
Initial auditing tools include .... :

  a. meetings, surveys, interviewing people and evidence evaluation.
  b. workshops, surveys, interviewing people and evidence evaluation.
  c. workshops, instructions, interviewing people and evidence evaluation.
  d. workshops, surveys, questionnaires and evidence evaluation.

2. Select the most appropriate sentence.
a. We have said several times that auditing for managers, or what we have also called internal auditing, is about giving power back to the front line.
b. We have said several times that auditing for managers, or what we have also called initial auditing, is about giving power back to the manager.
c. We have said several times that auditing for managers, or what we have also called external auditing, is about giving power back to the front line.
d. We have said several times that auditing for managers, or what we have also called initial auditing, is about giving power back to the front line.

3. Insert the missing word.
The type of audit in question really needs to be determined at the outset, as this will have an impact on the approach, ... and whether it will result in sensitivities for the business and people concerns.

a. standards of evidence.
b. standards of interviewing.
c. compliance checks.
d. fear factor.

4. Insert the missing phrase.
Good .... is about good organizations that are able to isolate and deal with anything that presents a threat to their continuing good name.

a. security.
b. planning.
c. governance.
d. ethics.

5. Select the most appropriate sentence.
a. It is important that the disciplinary action aspect of the inquiry is built into the terms of reference.
b. It is important that the lessons learnt aspect of the inquiry is built into the terms of reference.
c. It is important that the lessons learnt aspect of the inquiry is left for another day.
d. It is important that the naming and shaming aspect of the inquiry is built into the terms of reference.

6. Select the most appropriate phrase.
The POAC model is about:

a. pride, ownership, accountability and capability.
b. power, ownership, accountability and capability.

c. pride, ownership, accountability and composure.

d. pride, ownership, access and capability.

7. Insert the missing phrase.
Everything starts with the corporate mission and this needs to be ....
by all before we can make progress.

a. in place and documented.

b. standardized and understood.

c. in place and understood.

d. standardized and documented.

8. Insert the missing phrase.
There is one model that can help consolidate this viewpoint where we assess
the impact of three Es:

a. economy, efficiency and effectiveness.

b. economy, effort and effectiveness.

c. economy, efficiency and effort.

d. e-commerce, efficiency and effectiveness.

9. Insert the missing word.
The .... risk is okay and can be tolerated if it fits within the corporate risk appetite and is accepted by the key stakeholders.

a. inherent.

b. residual.

c. respite.

d. real.

10. Which is the odd one out?
One way of getting a perspective on the above matters is to categorize the audit
concept into three main approaches:

a. management investigations into specific events.

b. managers' audit of systems of internal control.

c. control risk self-assessment workshops by work teams.

d. management surveillance of staff activities.

Newsflash – read all about it

There is so much behind the move towards effective governance and risk
management in all walks of life, and a small selection of relevant examples is
provided to illustrate this new way of thinking.

10 new dimensions

Old thinking	New dimensions	A suitable example
Mind your step.	We will take all available steps to ensure you do not slip.	In the interests of 'public safety' the floor at a town hall has been coated with a nonslip substance – which puts an end to carefree whisks, locks, swivels, pivots and hip twists for dancers of a weekly dance class.[2]
Where a system does not work, we can expect some degree of failure; unfortunately, it's just a fact of life.	Where a system does not work, we can expect some degree of failure; unfortunately it can be a matter of life and death.	Two of the world's most powerful medical organizations have been accused of medical malpractice for knowingly promoting useless drugs that have led to the deaths of hundreds of thousands of children.[3]
There are no guarantees when it comes to pensions.	Organizations must bear some responsibility for the future welfare of their employees.	Protests were held in Scotland Yard (HQ of the London Metropolitan Police) to reinforce the view that pensions robbery was happening in many companies.[4]
The doctor knows best.	So-called experts may not be right all the time – and when they are wrong, it can be traumatic.	A leading children's doctor is immersed in a scandal over claims that he wrongly accused parents of assaults. The suggestion is that a few medical experts followed a set dogma rather than assess each child's symptoms properly.[5]
Schools are places and not procedure-bound businesses.	Those responsible for resources should be made to account for the way they discharge their responsibilities.	A headmistress was found guilty of stealing up to £500 000 from school funds to live the high life. One staff member said, 'People went in absolute fear of her. She brooked no opposition. Now we know why. She did not want anyone to interrupt her ride on the gravy train.'[6]
Common sense is all that is needed to get by in life.	Common sense is all very well, but where there is a real risk, we need to make sure it is properly addressed.	One writer questions why a council should decree that it takes up to four social care workers to change a light bulb: 'That means that when one staff member is changing the bulb there must be another on hand to hold the ladder. And a third, if the wiring is not up to scratch, to switch off the electricity and stand by while the bulb is being changed. And, should the client be at all frail or anxious, a fourth home care worker to keep him calm until this perilous operation is completed. Why not a fifth to drive the council people carrier? Or a sixth to feed the parking meter? Or a seventh to make them all a nice cup of tea?'[7]

(Continued)

Old thinking	New dimensions	A suitable example
Common sense is all very well, but where there is a real risk, we need to make sure it is properly addressed.	Common sense is all that is needed to get by in life.	I knew it. Turn my back for half a minute and Tony Blair is into my bathroom pointing at the basin and shrieking. There is terror in the taps, fear in the faucets, panic in the plugholes. He orders his Health and Safety Executives stormtroopers to my brass-necked weapon of mass destruction. They constitute a major and imminent threat.[8]
Vulnerable people such as the mentally ill receive all the care they need in a caring society.	People are not always aware of what goes on behind closed doors in sensitive areas such as mental health.	The mental health system is in disarray with psychiatric wards overcrowded, chaotic and unhygienic and people being prescribed out-of-date medicines, a report has found.[9]
If you want to make sure someone is competent just keep testing them.	Testing is a control that, like any other control, should be used with care – it can only do so much.	Pupils are 'punch drunk' with testing by the time they sit their GCSE exams, a teachers' leader said yesterday . . . during their schooling, youngsters will have sat more than 100 national tests – far more than any other country.[10]
There are many controls to protect a local community, including rigid rules for obtaining planning permissions.	For every rule, there is a loophole that may be exploited.	The latest outrage on the architectural scene is the growing practice by developers of hiring leading architectural names to obtain planning permission and then handing over the project to others – not necessarily even qualified architects – probably to save on costs. In the process the whole integrity and quality of the design can be lost or badly eroded.[11]

The key messages

The last section of each chapter contains a short story or quote that should provide an interesting format for illustrating some of the book's key messages.

Is red really red?

'Jack, how are you going to implement the new rationalization policy?'

'You mean the staff reductions. No problem. I'll delete all the South East Region posts and merge them with the South West site. Then we'll ask people to join the South West operation and those that do not want to can get off.'

'You mean, you'll set up a redundancy package?'

'Yes. We can relocate some of them, but there are too many faces for the numbers we need to have at the end of the day.'

'Are you going to delete the South West posts and then ask everyone to apply for what's left?'

'Not really. I'll concentrate on the South East, since that's the one we're shutting down. We did a risk workshop with the HR people and senior reps from both regions and we got a pretty good strategy from this. It's about shifting people and trying to get the good ones to stay and the poor performers to move on.'

'That's not easy, there's a risk that good people will leave and many others might complain. Even go on strike if we're not careful.'

'Ah...The UK board has set a risk tolerance and we used this in the workshop when we gauged what the big risks were.'

'What was their tolerance level?'

'The policy code says...Hold on, I've got it here. It says, "All risks should be contained within the amber spectrum and no red risks will be approved in any strategy document, until they are realigned to amber."'

'Did you have any red risks?'

'At first. We had loads of high-level risks but we got them all down to amber, after putting in a few safeguards.'

'Really?'

'I mean, the risk of compensation claims from South East staff was pretty big, but we will be putting in an appeals process to counter this.'

'So it went down to amber?'

'No problem. We talked it through and agreed that it was now amber.'

'How do you know something's red?'

'It's how we feel about it. Jenson – you know, the South West regional director – said that no one goes home until all reds are amber. So we all sat around and got there.'

'Why did Jenson insist on this?'

'He loses his bonus if he allows red risks to stay on the system for more than one quarter.'

'So you got rid of them?'

'Yes. We kept suggesting things until we could reassign all reds to amber. Jenson was very helpful and kept sending out for coffee.'

'So are you within the tolerance?'

'Absolutely.'

'What is a red risk to you?'

'Look. Why all the questions? Red is something that Jenson does not want. And if he doesn't want it, it goes.'

'So you're within the board's risk appetite?'

'I don't really know much about this. All I know is that we do not have any reds. In fact, Sharon came up with two new reds at around 6 pm but we decided that they could go down as amber.'

'Why?'

'Because it was getting late and you can't go on for ever and ever. We've all got real work to do – and we stopped after we got to our top ten risks.'

'So risk appetite is described as what?'

'It's what Jenson wants it to be, okay? Anyway, I'm sick and tired of talking about risk. We've done the risk register and Jenson's happy, the board's happy and I've sent a copy off to the global board and they're okay with it. So long as there are no reds, everyone's happy. So why don't you relax and leave well alone?'

'Okay, just checking. I've got to do my risk register tomorrow and I just want to make sure I come up with the right answers. I'd rather be dead than red.'

Notes

1. Committee of Sponsoring Organizations, Enterprise Risk Management, draft framework at July 2004, page 94 (www.coso.org).
2. *Daily Telegraph*, Saturday, April 10, 2004, page 3.
3. *The Independent*, Thursday, April 8, 2004, World News, page 22.
4. *The Mail on Sunday*, Sunday, April 11, 2004, page 15.
5. *Daily Mail*, Thursday, March 4, 2004, page 6.
6. *Daily Mail*, Wednesday, July 16, 2003, page 5.
7. *Daily Mail*, Monday, March 29, 2004, page 14, Keith Waterhouse.
8. *The Times*, Wednesday, January 7, 2004, page 16, Simon Jenkins.
9. *The Independent*, Wednesday, April 7, 2004, Home News, page 6.
10. *The Independent*, Tuesday, April 6, 2004, Home News, page 7.
11. *The Times*, Monday, April 19, 2004, The Register, page 52.

5 The manager's initial audit

A friendly eye could never see such faults.

William Shakespeare, *Julius Caesar*, Act IV, Scene 3

> **A4M Statement E** *An annual A4M.99 management initial audits (MIA) programme should be planned and applied by all managers to ensure the best application of this technique throughout the organization.*

Introduction

> **A4M 5.33** *A contact point should be available to managers that may be used for giving timely help and advice concerning the manager's initial audit process.*

Figure 1.1 in Chapter 1 shows how the book is put together. Chapter 5 describes the way managers can carry out their own reviews. We have discussed the way risks drive a business, in that it has to reposition itself to meet the challenges that are provided by new and changing risks. Likewise, internal controls have to shift to keep up with these changes. Since each manager should contribute to the entity's published statement on internal controls, there needs to be a review of controls to make this statement meaningful. One approach is for managers to carry out an initial audit of controls and present the results to the internal auditor for some form of validation. Our view of the manager's initial audit is not just a question of each manager sniffing around and asking staff whether everything is okay, it is more about having a set of standards derived from something such as the A4M.99 values that means the review will live up to external assessment. The idea is that the manager can do whatever works best so long as these values are observed and the standards for such reviews are used as guidance (see Appendix A).

Initial auditing

The manager's review of internal controls in line with the principles of A4M.99 is seen as an initial audit. This means that instead of the auditors turning up to review the controls in a particular part of an organization, we are asking managers to review their arrangements for dealing with risk, and then present these results to the company auditors if necessary. The auditors may assess this initial attempt to make sure controls work and are being used properly before they in turn carry out their own work. The hope is that auditors will focus on the reliability of these initial audits and then decide whether they need to carry out any further work.

In short

Empowering business managers to deliver is happening everywhere. But when we start devolving the real taboo things like meaningful audits, empowerment takes on a whole new meaning – it gives a licence to our front-line people to exercise real power and control over their work.

Leading with risk

> **A4M 5.34** *The manager's initial audit process should focus on high levels of residual risk and the way in which business controls are actually operating in response to changing risks.*

We start with risk, since this has been a theme of the book. The focus of the initial audit process is well described by COSO ERM:

> Often evaluations take the form of self-assessment, where persons responsible for a particular unit or function determine the effectiveness of enterprise risk management for their activities.[1]

In pursuit of this sentiment, the initial auditing equation is simple:

1. Managers are responsible for delivering objectives.
2. There are risks that create uncertainty, which mean this is not always straightforward.

3. The implications of these risks brings out the need for effective controls to establish an acceptable degree of certainty.
4. Managers have to establish controls to ensure their people have a reasonable chance to deliver the goods.
5. Meanwhile, the manager has to tell senior executives whether the controls are working well.
6. The auditors review the more significant controls to confirm whether or not they are working well.
7. The executives in turn publicize the fact that organizational controls have been reviewed.
8. And everyone is happy.

It is point 5 above that is the issue. Managers need to carry out regular reviews of their controls to make sure they are working well. In our world, point 6 changes to: 'the internal auditors will judge whether management's review of their controls (and therefore assurances that these managers are giving to the board) is reliable or not.'

Meanwhile, the gap between points 4 and 5 above can represent the distance between what staff are supposed to be doing, what we believe controls are achieving, and how we believe staff are applying these controls – and the reality. The initial audit is about checking that controls have been designed well and that they are being used properly. The first thing to do is to get to grips with the real issues and Figure 5.1 illustrates this point.

Murky waters

The first thing a manager needs to do is to look into the murky water and find out what is really happening in the business unit in question. The traditional

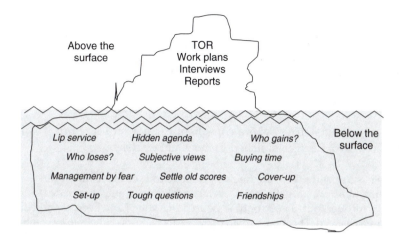

Figure 5.1   Murky waters

points of contact and performance framework rely on work plans, performance targets, annual appraisal interviews, staff meetings and progress reports from each team. In this world, there is a clear picture of the issues at hand. The real picture in terms of how people perceive risk and how they ensure prescribed methods for managing these risks is often hidden and this hidden world is much more difficult to grasp. Many people pay lip service to the policies in place and some even have a hidden agenda based on who gains from their action and who does not. For example:

> An occupying army that runs a prison for local detainees may operate a barbaric system of punishment and abuse in breach of the official authorized standards and this may be hidden from their superiors for some time.

Some teams have a very subjective interpretation of formal procedures and work as they please, covering up problems and taking sides in terms of supporting some colleagues and not others. Some intimidate weaker co-workers and even bully others. Meanwhile, they do favours for some customers and suppliers and are very strict with others.

> Senior management at a national chain of estate agents did not realize that staff in some local offices were trying to sell overpriced property to naive buyers while underpricing prime properties to their 'friends'.

The manager needs to know that what should be happening does happen.

> In one large retail outfit, the policy is that staff should open up extra tills whenever there is a queue of more than two people at one of the live tills. When the manager is out, the staff sit around in small groups and ignore the queues that build up on the few tills that are open.

There are some controls that are really important and where compliance is poor, there could be repercussions.

> In one government office, security staff are supposed to check badges and visitor identification before allowing people into offices where sensitive information is held. The front-desk people have not been told that the offices hold high-risk material and take a very lax view of this procedure, tending to wave people in whenever there is a large number of visitors or the visitor is well dressed.

There are some instances where compliance is not an issue but it is just that controls have not been established to meet all key risks.

> In one leisure centre there are frequent changes to exercise workout times and dates and the published programme of events quickly falls out of date. Many members turn up for workout classes only to be told that they have been cancelled or times have been changed. There is no control in place that allows changes to be communicated to members and people who enquire about classes. To make things worse, there is no

procedure to update printed programmes on a regular basis and make them available to visitors.

If the leisure centre manager commissioned an initial audit, it would be clear that there was a problem that called for better controls. Most managers are busy planning work, solving problems, getting resources in place and dealing with *ad hoc* issues that team members need sorting out. The manager also has to act as a contact with head office and ensure that changes and new strategies are properly implemented in the business unit, local office or project team.

The initial audit process is a chance for the manager to get someone to check that controls make sense and work. This is a chance for someone to take some time out and consider whether suitable procedures are in place. There are certain questions that the manager's initial audit will address, including:

- **Clear the air**. At times we need to find out what is happening in our teams so that nagging problems can be addressed.
- **What helps us**. The audit may come back with ideas for changes that may help people perform and help everyone deliver on time and to standard.
- **What hinders us**. There are issues that get in the way of progress and an audit can isolate them and suggest ways of overcoming constraints.
- **Assess forces**. Within an organization there are forces that act to promote positive change and those that work against it. The audit should take on board how these forces affect the way risks are being managed.
- **Public face – and real happenings**. One major benefit from the audit will be a view of what is really happening at work. This is about the way controls are working and whether there are any inherent risks that just cannot be kept at bay. This reality check should enable the manager to say with force, 'I have reviewed my system of internal control and am taking action to remedy any unacceptable positions due to unmitigated risks.'

In short

The manager's initial audit is not about checking on staff. If you need to know what people are doing, then go out and ask them. But if you need to check whether risks are being controlled properly, then this takes a bit more time and effort.

Overall strategy

> **A4M 5.35** *All employees should communicate any concerns they have with the state of organizational controls and the behaviour of people employed by or associated with the organization to their line manager or nominated person.*

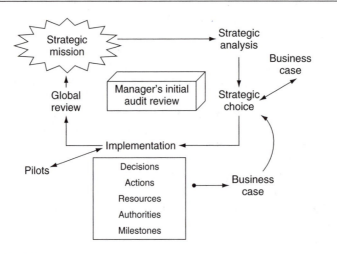

Figure 5.2 The MIA

We have said that the manager's initial audit (MIA) is not just about getting someone to sniff around a bit, it is a high-level attempt to meet business needs and formal disclosure requirements. It is an attempt to make sure the corporate reputation is not messed up by poor operational standards. The initial audit may concentrate on financial, operational, compliance or change issues or be a combination of these. It is also necessary to fit the initial audit into and inside the strategic framework. One version of this relationship is shown in Figure 5.2.

In this way the audit is seen to sit within the overall strategy and comment on the way risk assessment and internal control is built into the way strategy is analysed and implemented. Likewise, the manager should take a strategic approach to reviewing risk, controls and compliance by developing the following ten standards:

1. **Charter**. There should be a charter approved by the executive directors that states that each business manager should perform regular audits across their areas of responsibility. The charter should say something about the work being performed in line with set standards (see Appendix A).
2. **Strategy**. The manager should ensure that the audits fit the strategic framework, as suggested by Figure 5.2.
3. **Annual plan**. The manager should develop a plan of audits that sets out the reviews that should be carried out for the year in question. It is important that high-risk systems are checked at some time during the year.
4. **Programme of audits**. The annual plan should be broken down into a programme of audits for each quarter. The quarterly period is quite important in terms of disclosure reporting, as regulators need annual statements and the quarterly period also features in many codes.

5. **Audit preparation**. Some background work should be done before the field work commences. This involves setting the terms of reference, times involved and who will do the work and how.
6. **Field work**. This is the main stage and involves checking the way risks are addressed and whether smart controls are in place. We will be looking for things like errors, poor procedures, poor awareness and control failure.
7. **Assessing results**. The results should be got together and used to note any changes that are required to current actions.
8. **Amend risk register**. The whole point of the exercise is to ensure that the risk registers reflect a true position by double checking whether they need to be amended at all.
9. **Reporting**. Reports should be prepared to reflect any actions required and to provide formal disclosures each quarter and get this information to the board, auditors and audit committee.
10. **Follow-up**. The manager needs to keep an eye on everything that spins off from the review to make sure that what is supposed to happen does happen.

Note that many of the above 10 items will be discussed later in this chapter.

In short

In future, someone starting work in a section will automatically ask their new manager, 'How do you audit your systems in this section?' When we get to this stage, the quarterly and annual statements on internal control will start to make sense.

Planning

> **A4M 5.36** *Each manager should submit an annual plan of MIA activities for approval by senior management and/or the board.*

When setting up an initial audit process, the manager needs to take care. The starting place is to set out in writing what is meant by the manager's initial audit. Such a document may well include reference to:

1. **The aims of initial auditing**. This could run along the lines of: to oversee a programme of reviews of the extent to which internal controls are adequate and effective, and report on such reviews to inform the board's statement on internal control.
2. **Respective roles and responsibilities**. Here we need to make it clear that the manager should use this technique or an approved alternative way of

assessing controls in their area of responsibility. The person chosen to carry out a particular review has a responsibility to perform such work to the standards set out by the organization. There is an additional responsibility to bring to the manager's attention anything that interferes with the ability to deliver an effective audit. All employees have a duty to cooperate with any audits and contribute to ensuring controls are sound, which includes informing their manager of any control weaknesses directly or via the audit.

3. **Access**. The person who is asked to conduct the initial audit should have access to all books, records, information and explanations needed to complete the work. All such information may only be used in the discharge of the set objectives of the audit and must conform with corporate standards for document confidentiality, storage and retention.

4. **Scope**. The scope of all initial audits should be approved by the appropriate business manager and should be geared towards providing assurances on risk management and internal control.

5. **Independence**. The manager should take all reasonable steps to ensure that initial audits are carried out without fear or favour; that is, in as objective a manner as possible. The fact that the manager is reviewing systems that they are responsible for means that it cannot be done independently, in the full sense of the word. Nonetheless, the work should be conducted as objectively as possible.

6. **Professionalism**. The charter should note that all initial audits should be carried out to the standards set by the organization, and that the manager is responsible for ensuring that this is the case in all reports that are submitted.

7. **Fair and balanced**. All initial audit work should be done in a fair and balanced manner and any complaints should be submitted to the business manager in question, who will need to respond to any matters that are raised.

8. **Methodology**. The initial audit work should be carried out in a methodological manner that ensures they are planned, controls assessed and tests made where appropriate.

9. **Quality assurance**. The manager should establish a process for ensuring that the quality of initial audits have been carried out to acceptable standards.

10. **Reporting**. All reports resulting from the audit should be distributed in line with set standards.

The annual plan of initial audits

The business manager needs to formulate an annual plan of reviews that tackle high-risk aspects of the business. Planning is important because it means that resources may be committed to the work and applied in the best way possible.

It is a good idea to interface the initial audit process with the risk management process to address high-risk areas. One approach follows:

1. Establish a risk assessment process where staff are able to identify and assess risks to the achievement of their objectives.
2. Get them to formulate a risk register to reflect the work done and action needed to tackle weak controls and known problems.
3. Take the risk registers and work out where the high-risk areas are and where there are key controls in place to tackle these risks.
4. Formulate an annual plan of initial audits where the high-risk areas are further reviewed. Where there are key controls in place, they can be checked to find out to what extent they are being applied in practice.
5. Assign audits to specific quarters in the annual plan and allocate each one to an appropriate person.
6. Prepare a short brief for each audit that sets out what should be done, by whom, when and how.
7. Review and update the annual plan whenever there are significant changes to the risk profile or the risk register.

It may be possible to plan for each material part of the business group to be reviewed over the course of the year. This will enable the management team in question to report that they have reviewed all significant controls over their part of the business and have addressed the need to ensure that effective risk management is in place.

Preparation for each audit

There are some important considerations before we launch into a live audit. The four main questions to ask are:

1. What are we trying to achieve?
2. How do we do it?
3. How long have we got?
4. Who should do it?

1. What are we trying to achieve?

This is about setting really tight terms of reference, which should identify exactly what will be considered and to what extent. For example:

> To confirm whether the risk of managing temporary staff in section X is being conducted in line with divisional guidelines covering value for money, security vetting and attendance monitoring.

2. *How do we do it?*

The next matter to be addressed in planning the audit relates to the way such work is performed. For example:

> The audit will involve checking the procedures for:
>
> - employing temporary staff in section X,
> - security vetting and reference verification,
> - time-sheet monitoring and payment authorization.
>
> This will involve a consideration of a random sample of 10% of temps employed during the last quarter.

3. *How long have we got?*

A time budget should be set. For example:

> The audit will require one person spending two days, starting from A to B.

4. *Who should do it?*

This is a major consideration. The manager's review means that a resource has to be committed to the performance of regular audits of high-risk parts of an operation. There is no way a manager can sign a statement that internal controls have been reviewed and they are satisfactory, if there is no budget to perform this work. In the past the argument was that internal control design was something that was incorporated into the job. Where controls needed fixing, they got fixed. The new era of accountability and transparency means that where there are major risks that mean certain controls are fundamental to success, we need to expend an extra effort in making sure they are okay. Since the internal auditor cannot be everywhere and do everything, we are now asking business managers to have a go.

The manager can actually do the audits and in a smaller unit this may well be the answer. In the above example, the manager may spend a day reviewing the arrangements for employing temporary staff to make sure they are robust and work. In a larger section, the management team can choose someone to perform the work and report directly back to them. It may be that a supervisor or team leader may be taken off-line for a few days and asked to perform the work. If A4M.99 and the initial audit approach are to be successful, there must be a belief that the extra effort required to stand back and review controls is worthwhile. It will not work if this basic premise is not in place. For example:

John Brown has completed his basic A▲M.99 training and will be assigned to the two-day initial audit from periods A to B.

Preliminary survey

For really large sections with a lot going on, it may be necessary to engage in fairly detailed audits. For example:

> Manual file security (high-status customer accounts) has a significant risk rating and a manager's initial audit will be assigned to Sarah Brown for a one-week project starting ABC.

Instead of launching into the work using vague terms of reference such as 'to assess whether there is adequate security over the use and storage of high-status customer manual files', we may be better off doing a 'quick and dirty', one-day check on whether the audit needs doing and if so what terms of reference may be set. This preliminary survey would involve assessing:

- How the system works in outline.
- What level of risk is involved.
- How much attention has been paid to controls so far.
- Whether formal review teams (e.g. internal audit) have carried out detailed work recently.
- Whether there is much scope for a useful initial audit.
- What we should be looking at.
- Any known problems that have come to light so far.
- When it would be best to do it.
- How it should be done.
- Whether it would really be worth the effort.

A briefing note to the management team would address these and other relevant questions and as a result we would work out whether to proceed and if so how. For really large audits, say of the entire staff bonus system in department X, it may be worthwhile holding a short workshop with key players to work out the terms of reference for the work.

In short

The initial auditing concept needs to be worthwhile. Some thought given to planning the audits will help ensure that only valid projects are undertaken and high-risk issues are duly considered.

Field work

> **A4M 5.37** *The MIA process should involve testing the way in which corporate and operational controls are perceived and employed in the area under review.*

The COSO ERM sets out an important challenge for all organizations. For us, the 'evaluator' is the person who has most to lose and who is closest to the action; that is, the manager:

> The evaluator must determine how the system actually works. Procedures designed to operate in a particular way may be modified over time to operate differently or may no longer be performed.[2]

The fieldwork stage of the audit is simply about gathering evidence on the operation of internal controls. We know that controls are needed to manage risks and everyone in the outfit will be doing their best to ensure these are properly in place. The problem is the potential gap between two worlds:

- What should be happening.
- What is actually happening in the field.

Documenting the system

Before controls can be evaluated to judge whether they are well designed and working as intended, it may be necessary to prepare an outline of the system that is being reviewed. It is possible to prepare a simple block diagram or a short narrative that describes the steps involved in the systems in question. It is also possible to prepare a basic flowchart to trace the movement of documents and information and in this way assess the strength of specific controls. If a project approval system is being audited by a manager, a basic flowchart may be used to record key aspects of the system. To illustrate this point, Figure 5.3 gives an example of some flowchart symbols. Figure 5.4 traces part of a project approval system.

Internal control surveys

One short-cut way of performing an evaluation is to use a survey to assess whether the types of controls that should be in place are actually present. For an audit of something simple such as travelling to meetings, we would pose a

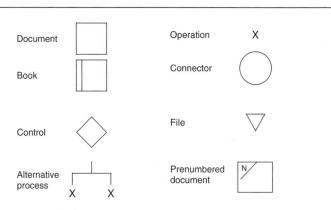

Figure 5.3 Flowchart symbols

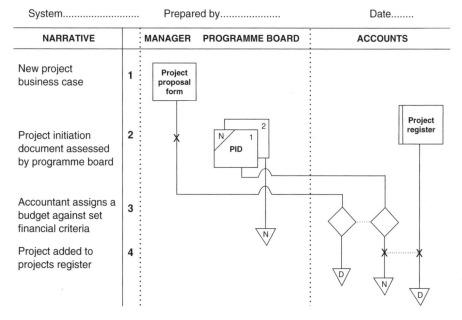

NARRATIVE		MANAGER	PROGRAMME BOARD	ACCOUNTS
New project business case	1	Project proposal form		
Project initiation document assessed by programme board	2		PID	Project register
Accountant assigns a budget against set financial criteria	3			
Project added to projects register	4			

Figure 5.4 Project approval process

series of questions in an internal control questionnaire (ICQ) that is related to the type of controls that should be in place and as a result indicate whether the control is present or not (Yes/No). For controls that are marked 'No', we would explore the consequences and may end up recommending the missing control is put in place, as per Table 5.1.

Field work is about deciding what standards provide our reference point and then working out to what extent these standards are being achieved. The ICQ can be a little rigid in setting out standards and checking that they are being applied.

Table 5.1   ICQ: Travelling to meetings

Question	Controls	Yes	No	Action
Q1	Trips planned in advance or early notification of trip wherever possible	✓		N/A
Q2	All information needed is available and up to date	✓		N/A
Q3	Map downloaded from Internet		✓	Recommend use of Internet in future
Q4	Train tickets bought in advance	✓		N/A
Q5	All information needed is available and up to date	✓		N/A

Internal control matrices

Using the ICQ approach, there is less chance to build in the concept of changing risk profiles and a more dynamic approach is to try to work out the following:

- The objectives for the operation in hand.
- The way risk has been identified and assessed.
- The type of controls that have been designed to mitigate risk.
- Whether these controls are working well.
- The level of residual risk and whether this is acceptable or not.

Using this approach, the field work for a manager's initial audit may consist of the following:

1. Establish (or confirm) the objectives for the operation under review.
2. The stages we go through in this operation.
3. The risks that appear at each stage.
4. The controls we have put in place to mitigate these risks.
5. The tests applied to these controls to judge whether they are working well or not.
6. An opinion on the overall adequacy of internal controls.
7. Any recommendations for improving controls where appropriate.
8. Report on the above.

Going back to our example of travelling to meetings, we can illustrate how this assessment process works through the preparation of a basic internal control evaluation matrix (ICEM). In terms of travelling to meetings, we may set an objective as:

Objectives – to arrive at the right destination at the right time in a relaxed and unhurried manner.

Table 5.2 Internal control evaluation matrix

Stage	Risks	Controls	Tests	Opinion	Recommendations
Need for nonstandard travel arises	Trip not needed	Trips planned in advance or early notification of trip wherever possible	Diary used but not all appointments are confirmed beforehand. Two trips made when not required	Sound controls but the occasional unnecessary trip. No clear criteria for determining whether phone contact is sufficient	Criteria for meetings and confirm all meetings before travelling
Available options considered	Expensive, slow or uncomfortable	All information needed is available and up to date	Internet used to assess all alternatives, but at times train timetable is out of date	Good risk management arrangements – but not all information is up to date	Check train times and road traffic alerts given by Internet sources
Travel route and plan selected	Get lost or take longer than planned	Map downloaded from Internet	Journey plans have been accurate	Good risk management arrangements in place	N/A
Payment made	Unable to obtain a ticket easily	Train tickets bought in advance	Some tickets bought too early and when meeting cancelled, not all funds can be recovered	Timing of purchases not adequate	Need to ensure meetings confirmed before buying train tickets
Travel	Expensive, slow or uncomfortable	All information needed is available and up to date	Some train journeys are crowded and uncomfortable, while 20% of car trips lead to delays and late arrivals	Insufficient attention given to travel conditions at different times of day	Try to arrange meetings and events to minimize overcrowding and road congestion

Stages 1–8 would appear on the internal control evaluation matrix in Table 5.2.

By going through this systematic ICEM process, we can judge whether the current arrangements for travelling to meetings need to be improved, but this time in terms of the actual risks in question.

Testing

The testing column of the ICEM is about looking for evidence of the way risks are being responded to; that is, controlled. To work out whether the 'What should be happening' fits with the 'What is actually happening', managers need to dig into the murky waters (see Figure 5.1) and find out what people really do when arranging their meetings. Testing applies many techniques of discovery, including:

- **Interview**. This is a structured method of asking questions about the operation of risk management and internal control.
- **Examination**. This involves looking at relevant documents and procedures to determine whether they fit with the understanding of what they are supposed to do.
- **Inquiry**. This is exploring a specific issue by researching it further.
- **Observation**. This involves looking at physical occurrences to determine whether what should be happening is happening.
- **Inspection**. This involves checking that specific features of an item are present and correct.
- **Reconcilation**. This involves checking that one set of transactions is consistent with another related set of transactions.
- **Analysis**. This involves scrutinizing an item to determine its true properties.
- **Confirmation**. This involves asking a third party to provide information regarding the existence and accuracy of an item.
- **Verification**. This involves checking that something exists and is presented in a way that is anticipated.
- **Reperformance**. This involves redoing a transaction to judge whether it was properly processed in the first place.
- **Vouching**. This involves comparing one document (or statement) with another document (or statement) to determine that they are accurate or that they are derived from the same source.

Travelling to meetings – testing procedures

Table 5.3 outlines the types of tests that could be applied to the travelling to meetings example.

Table 5.3 Testing procedures

Type of test	For example
Interview	Ask people how they travel to meetings
Examination	Check the diaries to determine whether meetings are booked
Inquiry	Find out whether the Internet provides user-friendly maps
Observation	Take a rush hour train trip and find out how comfortable it is
Inspection	Attend a regular meeting and find out how useful it is
Reconcilation	Compare train tickets issued with train journey approved
Analysis	Plot the trend of cancelled meetings and unnecessary journeys
Confirmation	Find out whether admin team give advice on travelling as claimed
Verification	Check a batch of tickets to see if they match approved trips
Reperformance	Re-calculate travel expenditure claims to see if done properly
Vouching	Tick off train tickets issued with payments made for train journeys

Interviewing

If we need to know how controls are functioning, then rather than spend too much time on the above testing techniques, the best thing to do is ask someone. All the techniques other than interviewing are only relevant when we are dealing with a difficult and high-risk matter where we really need to explore something further. Everything else is covered by simply performing a suitable range of interviews. There are many benefits of carrying out interviews regarding the state of controls, including the following:

- Information comes 'from the horse's mouth'.
- The matter can be confidential if necessary.
- We can explain why the review of controls is being carried out and our approach.
- We can get opinions from the interviewee.
- It is better to ask people about the way controls work rather than analyse and surmise.
- We can get straight to the point and ask direct questions about what works and what does not.
- It is possible to get people to open up and talk about problems.
- People can express any concerns they might have.
- We can get people to answer previously unasked questions.
- It can be a rewarding experience if done properly.

The important thing to remember is that the interview is not a trial by examination. It is just an attempt to find out a bit more about controls and how they are used. The interview process may follow this 10-point format:

1. State the objectives of the interview.
2. Prepare an agenda of things to cover.

3. Establish rapport.
4. Ask for any questions.
5. Manage time properly.
6. Take charge of the process and try to get to the bottom of any concerns by asking questions.
7. Take notes and explain why this is happening.
8. Tell the person how the audit is getting on.
9. Ask for any questions.
10. Close with a summary and a note of thanks.

Documentation

The manager's initial audit needs to stand up to external review and satisfy auditors, the board, the audit committee and anyone else who wants to know how managers are able to sign off their statements on internal control. As such, it is important to prepare sound documentation that records the work carried out in reviewing controls and checking that there is good compliance. There are many items that should be documented, including:

1. **The terms of reference and plan**. This should contain what was agreed with the manager and the planning arrangements that we discussed earlier. A basic A4 form may be used that captures the following details: audit, objective, scope, timing (start and finish), assigned person, reporting lines, time assigned to job.
2. **The interview records**. This record may indicate how the system is operated. All interviews and meetings should be noted and set out in the file. A basic A4 form may be used that captures the following details: audit, interviewer, interviewee, date, times, reason for interview, record of interview, summary of key points.
3. **The ICEM or ICQ**. In fact the ICEM is the cornerstone of the audit file. It records the objectives, risks, controls, evaluation, any testing carried and the opinion and points for the report. A basic spreadsheet may be used that captures the following details: audit, objective, stage, risks, controls, assessment of adequacy, test results summary, final opinion, actions required, by whom, review dates.
4. **Testing records**. This contains the results of all the tests carried out and key findings may be summarized in the ICEM. A basic A4 form may be used that captures the following details: audit, test objective, technique applied, sample used, approach, summary results of the test.
5. **A report on the audit**. A short, one-page report of the work carried out should be held on the audit file as well as distributed to the relevant parties. A basic document may be used that captures the following details: audit, terms of reference (objective and scope), approach, main findings, action recommended.
6. **Action plans**. Any actions that result from the audit should be appended to the report and also held on file. A basic A4 form may be used that captures

the following details: audit, objective, action, by whom, key dates, impact on risk register.

7. **Quality assurance checks by the manager**. The manager should hold a briefing with the reviewer and, before the report is accepted, needs to make sure the work has been done properly and the file contains all the necessary records. A basic A4 form may be used that captures the following details: audit, list of matters checked by manager, any outstanding points, signed off by manager and reviewer.

8. **Subsidiary matters such as general correspondence**. Anything else that is important to the audit should be placed on file or the file can simply be cross-referenced to the source documents in question. A basic A4 form may be used that captures the following details: audit, reason for document, summary of attached paperwork.

We have seen how clear and careful documentation is needed to ensure we can meet our disclosure requirements. Formal audits are the basis of MIAs and they must stand up to examination. Likewise, the disclosures going up through the organization must contain a full management trail so that each decision can be tracked down to the review of internal controls.

Why bother? The 10 As

The manager's review is driven by the need to make sure controls are reliable and there is a useful framework for assessing what is done and what matters are deemed important. These are the 10 As. What we really want from the audit includes:

1. Awareness of controls increased for all staff.
2. Assurances provided to the board and audit committee.
3. Adherence to standards checked and also encouraged.
4. Alerted to problems that need addressing.
5. Advice where required on improving controls.
6. Action needed to address problems.
7. Assistance where possible in redesigning controls to make sure they are risk smart.
8. Answers to key questions contained in terms of reference.
9. Accountabilities established and related to risk ownership and controls.
10. Adding value to the business through the initial audit work so that overall performance may be improved.

Follow-up

The manager needs to make sure all actions resulting from audit work are carried out and this can be done by placing a need to respond to control reviews into the definition of work duties. It is also helped by setting action points within performance targets for team leaders, supervisors and team members. The manager will want reports back from the teams on how they are getting on with changes that are recommended by the audit. It is helpful if the managers turn recommendations from the audit into direct instructions to make changes to control design and even take a lead on this activity. The idea is to ensure that residual risk is acceptable and problems should be accelerated through the business line, so that red risks will go up to sub-board level for effective monitoring, if appropriate.

Concept mapping

When an audit has been completed it is often not possible simply to come up with a list of recommended control improvements and present these to the manager for endorsement and implementation. More likely, we will discover control weaknesses and report a need to redesign our procedures to make them better and more risk focused. This is something that needs to be put back to the team to look into. In seeking to redesign controls we need to move from the 'actually is' world to the 'really should be' world; in other words, from excessive residual risk to acceptable residual risk. Much of this is about the concept of risk and how this sits with various parties in the business area. In searching for better controls as a result of a manager's audit that has identified problems and weaknesses, it may be necessary to get the team together and talk through the issues and ideas for improving things. One model that can assist significant control redesign is set out in Figure 5.5.

Here we focus on the action plan to improve controls and get people together to generate ideas that might help. The ideas are rated and a new map

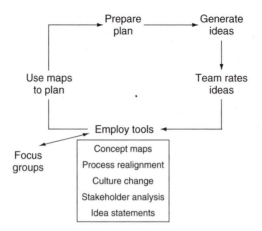

Figure 5.5   Mapping change

drawn of the procedures that incorporate views of stakeholders, team culture and the need to align the process to business needs. Once we have a set of good proposals we can use a small focus group to assess their value and go back to the map to see whether we have been able to achieve better and smarter controls.

In short

When we ask someone to review controls, this entails a formal task that needs to be done properly, recorded properly and meet high quality standards to be of any real use.

Reports and the risk register

> **A4M 5.38**   *Interviews and/or facilitated discussions should be held where it is necessary to secure specific information or viewpoints from defined persons.*

The manager's initial audit provides an opportunity for managers to set out how they may review controls over the various activities that they are responsible for. This approach is about getting someone to do the work and report back on controls that are keeping up with the business and those that may need amending or strengthening. In fact, there may be certain controls that can be discarded because they slow things down too much and the risks in question are not really significant. What we have not mentioned yet is the fact that each part of the business group may have already made a good start on keeping their controls in check. The secret here is to focus on their risk register. If we provide an amended version of the control evaluation process that has already been discussed in Table 5.2, it can be redrawn as Table 5.4.

In this scenario the manager's audit will consider the way the risk register has been put together by work teams and how well it reflects business realities. Instead of performing the audit from start to finish, a more appropriate approach would be to review the way the risk register has been developed and seek to confirm some of the matters that have entered into the frame. It is the '?' column that gives us most concern. The team's assessment of risk enables them to complete all the columns of the risk register except the one that the audit would produce relating to 'testing'. The testing column records the results of all the testing techniques applied to the state of controls, particularly relating to whether the controls in question are being adhered to. This evidence is used to support a view that controls are okay or that they are not doing a good job. The manager's audit may then focus on confirming that the premise on which the register is developed is sound, and look for evidence to substantiate this state of affairs.

Table 5.4   Internal control – risk register

Business activity objective...

Risks identified	Rating I and %	Adequacy of current controls	Testing	Opinion	Action plans
All the risks to the achievement of business objectives that the business team has been able to identify to date	Assessment of each risk for I (impact) and % likelihood of materializing if no controls are put in place	Assessment of adequacy of current risk management strategy and systems of internal control	?	Formal assurances on the state of controls available to senior management and others	Actions needed to remedy weaknesses, deal with high residual risk and ensure that compliance happens across the unit

For example, where the register records a key control over writing off balances on existing customer accounts – say, authorization by two senior managers of a report confirming nonrecoverability of balances – then the audit may test the effectiveness of the control in question. This may mean checking the files and authorizations for a sample of recent write-offs.

Figure 5.6 demonstrates how the MIA documentation process may be designed. In this way the internal control evaluation matrix can be used as a high-level summary of the MIA work, which is supported by various other documents. All findings, opinions and recommendations resulting from the MIA, including the manager's controls assurances that feed into the statement on internal control, can be traced back to their original source.

In short

The manager's initial audit is about the management team asking, 'Are our controls sound and can we report that they are okay? Are these risk registers that keep popping up from our section heads worth the paper they are written on? Please check these things out. When the auditors turn up I want to show them what you have done and see if this keeps them happy.'

Common mistakes

> **A4M 5.39**   *The MIA process should adhere to formal MIA standards and guidance.*

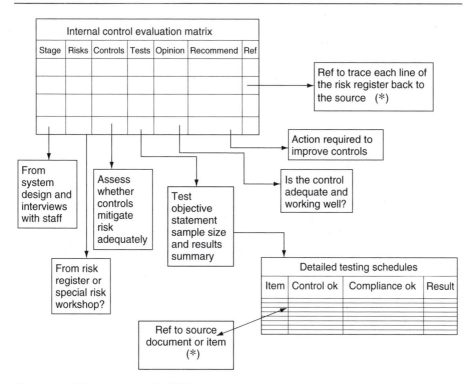

Figure 5.6 Documenting the MIA

Figure 5.7 Making a start

Scenario one

The divisional management team members get their risk register from the section heads and wait for the dreaded day when the auditor turns up looking for errors, abuse and failings. Hopefully, they will not have enough time to find too many faults before they have to get off and hit the next division.

Scenario two

The A4M.99 process turns much of this on its head by suggesting that the scenario should change to the following:

The divisional management team members will need to commission a programme of reviews to ensure their controls are really robust and reliable, using the current risk register as a starting place, which will help support the process by which each work team produces their risk registers.

Is it that simple?

There is much that could go wrong in moving from scenario one to scenario two:

- **The manager cannot see the value in commissioning audits of internal controls**. Where there is no track record of design and redesign of internal controls, there will be less gained from MIA.
- **The manager's initial audit process is mainly used to look for abuse among staff**. Where the MIA is used to check on staff, it will fast become a weapon of mass destruction and be seen by most as highly dangerous.
- **The manager is not competent to carry out the work**. Where the manager has no real grasp of the audit process, the results will be rather hit or miss.
- **There is no effective quality assurance aligned to the audit**. Where the MIA process is not validated in any way, there will be less credibility attached to the documentation and decisions made as a result.
- **The manager's audit is not recognized by the internal and external auditors**. Where the auditors do not use the MIAs as a platform for their own audit work, there will be little credibility given to the managers' efforts to get their controls right.
- **The audit process does not involve proper testing or evidence gathering**. Where the MIAs have no regard to evidence and substantiating claims made, they will have less standing as a valid assessment tool.
- **The audit process fails to take on board the current risk register**. Where there is no interface between MIAs and the business risk register, there will be less reason to invest in this type of audit work.

- **The audit process is drawn out and costly.** Where the MIA process is time consuming and expensive, there will be less support for it among managers and front-line staff.
- **There is no attempt to look into the murky waters of real-life practices.** Where there is little appreciation of the reality of internal control and how it is removed from the documented procedures, the outputs from MIA work will have little meaning to the business.
- **The documentation attaching to the manager's audit is poor.** Where there is little documentation to support all the activity of the audit work, it will not be possible to substantiate the results.

Helpful models for overcoming problems

There are several models that may help with some of the problems noted above. The first one addresses the role of the MIA process within the wider corporate picture, as noted in Figure 5.8.

The audit is about helping establish accountabilities, improving procedures and giving assurances about controls. The review will focus on risks and controls that affect the systems for achieving the set objectives, while these objectives are devised within the context of the expectations of corporate stakeholders.

The next model is in Figure 5.9. This suggests that in terms of residual risk, it is not a question of letting teams devise their own controls unilaterally. Everyone must adhere to basic corporate controls, but local managers should be allowed to develop controls that reflect their local risk profiles. The manager's initial audit will be concerned about the level of compliance with corporate controls such as IT security, employment practices, performance management, values and ethics, project management, financial regulations and so on.

The final two models demonstrate the movement from the emphasis on formal audit assurances (Figure 5.10) to a view that primary assurances from

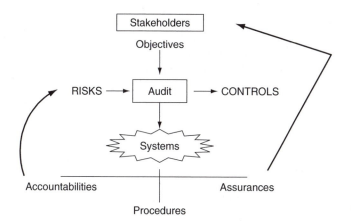

Figure 5.8 Audit and accountability

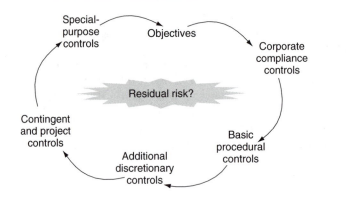

Figure 5.9 The residual risk cycle

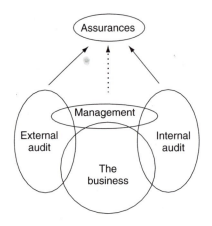

Figure 5.10 Initial audit – old-fashioned auditing

the manager's initial audit should hold much more sway than they currently do (Figure 5.11).

The new position in Figure 5.11 shifts the formal audit (internal and external audit) towards a review of the initial audit process rather than just delving into the detailed operations. In this way, what may be a two-week formal audit can become a two-day review of the management's initial audit, if the initial audit proves to be sound and reliable.

In short

An audit not done to proper auditing standards is a lot like nonalcoholic beer: it may sound like a good idea, but it's really pretty pointless.

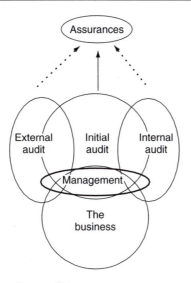

Figure 5.11   A new approach to auditing

Check your progress

> **A⬛M 5.40** *All managers should have access to a set of standardized documentation that can be applied to the MIA process.*

One tool that can be applied to track your progress is to test the extent to which you have assimilated the key points raised in this chapter. The multi-choice questions below will check your progress and the answer guide in Appendix D is based on what is most appropriate in the context of this book. Please record your answers in the table at Appendix D. You may also record the time spent on each test and enter this information in the 'Mins' column of Appendix D.

Name ....

Start time ....   **Finish time** ....   **Total minutes** ....

Multi-choice quiz

1. Insert the missing word.
The hope is that .... will focus on the reliability of these initial audits and then decide whether they need to carry out any further work.

a. managers.
b. auditors.
c. work teams.
d. stakeholders.

2. Insert the missing words.
The first thing a manager needs to do is to look into the .... and find out what is really happening in the business unit in question.

a. murky water.
b. clear water.
c. crystal ball.
d. abuses and scams.

3. Select the most appropriate sentence.
a. The manager's initial audit is about checking on staff. If you need to know what people are doing, then ask them to attend an interview.
b. The manager's initial audit is not about checking on staff. If you need to know what people are doing, then watch over them.
c. The manager's initial audit is about checking on staff. If you need to know what people are doing, then go out and ask them.
d. The manager's initial audit is not about checking on staff. If you need to know what people are doing, then go out and ask them.

4. Insert the missing phrase.
The business manager needs to formulate an annual plan of reviews that tackle .... aspects of the business.
a. high-risk.
b. highly embarrassing.
c. low-risk.
d. people-problem.

5. Which is the odd one out?
There are some important considerations to be had before we launch into a live audit. The three main questions to ask are:

a. What are we trying to achieve?
b. Do we rock the boat?
c. How long have we got?
d. Who should do it?

6. Insert the missing phrase.
For an audit of travelling to meetings, we would pose a series of questions in an .... (ICQ) that is related to the type of controls that should be in place and as a result indicate whether the control is present or not (Yes/No).

a. In-house control questionnaire.
b. Internal compliance questionnaire.
c. Internal control questionnaire.
d. Internal control quiz.

7. Insert the missing phrase.
By going through this systematic ICEM process, we can judge whether the
.... arrangements for travelling to meetings need to be improved, but
this time in terms of the actual risks in question.

a. past.
b. future.
c. basic.
d. current.

8. Select the most appropriate sentence.
a. The testing column of the ICEM is about looking for evidence of the way
   controls are being responded to; that is, risk management.
b. The testing column of the ICEM is about looking for evidence of the way
   risks are being responded to; that is, controlled.
c. The testing column of the ICEM is about looking for errors in the way risks
   are being responded to; that is, controlled.
d. The compliance column of the ICEM is about looking for evidence of the
   way risks are being responded to; that is, controlled.

9. Which is the odd one out?
There are many benefits of carrying out interviews regarding the state of controls, including the following:

a. information comes 'from the horse's mouth'.
b. the matter can be confidential if necessary.
c. we can explain why the review of controls is being carried out and our
   approach.
d. we can put pressure on the interviewee.

10. Insert the missing word.
The idea is to ensure that residual risk is acceptable and problems should be
accelerated through the business line so that .... risks will go up to sub-board
level for effective monitoring, if appropriate.

a. red.
b. amber.
c. green.
d. all.

Newsflash – read all about it

There is so much behind the move towards effective governance and risk management in all walks of life, and a small selection of relevant examples is provided to illustrate this new way of thinking.

10 new dimensions

Old thinking	New dimensions	A suitable example
Strawberries and cream go hand in hand with tennis at Wimbledon.	Before you eat the fruit, it may be a good idea to ask whether Friends of the Earth endorse the levels of toxicity used in its production.	One writer argues that the fruit is now associated with intensive farming, artificial stimulants and noxious chemicals.[3]
If, for one reason or another, staff are not up to the job, then it is best to get rid of them.	When dealing with staff it is important to stick to the legislation that protects employees. There are no short-cuts to this.	A solicitor axed two hours after announcing she was pregnant accepted an estimated £250 000 from a city firm yesterday.[4]
Once we have assessed risks we can ensure they are addressed and get on with our real business.	It is not so much a question of assessing risk, but more a matter of ensuring we have a radar system in place that means emerging and new risks are addressed during the normal course of doing business.	What is dangerously risky one year can be as safe as houses – or safer – the next. Equally, what is this year's safety-first strategy can, with a bit of market volatility, unforeseen currency weakness or a few changes in interest rates, become a serious headache a very short time later.[5]
What the railways need is new trains to replace the old rattlers that are still in use.	The railway network is a system and when improving one aspect of the system it is as well to consider how the rest of the system will fit in with the new arrangements.	Thousands of London mainline rail commuters are today condemned to travelling on overcrowded and 'grubby' 40-year-old slam-door trains after a 'catalogue of blunders' by industry chiefs. Up to 300 new £1m carriages for the capital's busiest routes will be left in sidings because rail chiefs failed to realize there was not enough power in the tracks, an official report concludes.[6]

It's only cowboys who fill their product with hidden charges.

You really have to be very careful about hidden costs in all aspects of life.

Patients phoning their doctors are being secretly charged under a controversial deal between family doctors and a telecoms company. Callers are not told that they are paying over the odds and have no idea of the extra cost, until they get their phone bill.[7]

Procedures are important because they make it clear who does what and how the task is performed. Without them we would be lost.

Procedures like all other controls must be set with regard to the risks that they are meant to guard against. They must be cost effective and make good sense.

Staff working at Hull Council have to follow a strict procedure that costs £50 and involves a minimum of 5 people to replace a 35 pence light bulb. The steps are:

1. Report the broken light to the superintendent's office.
2. Superintendent faxes details of the light bulb to the property service section.
3. Property services issues an order for a new bulb to the works department.
4. Job sheet issued by the works dept to an electrician.
5. Electrician replaces the light.[8]

The best way to find how people are managing their risks is simply to interview them. Just ask a few basic questions.

The best way to find how people are managing their risks is simply to interview them. Having said that, interviewing is a key skill and needs to be properly mastered.

Heather Mills McCartney (HMM) made a guest appearance as a stand-in for American chat show host Larry King and her interview with famous actor Paul Newman (PN) was described by critics as 'simply awful'. Some of the highlights follow:

'HMM: Good evening. Hi. I'm Heather Mills McCartney, filling in for Larry King. It's my great pleasure to welcome the multifaceted, rarely interviewed Paul Newman. Hi, Paul. Thanks for being here. How come you're such a philanthropist?

PN: Come on. Well, you start quickly don't you?

HMM: But you are. You're kind. You're generous. How come?

(Continued)

Old thinking	New dimensions	A suitable example
		PN: I have laryngitis, which is why I sound so. **HMM: So sexy?** **PN**: No. **HMM: We'll take a break now.**[9]
External inspections provide formal results and this should be the final word on the matter subject to inspection.	External inspections provide formal results that seek to reveal the true position of the matter subject to inspection. Great care should be taken with such work and if the resulting report is in any way inappropriate, the report should be remedied or withdrawn.	Popular and well regarded by locals, the Banham village community Primary School reflected the social make up of the rural area it served. The Ofsted inspectors' report accused the school of failing to promote race equality and failing in its statutory duty to pupils. Following furious complaints the report was retracted after an admission that its conclusions were deeply flawed.[10]
Evidence to support a conclusion must be compelling and obviously correct.	Evidence to support a conclusion must be compelling, but there is very little evidence that can be described as obviously correct.	Fingerprint evidence is much more unreliable than the public, police and courts think and rests on foundations that have never been rigorously tested, an investigation by *New Scientist* magazine has suggested.[11]
When the benefits of something are being investigated we need to discover whether the benefits are real and why they arise.	When the benefits of something are being investigated we need to discover as much relevant material as possible, although it is never easy to answer all questions.	The ancient martial art of t'ai chi has proven medical benefits, research published today says. But the medical establishment is still mystified as to how the slow-motion movements actually improve health.[12]

The key messages

The last section of each chapter contains a short story or quote that should provide an interesting format for illustrating some of the book's key messages.

Running the business

If you run a shouting regime, you have to be a police officer as well. You have to check, endlessly, constantly, that your wishes are being obeyed. Even if people do not cheat but genuinely try to do it right, they may not try so hard when you are gone; it is your wishes they are carrying out, your rules, your commands, and when you are no longer there, the wishes, rules and commands can easily disappear with you.[13]

Notes

1. Committee of Sponsoring Organizations, Enterprise Risk Management, Draft framework at July 2004, page 82 (www.coso.org).
2. Committee of Sponsoring Organizations, Enterprise Risk Management, Draft framework at July 2004, page 82 (www.coso.org).
3. *Daily Mail*, Monday, March 29, 2004, page 11.
4. *Daily Mail*, Wednesday, March 31, 2004, page 7.
5. *Evening Standard*, Tuesday, January 20, 2004, page 37, all quotes taken from column by Anthony Hilton.
6. *Evening Standard*, Wednesday, February 4, 2004, page 20.
7. *The Mail on Sunday*, Sunday, March 28, 2004, page 43.
8. *Daily Mail*, Tuesday, January 13, page 25.
9. *Daily Mail*, Monday, April 19, 2004, page 15, 'Heather, talking her way out of a chat-show career', Mark Reynolds.
10. *Daily Mail*, Saturday, April 17, 2004, page 19.
11. *The Times*, Thursday, January 29, 2004, News, page 10.
12. *The Independent*, Tuesday, March 9, 2004, Home News, page 5.
13. Charles Handy, *21 Ideas for Managers: Practical Wisdom for Managing Your Company and Yourself*, Jossey-Bass, San Francisco, 2000, page 75.

6 The team's initial audit

All the world's a stage, and all the men and women merely players.
They have their exits and entrances; and one man in his time plays many parts.
William Shakespeare, As You Like It, Act II, Scene 7

A4M Statement F *The A4M.99 approach should include the use of team workshops or facilitated meetings designed to ensure that those closest to the business risks are able to design and report on internal controls that mitigate these risks where appropriate.*

Introduction

A4M 6.41 *Team initial audits that utilize the workshop approach should be based around groups of people who are brought together because they are best able to identify, assess and manage the risks in the area in question.*

Figure 1.1 in Chapter 1 shows how the book is put together. Chapter 6 describes the team's initial audits (TIA), which have been developed to reflect the growing popularity of self-assessment of risks and controls. The manager's initial audit detailed in the previous chapter is an attempt to enable managers to review their systems of internal control and assess how controls are being applied by staff in operational areas. This is quite important in command-and-control type organizations that emphasize the authority of management and the need to set formal standards for employees. A complementary approach to addressing risk and controls argues that it is the front-line staff who should be

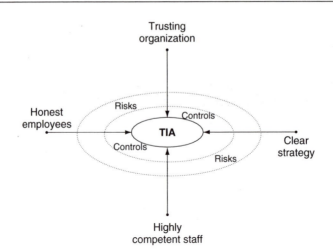

Figure 6.1 Auditing at the centre

most involved in assessing risk and developing good controls. Figure 6.1 puts this point into perspective.

In Figure 6.1 we argue that good staff, working in a trusting organization with a clear sense of direction, are well placed to be given the task of assessing their own controls. Where these people are essentially honest and there are high standards of conduct and vetting procedures in place, more reliance can be placed on their work in promoting suitable controls. One response is to ask people to get together and embark on team initial auditing. This contrasts with the manager's initial audits dealt with in the previous chapter. Team initial audits are based on control risk self-assessments, which is one well-known tool for getting people involved in this debate, and is supported by A4M.99. Note that there is a set of standards covering the TIA approach in Appendix B.

In short

As well as reviewing how staff are applying controls, it is a good idea to give people who know most about the day-to-day business the ability to review their own controls and therefore achieve more ownership and commitment to the risk and control debate.

The team initial audit concept

A4M 6.42 *The TIAs that involve representative groups may be conducted using short facilitated discussions where it is appropriate.*

The team's initial auditing concept is about encouraging people at the front line to take responsibility for ensuring that their controls work. The wider canvas may contain segments of the following items:

- **Board policy**. A corporate risk assessment and high-level policy should drive the TIA programme, along with sponsorship from the board itself.
- **Awareness initiatives**. People should be told about TIA and how they can use it to enhance both performance and adherence to regulatory requirements.
- **Approach**. The programme may be used in projects, teams, processes and new developments.
- **Preparation**. General surveys, interviews of key staff, training for facilitators and development of the workshop theme should all occur before the programme is launched.
- **Process**. The process may involve clarifying issues such as team objectives, stakeholders, performance criteria and change programmes.
- **Risk management**. The team should work through risk identification, risk assessment, risk management, internal controls, risk registers and formal assurances on business controls.

The idea is really simple in theory: to get people together to sort out and improve their controls. An example illustrates how flexible this technique can be:

> A team of divisional managers in charge of site inspectors asked for training in audit techniques so that they might control their inspectors better. They ended up getting the trainer to run a risk workshop to identify what could go wrong in terms of managing the inspectors and the type of techniques they needed to apply to help them develop a high-quality and successful inspection process.

The TIA process fits well with the concept of self-managed work groups (SMWG), as suggested in Figure 6.2.

The SMWGs work within corporate policies and are responsible for a whole range of work-related issues such as improving systems, promoting values,

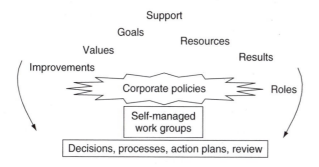

Figure 6.2 Self-managed work groups

achieving goals and so on. The groups are then empowered to make decisions, design local processes and develop action plans and targets to review their performance. TIA allows them to review their risk and controls and rather than such an audit being 'done to them', they 'do it for themselves'.

There are many benefits of TIAs, as the system incorporates both the formal group roles and the informal group's personal relationships and social ties. The group can develop better controls that recognize the way they relate to each other and the drivers based on team tasks and group loyalty. While we give teams and groups freedom to help design controls, it is still important to ensure that the risk owner, such as the business unit manager, endorses their recommendations.

In short

Modern organizations use the team structure as the basis for a dynamic business. Giving teams responsibility for their own success, including risk management practices, is one way of endorsing this concept.

Establishing the programme

> **A4M 6.43**   *The TIA process that uses groups and team workshops should be piloted and formally assessed before it is applied across the organization.*

It is not a good idea simply to set up a series of risk workshops and ask people to start assessing their risk and controls. We need to build and establish a programme that has a good chance of success. This means putting in the necessary infrastructure, including someone who understands the need for a commercial return and the benefits and difficulties of designing and implementing a worthwhile programme. Figure 6.3 has a go at explaining the building process.

Figure 6.3 suggests that the first thing to do is get what some organizations call a 'risk map' together. This is a map of the organization in terms of the way risks will be identified and managed, set at a corporate level as an overview of the business. Then work out where TIA will be focused in terms of applying this technique to:

- Team workshops.
- New projects as part of the project management methodology.
- Compliance reviews, where workshops can be used to assess control compliance.
- Staff directives, where the way corporate procedures are designed can be assessed using risk assessment.

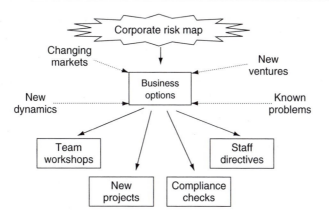

Figure 6.3   Corporate risk mapping

Why team audits?

The background to using TIA is provided by factors such as shifting markets, known problems and so on. In this way TIA can be seen as a tool to be adapted and applied in whatever way best suits the situation. TIA is about achieving:

- Better risk management.
- Review of controls.
- Better understanding of objectives and priorities.
- Better ways of working.
- Better delivery of products and services.
- Supportable disclosures on reviewing internal controls.
- Better team working.
- A more successful organization.

As a technique, TIA can be applied in any part of the organization, including back-office teams. The key is to define what the outfit is trying to achieve. Even if the activity has a support role rather than being part of customer delivery, there is still no reason why it should not be applied.

Adapting team audits

The TIA approach should be adapted to suit the organization. Those that have a mature risk management process in place may see TIA as a way of getting people to endorse the risk registers that have been prepared throughout the organization. A brand new organization, or a newly merged entity, may want to spend a great deal of time in 'blue sky thinking' and develop controls that it can rely on. An organization that has been trotting along nicely and become a little stagnant may get swept up in a TIA tidal wave and set up many workshops – probably because the average employee has never been able to get together with colleagues and talk about the business and where it is going.

Some organizations start at the top and get the board to carry out a corporate risk workshop and then use this to set the tone for the rest of the organization. Workshops in this environment may be short, sharp, one-hour events, rather than an exercise that runs on all day. Public-sector bodies tend to spend more time in workshops than private-sector businesses, which simply cannot find the time and logistics to get together very often. The other thing that happens with TIA is that people in one part of the organization start to see what people in other parts want and where their priorities lie. After a few workshops, the workshop leader eventually gains a great deal of knowledge about the way different parts of the entity operate and can start to move into enterprise risk management as walls are broken down and people start working to a common standard. In reality, much depends on the risk appetite that was discussed earlier on in the book.

In short

TIA can be a great success or an annoying series of stressful workshop confrontations that become tiresome. Much depends on the way it is organized and run. It's very easy to mess it up and bury what could be a useful business improvement tool.

Running workshops

A4M 6.44 *Where team workshops are used to support TIA, the facilitator should have undergone suitable training in the use of facilitation skills and techniques and possess a good understanding of the pros and cons of the team approach to TIA.*

Workshops tend to be the lifeblood of TIA. A great deal of interaction happens when people come together face to face, and it is here where great strides can be made in finding out how people think and how they behave. However, the workshop takes people off-line and it occupies time and energy that could otherwise be applied at their desks. The reality is that the workshop approach comes and goes, as illustrated in Figure 6.4.

As risk management kicks into an organization, there are several different strategies that can be adopted in terms of applying TIA workshops:

A. This approach is to run a greater and greater number of workshops as more parts of the organization come together and get involved in the programme.

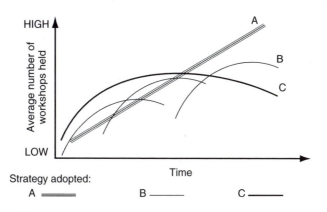

Figure 6.4   Workshop activity levels

B. In this situation the workshops appear in fits and starts. They take off, then die down until a memo comes around saying more are needed.
C. This scenario means the workshop approach is kick started and then diminishes as people get to understand their risk portfolio and only need to get in workshop mode to update or confirm their risk registers.

The **A** approach can bring 'death by workshop' to staff and reflects a tick-box attitude where the board can report on the high volume of risk events. Style **B** is a 'kick-in-the-pants' approach where events are put on when people get bored and start to slow down. The **C** version is quite useful. It suggests that we need to get people together to work through their risks and controls, but thereafter we will only use this approach where a 'quick chat' is needed to update things or when there is a new development.

The above parallels the way groups behave when they come together to work on a new initiative or fresh approach. A great deal of work is needed to move through the seven stages of:

1. Coming together and jostling for position.
2. Ground rules being eventually set on who does what.
3. Focusing on the real issues.
4. Going into problem-solving mode and focusing on solutions.
5. Identifying new challenges to avoid boredom with the whole process.
6. Deciding what to do next.
7. Getting back to the day job.

At stage 5 when the group members are in action mode, we need not put them straight back to stage 1. It is better to leave the workshops until there are another set of real issues to address, before they fall into boredom, stage 6.

We have said that workshop activity declines as the risk management process matures and Figure 6.5 sets out this trend.

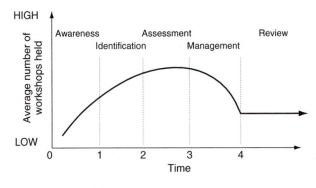

Figure 6.5   Risk maturity model

How many workshops?

As outlined in Figure 6.5, people become adept at identifying and assessing their risks and there is less need for long workshop sessions. When over time managers move into the risk management and review stage, workshops can become much more focused on reviewing and updating. The argument applied to this trend is that there are four main stages to the process and we should expect to see this reflected in the way workshops are resourced and allowed to develop. In fact, each of the above stages may be seen as milestones and the board can set targets for getting to stage 1, 2, 3, then 4 across the organization.

   A key stage that may be aimed at would be to get risk assessment and control redesign integrated into the way people tend to work anyway. Control design is not about working in special workshops, but is more about the way people normally communicate and make decisions at work. Workshops suggest an alien climate that is outside the office and outside normal business. The problem is that we have to go through the various stages before we can move into full integration.

The workshop stages

When we are running a risk workshop it is an idea to go through a series of set stages to ensure the event is worthwhile, which in summary can be described as follows:

1. **Preparation** – set objectives and timing, contact participants and get their initial views.
2. **Planning** – think about refreshments, location, format, the agenda and note taking.

3. **Run the event** – facilitate, describe aims of the workshop, introductions, agenda, voting, terminology used, ground rules, active participation and closing.
4. **After the event** – check the notes, prepare a report, think about follow-up and review the success of the event.

Facilitation

The TIA approach is not as simple as basic facilitation. It covers a number of different facets. The workshop leader will need to perform several roles:

- Explain the risk policy and respective roles and responsibilities.
- Explain where TIA fits into the enterprise risk management process, risk policies and the way risk appetites are established.
- Describe how TIA events come together to provide better business and underpin business controls assurance.
- Energize the group and get them to appreciate how good controls can help them.
- Allow them to decide how they want to work through the risk process from start to finish.
- Encourage the group to work together, listen to each other, brainstorm risks and come up with good ideas for moving forward.
- Promote the active engagement of all persons present.
- Encourage a move away from any blame cultures that may impair open communication.
- Ensure that people understand the concept of accountability.
- Seek to get people to see the way TIA fits into planning, performance management, decision making and other corporate business systems.
- Convince the group that TIA is also a learning process where we need to fit into the organization's search for continuous improvement.
- Help make decisions about the role of the team's supervisors and line managers in the workshops and the need to balance open communications with the need to reinforce the manager's responsibility to make decisions about control arrangements.
- Develop an understanding of the difference between active facilitation and passive facilitation and the way control can be handed over or partly withdrawn from the group during a risk workshop.
- Demonstrate an appreciation of the way voting technology can be applied to a workshop event and the pros and cons of this approach.
- Think about the way consensus can be managed through debate, discussion and good teamworking.
- Discuss the practicalities of the business in question and constraints that the teams work under.

In short

Workshops take time and money and it requires a true professional to make the best use of this forum as an active ingredient of the initial auditing process.

A short example

> **A4M 6.45** *Formal TIA workshops may consume a great deal of resource and should therefore only be used when there are clear benefits from using this forum for auditing an area of the business.*

TIA is about giving responsibility to work teams to develop better ways of working within corporate policies and this needs to be done carefully. There should be a good business case attached to the use of this technique. An example follows in Table 6.1 of the output from a workshop and how it can be applied to developing a better system for filling regional job vacancies in various divisions, and managing the risks that can arise from this task.

Table 6.1   Recruiting staff
Objectives: To get the right people, at the right time and rates into vacant posts, in line with laws, commercial needs and corporate policies.

Stage	Risks	Controls	Tests (*)	Opinion	Recommendations
Vacancy	New recruit not needed	Needs test applied	Selection of vacancies examined for commercial viability in each division	Division X not applying criteria properly	Human resources manager needs to address noncompliance
Job description and specification reviewed	Incompetent people employed based on poor job specification	Panel reviews job description and specification, including line and personnel staff. Adjust for new challenges	Examine panel review for impact	25% of post specifications not reviewed	Reinforce review procedure and no recruitment until carried out
Advertise job	Suitable people not aware of vacancy	Adverts go to agency and newspaper	Review current exposure – reaching the right people?	Current procedure inefficient, people missing out	Place ads on intranet and use university open days and contacts

Sifting applicants and shortlisting	Wrong people get through	Set criteria agreed and applied by panel	Examine past cases over last three months	Very tight criteria applied	N/A
Test candidates	Good people knocked out	Tests drawn up by personnel unit	Examine testing applied per job specification	At times tests not aligned to jobs in question	Panel reviews type of tests – casting vote by line manager
Interviews	Unfair and against equal opportunities	Panel agrees questions and asks all of them	Check complaints level and notes	No complaints and panel appears well balanced, but other companies have had problems	May still need to provide training for panel members
Selection process	Not objective	Panel declares any conflicts of interest and sets points criteria	Check some key posts	No clear records explaining choices	Design clear points criteria form for use by panel
Contracts and setting up postholder	Wrong conditions applied	Personnel sets up standard contract for post	Check all appointments in last month	New post contracts are made up by personnel and 20% of contracts unsigned	Formal sign-off procedure for all new starters. Legal department to be involved in drawing up new contracts

* Note that detailed tests are not normally carried out in TIAs and any checks may need to be followed up in subsequent management initial audits.

In short

TIA is a real business tool and it's about real issues and real improvements to the way controls are established and kept sharp.

Getting the best out of people

> **A4M 6.46** *The TIA approach is based on the premise that people are the most important aspect of any business and it is the way they perform, communicate and interact that is fundamental to promoting good risk management and control.*

TIA is about getting the best out of people in a way that is directed at their targets. Many workshops start with the team objectives and it is also a good idea to explore the way people define their work priorities, as in Figure 6.6.

One person's goals are affected by many things. All the items surrounding the personal goals have an impact on the final position. TIA workshops that fail to recognize the effect of these factors for each individual will have less chance of being successful.

There are several ways in which TIA can be designed to get the best out of teams:

- Build risk into staff meetings and where teams get together for impromptu problem-solving sessions. In this way it may be possible to get people talking risk and controls as a way of doing business.
- Link the TIA approach to wider events such as the annual work conference. A short account of some of the quick gains from risk workshops can be presented at these conferences along with the corporate publicity material.
- The TIA leaders can use the phone to keep in touch with team members who have attended or plan to attend any workshops.
- One-to-one meetings may be possible with people who are planning to attend a workshop to get across any issues that are relevant to the coming event.
- Tell people that they should carry out risk identification and assessment exercises whenever they are going to make significant decisions, and ensure that the results are recorded.
- Build TIA sessions into change management programmes to ensure that future risks are considered.
- Watch out for teams that produce, say, hundreds of key risks – this suggests that there is a need to aggregate and scale down into key aspects and reduce to, say, up to 10–20 main risks linked to key objectives.
- Perform awareness presentations on controls and control frameworks whenever this would be appropriate. Fit the presentations to the needs of the

Figure 6.6 Goals within goals

people in question. Link these presentations to the TIA workshops that may be planned.

- Build risk assessment into all process redesign projects and brainstorm threats. Checklists may be used to stimulate discussion on the impact and likelihood of risks to achieving set tasks.
- Demonstrate the value from risk registers and explain the need to capture key information in workshops, meetings and special events.
- Link TIA events to corporate values – that is, what is important to each person and the team as well as the organization.
- Where there is a highly trained facilitator, the workshop may be used to encourage people to discuss their concerns and some of the nagging issues that get in the way of good performance.
- Promote the view that a good team is one that understands and manages its risks well – that the two concepts go hand in hand.
- Ensure that TIA has an in-built challenge element and tease out teams that feel threatened by external events to find out why this is so. Try to stay away from basic voting averages, since this may become stagnant as a middle ground is always sought for very real problems that require decisive action.
- Appreciate that time spent away from the office is at a premium and that clear benefits are needed to ensure a pay-off.

In short

TIA is a people tool. It's about recognizing the people aspect of internal controls. If we get that right, most everything else will fall into place.

Common mistakes

> **A4M 6.47** *The TIA group workshop approach is more useful where the group, or team members, have clear team objectives and operate as a team. Where the team does not work well, TIAs may be used to promote better communications and relationships between team members.*

Scenario one

People in an organization are told what to do by their managers and, so long as they follow instructions, all should be well. The reason internal controls work is because discipline, standards and set rules ensure we are all working in the same direction.

Figure 6.7   Communicating well

Scenario two

The A4M.99 process turns much of this on its head by suggesting that the scenario should change to the following:

People in an organization generally know what they need to do to be successful and, so long as they are given the tools and space to grow, all should be well. The reason internal controls work is because they make sense to the people who operate them.

Is it that simple?

There is much that could go wrong in moving from scenario one to scenario two:

- **Managers rely on their own audits as the main means of receiving assurances about the state of internal controls**. Where the manager's audit is prioritized over team audits, there will be an imbalance and less trust from both managers and work teams.
- **The TIA process sits outside the organization's main business systems**. Where the team efforts to review controls do not lead to any real change, there will be less incentive for people to get involved and contribute.
- **TIA workshops are held without regard to a high-level risk map of the organization**. Where the policy is to hold many workshops at random across the organization, a holistic approach to enterprise risk management will be less likely to arise.
- **A large number of workshops are held mainly to enable the organization to report high volumes of these events for published disclosures**. Where the focus is on volume and not quality outcomes, any workshops held will become more of a paperchase than a real business change process.
- **Workshops are held without support from trained facilitators who understand the TIA process**. Where the facilitators are not properly trained, any workshops held may become boring and achieve little improvement in controls.

- **TIA programmes are not supported by a business case**. Where there is no convincing reason to develop team audits, there will always be a suspicion that the effort is not worth expending.
- **The TIA process is based on the assumption that team and personal objectives are clear and are not complicated by other factors**. Where there is insufficient time spent on considering team objectives, the ensuing risk assessments may not be attached to any real decision making.
- **The TIA process is not based around any real understanding of controls and control frameworks**. Where the team's efforts do not include a presentation of internal control frameworks, there may be a gap in understanding that reduces the value from the audits.
- **TIA workshops are held without regard to the way people go through various stages of maturity before arriving at a stage where they can perform well**. Where the team audits do not take on board the way team members work together, there may be less scope to build an action plan that all team members are committed to.
- **The TIA process tends to result in an abundance of significant risks that run into the hundreds**. Where there is a large number of risks that feature in the audit, there will be less scope to address real priorities.

Helpful models for overcoming problems

It is possible to widen the assessment of aims and goals, as in Figure 6.8.

Here we are trying to make a beeline for reconciling people's own personal goals with what the organization is trying to achieve via its corporate goals. A strategy where we get teams together to discuss what they are trying to achieve needs to take on board these factors. That is, what makes someone tick? And how do we get everyone pulling together in the same direction?

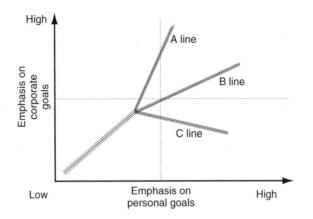

Figure 6.8   Goal congruence

In short

Workshop after workshop does not mean all is well. We need to make sure we have a way of measuring progress in setting up the TIA process – for most people, that is better risk management and a stronger control environment.

Check your progress

> **A4M 6.48**   *People who are embarking on TIA workshops should take part in suitable awareness events before the actual workshops are held.*

One tool that can be applied to track your progress is to test the extent to which you have assimilated the key points raised in this chapter. The multi-choice questions below will check your progress and the answer guide in Appendix D is based on what is most appropriate in the context of this book. Please record your answers in the table at Appendix D. You may also record the time spent on each test and enter this information in the 'Mins' column of Appendix D.

Name ....

Start time ....   **Finish time** ....   **Total minutes** ....

Multi-choice quiz

1. **Select the most appropriate sentence.**
a. A complementary approach to addressing risk and controls argues that it is the front-line staff who should be most involved in assessing risk and developing good controls.
b. A complementary approach to addressing risk and controls argues that it is the support staff who should be most involved in assessing risk and developing good controls.
c. An unheard-of approach to addressing risk and controls argues that it is the front-line staff who should be most involved in assessing risk and developing good controls.
d. A complementary approach to addressing poor staff argues that it is the front-line staff who should be most involved in assessing risk and developing good controls.

2. Insert the missing words.
While we give teams and groups freedom to help design controls, it is still important to ensure that the risk owner (e.g. the ....) endorses the recommendations.

a. internal auditor.
b. chief risk officer.
c. business unit manager.
d. legal officer.

3. Which is the odd one out?
The first thing to do is get what some organizations call a 'risk map' together. Then work out where TIA will be focused in terms of applying this technique to:

a. the well-known team workshops.
b. new projects as part of the project management methodology.
c. compliance reviews, where workshops can be used to assess control compliance.
d. management checks on staff absences.

4. Insert the missing words.
After a few workshops, the .... eventually gains a great deal of knowledge about the way different parts of the entity operate. Here we can start to move into enterprise risk management as walls are broken down and people start working to a common standard.

a. security staff.
b. workshop leader.
c. external consultant.
d. external auditor.

5. Select the most appropriate sentence.
a. As people become adept at identifying and assessing their risks there is less need for long workshop sessions.
b. As people become bored with identifying and assessing their risks there is less need for long workshop sessions.
c. As people become adept at identifying and assessing their risks there is more need for long workshop sessions.
d. As people become adept at identifying and assessing their risks there is less need for shorter workshop sessions.

6. Insert the missing words.
Workshops take .... and it requires a true professional to make the best use of this forum as an active ingredient of the self-assessment process.

a. time and accommodation.
b. funding and money.
c. time and money.
d. risk and controls.

7. Insert the missing word.
There should be a good .... attached to the use of this technique (TIA).

a. business manager.
b. audit review.
c. social reason.
d. business case.

8. Select the most appropriate sentence.
a. Watch out for teams that produce key risks only – this suggests that there is a need to aggregate and scale down into key aspects and reduce to, say, up to 10–20 main risks linked to key objectives.
b. Watch out for teams that produce, say, hundreds of key risks – this suggests that there is a need to aggregate and scale down into key aspects and reduce to, say, up to 10–20 main risks linked to key objectives.
c. Watch out for teams that produce, say, hundreds of key risks – this suggests that there is a need to aggregate and scale down into key aspects and reduce to, say, up to 200 main risks linked to key objectives.
d. Watch out for teams that produce, say, hundreds of key risks – this suggests that there is a need to aggregate and scale down into key aspects and reduce to, say, up to 10–20 main risks linked to 50 key objectives.

9. Insert the missing word.
Ensure TIA has an in-built .... element and tease out teams that feel threatened by external events and why this is so.

a. challenge.
b. fun.
c. threat.
d. teasing.

10. Insert the missing word(s).
The reason internal controls work is because they .... to the people who have to operate them.

a. belong.
b. are special.
c. make sense.
d. are forced on.

Newsflash – read all about it

There is so much behind the move towards effective governance and risk management in all walks of life, and a small selection of relevant examples is provided to illustrate this new way of thinking.

10 new dimensions

Old thinking	New dimensions	A suitable example
Where there's blame, there's a claim.	Suspect business practices will eventually be found out.	The Accident Group collapsed amid allegations that claims were being filed with little or no regard for the true circumstances of the case. One story suggested that a salesman loaded five friends into a car, drove over a pothole and filed claims for whiplash.[1]
Risk management means one should always expect the worst.	Risk management is not a science and the most unlikely things, both good and bad, can sometimes happen.	A sixty-seven-year-old grandmother had a heart attack while flying with her family to Florida. After an announcement was made asking whether there was a doctor on board, 15 cardiologists (who were on their way to a conference in Orlando) rushed to her aid and saved her life.[2]
We have the best people taking care of security.	High-risk targets need a commensurate degree of vigilant security.	The comedian who gatecrashed Prince William's 21st birthday party wandered unchallenged into Windsor Castle and ended up kissing the prince on both cheeks.[3]
		In another case an undercover reporter got a job as a royal footman at Buckingham Palace using fake references, naming a pub in Wales as his previous employer. When the Palace personnel staff checked the reference they phoned the pub and asked if anyone recognized the job applicant's name. When the journalist's name was shouted out by the barmaid a customer replied, 'Yes, I know him.' After that he was offered the job.[4]

(Continued)

Old thinking	New dimensions	A suitable example
Compensation claims happen when one person behaves totally out of step with everyone else in an organization.	An organization needs to make sure its current practices do not leave it open to compensation claims. As the public attitudes to transparency change, so the need to respect people's wishes becomes more paramount.	The NHS faces a multimillion pound compensation bill over the scandal of doctors who removed organs without the families' knowledge. In a landmark decision, a judge ruled yesterday that doctors have been acting illegally for 40 years by keeping children's body parts without their parents' permission after hospital post-mortems.[5]
As long as you get the build specification right in a big contract, everything else should be okay.	Really good project risk management starts with taking a wide view of all potential risks that could affect the project.	The programme to build Airbus's A380 superjumbo is descending into farce, with the first set of wings for the world's largest passenger plane having to be dismantled for transport as soon as factory assembly in Wales is complete. The debacle could put off companies thinking of making large-scale investments in Britain, MPs say ... a specially made ship for the giant wings ... has been denied access to the port of Mostyn, forcing Airbus to scramble a smaller ship that is not large enough to carry the wings intact.[6]
Sometimes we need to take short-cuts to get the job done. If it's good enough for our allies it's good enough for us.	Each project is different, and it is essential that, in terms of managing risk, whatever is being developed does the job and does it well.	Helicopters built specifically for the SAS at a cost of £259 million cannot fly on a cloudy day, a damning report has revealed. The eight Chinook Mark 3 aircraft are crippled by such massive technical problems that they are still idle six years after they should have entered service ... The cockpit layout is so bizarre that it cannot be given UK safety clearance, so the helicopters are only allowed to fly on cloudless days, above 500ft and for a limited time.[7]
There are always some annoying aspects of work, and while they can drag us down, we need just to accept them.	Risk management is a really versatile tool. Sometimes it is a good idea to identify and tackle the little things that make going to work unappealing.	There is one view that suggests staff can get together and identify all the things that make life difficult at work and then try to deal with as many as possible.

High-risk items such as cash attract a high degree of controls to ensure nothing untoward can happen.	High-risk items such as cash attract a high degree of controls, but there can never be cast-iron guarantees that nothing untoward can happen.	The villagers of Wooler were still wearing broad smiles yesterday as they fondly recalled Golden Wednesday. It was only seven days ago, but it was the busiest night in living memory and they will talk about it for years to come. It was the night the Barclays cash machine in the Northumberland village paid out twice as much money as every customer asked for. News travels fast in rural communities and within an hour there was a queue the length of the high street. One woman arrived at the machine by taxi in her nightdress and curlers.[8]
Senior people are different from lowly workers. There is one rule for them and one for us. That's the way it's always been.	The new vision of society is that rules apply to everyone and the more senior the figure the more important it is to set high standards.	A prominent member of the Irish parliament has been sacked for breaking the country's ban on smoking in the workplace. He is the first person to be penalized publicly since the law came into force Monday.[9]
As long as staff are kept busy then we will make good progress.	Progress is achieved by positive people working in positive ways, with enough space to develop.	People react much more positively to a supportive management style where it is made clear what is expected of them. You should have a strong sense of values to guide behaviour. If staff are regularly involved in decision-making then managers don't have to micro-manage while on the move ... Companies ought to measure people's performance by what they achieve rather than the visible effort they put into it.[10]

The key messages

The last section of each chapter contains a short story or quote that should provide an interesting format for illustrating some of the book's key messages.

Organizing a dinner party

The next day saw the final push in organizing the furniture and various items that had been dumped around the house as the couple and their friends finally moved into their new home in the small rural village. After such a great deal of manual effort, it was agreed that lunch at a pub they had spotted yesterday, some 10 miles away, would go down well. This proved a good idea as the four of them sat round a table in the attractive garden at the back of the pub, which overlooked a winding stream that trickled past. The two children tackled the play area just a few feet way and while one used the swings, the other ventured onto the climbing frame. John, satisfied that the children were okay, reached for his pint of real ale and said, 'I guess we're not going to make much progress on our dinner do, if last night's anything to go by.'

Stephanie stretched her long legs out towards the stream and in the silence that followed sipped her drink, frowned and, since she was normally very quiet, drew the attention of the other three who were longing to hear her speak without being prompted. She said in a gentle voice, as if talking to a group of small children, 'Going back to the dinner party that we said we'd organize to introduce ourselves to our neighbours. You know we couldn't agree last night whether it should be formal or not and that it could end up a complete disaster. We could always carry out a proper assessment. You know, an audit with an agreed action plan. Review any risks and then determine how we can address them. I do it at work when advising my clients about risk management. We could do the same here if you like.'

'How will that work?' Anna asked.

'It's really quite simple. You do an audit when you are not sure about something and you need to check it out before you can move forward. So for us, we would do a number of things.'

Grundig looked at his wife with pride as she bristled with life and once again dispelled any idea that she was shy and retiring. 'List the steps we would need to go through and I'll write them down,' he urged, and Stephanie continued.

'Well. If it needs to be done properly, and if there is much that could go wrong, we would need to do a number of things. Okay, I'll list them if you like: We will need to agree and write out our objectives. Then we consider the types of things that can get in the way of our achieving our objectives. Next, we prioritize these risks and work out which ones are most significant. For the bigger risks we will need to put in place safeguards; that is, ways of addressing the issues that arise from the risks that we have identified. We assign action points to ensure any outstanding action is taken. Finally, we act and keep everything under review. That's it folks – an audit to ensure what we want to do has a good chance of happening. I mean, what we plan to achieve is more likely to be achieved.'

At this, one of the children slipped and rolled off the climbing rope and thereafter let out a soft moan as he examined a small cut on his knee.

Stephanie moved quickly to assist and after the application of a plaster and a quick cuddle, the child resumed his climbing adventure, having been told not to go too high up.

As Stephanie returned to the group, the others looked at her expectantly.

'What?' she asked. 'I've left my job and I'm not going to spend all afternoon lecturing about this audit stuff. John, I'll have another drink please.'

'Well,' Grundig said with gusto, 'I like it. An audit. Let's give it a go. Why don't we do it this evening? Steph, you can take us through your audit if you like.'

'All right. I don't mind. So long as we leave the wine for later and not before.'

The rest of the day went to plan as the remaining boxes were unpacked and items placed in what seemed to be acceptable locations, at least for the time being. A light snack sufficed for dinner as they had all eaten too much in the pub. At around 7 pm they assembled in the front lounge and gathered around Stephanie, eagerly awaiting the newly found game. Stephanie took up the challenge and pinned a spare piece of wallpaper to the back of the door and produced a large black marker.

'Right,' she said, totally immersed in her instructional work mode, which as a professional consultant allowed her to project an air of total confidence. 'Let's get down what we are trying to achieve by holding this dinner party. What are our aims?'

'To get to know the locals,' shouted John.

'To inform our neighbours that we are respectable people,' added Anna.

'To have a good feed and show these country folk that us townies know how to throw a good bash,' suggested Grundig. 'And,' he went on, 'to make useful contacts, with important people. For future reference. To get into high society...'

'Okay,' interrupted Stephanie, 'that's a good start. So it's about meeting people, meeting the right people and presenting a good image – and perhaps having a good time all round. Yes?'

'Absolutely,' John replied, feigning a salute.

Stephanie looked at the small group sitting around the oak coffee table. 'How can we best sum up our objective?'

Grundig was first to answer. 'To show what city folk can do – how to throw a bash to end all bashes, to make this little hamlet really swing...'

Anna interrupted. 'It's not really a competition. We don't want to make people think we do not fit in. I like Steph's description: to introduce us to the village by inviting a few local people around for a meal.'

'Yes,' John added, 'simply to say here we are and we would love to get to know you as neighbours.'

Stephanie started to write:

'Objective – to hold a small dinner party to:

1. Get to know some of the local people.
2. Show them that we are friendly and down to earth.
3. And at the same time make sure everyone has a good time.'

'That's it,' confirmed John.

Stephanie continued, 'Once we've set the objectives, everything else flows from this. This is not as easy as it seems. Right, the next step is have a look at our objectives and think about anything that affects our ability to deliver them.'

'You mean risks?' Anna asked.

'Absolutely. Risks are what could get in the way of our achieving our objectives. So we want a dinner party, with the right people, to show them we're not stuck-up and unfriendly and make sure we all have a good time. What could get in the way of this?'

Grundig scratched his beard, while John and Anna looked around for inspiration.

Grundig stood up as if addressing an audience. 'It may all go wrong. People may have a terrible time and then blame it on you. There might be arguments, and...er...unpleasantness...'

'Look,' Stephanie said as she guided Grundig back into his chair. 'Let's focus on our objectives. We said the first goal was to get to know some of the local people. So what could go wrong here?'

Grundig, this time while sitting, suggested, 'We could invite too many, not enough or perhaps a poor selection of guests. You know, one family and not others who live nearby.'

John waved his hands as he thought of a few contributions. 'For example, we might invite a chap and his ex-wife's lover. Or forget to invite someone who feels aggrieved...'

Stephanie wrote many of these ideas down and said, 'In short, for one reason or another we may come up with an inappropriate guest list. If we invite people at random, there is more chance of this risk materializing. Yes. Now, what about our next objective, show them that we are friendly and down to earth?'

John set the pace. 'We may appear too formal or in fact too rough and ready with our event. Bangers and mash as compared to haute cuisine. Both will be seen by some as either too basic or over the top.'

Anna added, 'That goes for the music as well. Heavy metal in contrast to classical music.'

Grundig completed the list, 'We may appear stuck up if we try to show off too much.'

'Again,' Stephanie concluded, 'we would have to plan the approach and leaving things to chance creates a potential risk, which may or may not materialize. The final objective was to make sure everyone has a good time. What could go wrong here?'

John stood up. 'We could hold a barbecue and it rains. Or we could fail to provide a vegetarian option. Or we could run out of drinks, say beer or for that matter wine...'

Anna joined in. 'The dinner may be poorly prepared. There may not be enough seating for everyone. Or someone may get drunk and insult everyone. Hey, gatecrashers may come in and spoil it all.'

Not wanting to be left out, John said, 'Perhaps loads of people fail to turn up and we are only left with one or two guests, who may feel odd.'

'Great,' Stephanie said. 'Now, out of all the risks that we have listed, which ones pose the greatest threat?'

Everyone had a go at scoring the risks to secure a revised list of significant risks. Stephanie then got them to work out which risks were more likely to

Table 6.2   The risks to the dinner party

Objective	Risks	Score Impact %	Things to do and by whom
1. Get to know neighbours			
2. Let them know we are friendly			
3. Have a good time			

arise if they took no specific action to address them. The list was rapidly becoming very detailed and ended up looking like Table 6.2.

'We are nearly there,' said Stephanie. 'Now, we can turn to those risks that we rated significant in terms of their potential impact and scored likely to arise if we failed to do something. We need to set out some way of handling the key risks if we are to achieve our goals. Or more correctly, if we are to have a better chance of achieving them.'

That said, the group looked at ways that they might tackle each key risk and after much debate, came up with ideas to complete each part of the list of things to do.

'The final thing to do is assign tasks to each of us to ensure that what needs doing is done. Any offers?'

John chose to research the guest list and talk to the postman, shopkeeper and others about preparing a guest list of geographically close neighbours. He would also find out what people in the village tended to do for such an occasion and the degree of formality that would fit the bill. The final task was to ensure everyone received their invitation in good time.

Anna would prepare the menus and ensure the food and drinks were purchased and prepared for the day. Grundig was given the task of preparing the dining room and back garden, as well as finding a local group of musicians to perform a suitable repertoire.

Stephanie had the less specific things to do and acted as coordinator, with the job of listing the various subsidiary tasks and ensuring they got done. One of her jobs was to watch the weather forecast and set up a contingency plan if it was likely to rain.

Notes

1. *Daily Mail*, Saturday, June 7, 2003, page 18.
2. *Daily Mail*, Thursday, January 1, 2004, page 7.
3. *Daily Mail*, Tuesday, June 24, 2003, page 1.
4. *Daily Mail*, Thursday, November 20, 2003, page 6.
5. *The Independent*, Saturday, March 27, 2004, page 6.
6. *The Business*, Saturday/Sunday, March 28/29, 2004, page 4.

7. *Daily Mail*, Wednesday, April 7, 2004, page 39.
8. *The Telegraph*, Wednesday, April 28, 2004, News, page 3.
9. *The Independent*, Friday, April 2, 2004, European news, page 30.
10. *The Times*, Friday, January 30, 2004, Effective Learning, page 8, Angela Baron, Chartered Institute of Personnel and Development, interviewed by Fred Silver.

7 The manager's initial investigation

Condemn the fault, and not the actor of it.

William Shakespeare, *Measure for Measure*, Act II, Scene 2

A4M Statement G   *The manager's initial investigation (MII) may focus on investigating past events where this is designed to clear the air and promote a healthier organization.*

Introduction

A4M 8.49 *The manager's initial investigation (MII) should secure reliable evidence that either supports or refutes the points at issue.*

Figure 1.1 in Chapter 1 shows how the book is put together. Chapter 7 describes how to establish and conduct a basic internal inquiry. There are times when the manager needs to carry out an inquiry into past events in line with formal terms of reference set by a commissioning party. The objective is to secure and assess relevant evidence, establish the facts and make helpful recommendations concerning the problem or situation back to the commissioning party. These types of audits are dealt with in this chapter and there is a set of standards in Appendix C that should also be referred to.

In short

Making a mistake is not the problem. It's making the mistake of trying to cover up problems that causes the real problem.

What is at stake

> **A4M 7.50** *All MIIs should be approved by an authorized commissioning party and include set terms of reference, lead investigator, review arrangements, access rights, reporting lines and quality assurance procedures.*

There are many times when controls fail to address a risk to an organization that can cause problems. The aim is to discover the truth and fix the controls, while managing the fallout. An investigation could result from a variety of reasons, including:

- Failing financial procedures.
- Errors in the accounts.
- Budget overspends.
- Accounts that do not reconcile.
- Unclear year-end accounting procedures.
- Projects that have failed.
- New acquisition that has crashed.
- Background to a trade union dispute.
- Breach of safety procedures.
- Serious complaints from customers.
- Claims of sexual harassment.
- Accidents at work.
- Unusual losses in a business unit.
- Staff misconduct.
- Appraisal of a company that may be taken over.
- Inaccuracies in management performance reports.
- Low staff morale in a section.
- High levels of sick leave.
- Product that has significant faults.
- Marketing campaign that has failed.
- Allegation of breach of procedure.
- Unfair manager promotion practices.
- Staff performance appraisal scheme that is not working.
- Aggressive sales techniques.
- Unethical work practices.

- Overpayments to suppliers.
- Abuse of privileges.
- Relocation costing three times more than planned.
- Poorly perceived performance management system.
- Allegations of minor employee fraud.

The above are all caused by failings in internal controls. Managers need to provide an initial response to these failings as part of their overall responsibility for establishing good systems of internal control. A manager's initial investigation (or MII for short) is an inquiry organized by a business manager that:

1. Is initiated by a commissioning party (CP).
2. Involves nonroutine aspects of work.
3. Involves the search and assessment of evidence.
4. May involve sensitive issues.
5. May not be supported by all stakeholders.
6. Can lead to reprimands.
7. Will probably examine past activities.
8. Should defend against interference.
9. Should be set within an ethical stance.
10. Concludes with a formal report that addresses any failings in internal control.

Each inquiry is unique but should follow a defined set of standards and methodology (see Appendix C for relevant standards). One way of viewing the MII is set out in Figure 7.1.

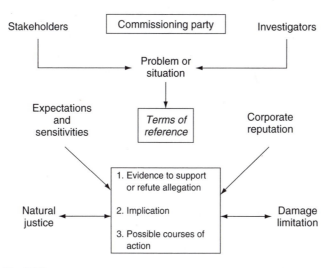

Figure 7.1   The MII process

Senior management will be authorized to commission an investigation and will have regard to the needs of stakeholders, as well as setting terms of reference to address these concerns. The principle behind A4M.99 is to give those most responsible for an activity an opportunity to provide an initial response to auditing this activity, and this includes working out where controls have failed. Once the terms of reference have been set, the work can commence against the need to cover all bases, including any expectations or sensitivities, and defend the corporate reputation. Huge problems can arise for an organization not because of a mistake or misjudgement, but more often because management has failed to respond to the problem in an acceptable manner. In fact, many criminal prosecutions for corporate wrongdoing end up with charges relating to concealing or destroying evidence or failing to cooperate with the authorities, rather than the original offence.

Specialist input?

Before line managers launch major investigations into significant problems, it is as well to consider when it is appropriate for the manager to review the events and when it is necessary to call in a specialist. Figure 7.2 helps clarify this matter.

Levels 1, 2 and 4 inquiries in Figure 7.2 should really be undertaken by the experts and there may be little to be gained from asking the manager to investigate. However, in level 3 issues it can be left to the manager to carry out an initial inquiry and it is these types of low-level issues that are addressed in this section of the book. Level 1 issues involve things like serious fraud, money laundering, legal claims, surveillance exercises, product liability, major security breaches, mergers and acquisitions, sabotage and health and safety breaches. An organization would be at fault if it did not use a specialist to work on these types of problems.

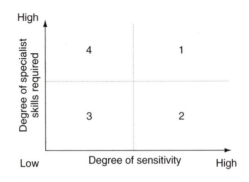

Figure 7.2   Bringing in the experts

In short

Really serious investigations need to be dealt with by people who are skilled at working at this level. All other matters should be part and parcel of a business manager's role.

Reputation management

> **A4M 7.51** *The MII process should include both immediate and longer-term measures to respond to issues that threaten to damage the corporate reputation of the organization.*

The manager is responsible for **promoting** the interests of the organization and also **protecting** it. This protection is about preserving the good name of the business or, in other words, the corporate reputation. Most people who have a dispute with a local business really only want an apology and a response that steps have been taken to strengthen controls. This is why all problems, issues, complaints, mistakes and oversights need to be cleared up properly and quickly. Figure 7.3 makes clear the link with corporate reputation.

It is generally a good idea to tell people about any obvious problems and rebuild any damage to corporate reputation. Figure 7.3 suggests that any issues such as failed projects and operational errors need to be remedied, as it will affect reputation if there are any gaps in the way they are reviewed and dealt with.

Avoiding a crisis

Where the problem is quite serious and can lead to a crisis, managers could take several drastic steps, including:

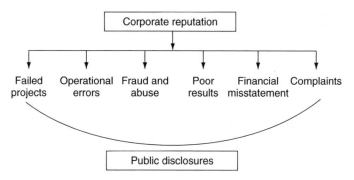

Figure 7.3   Reputation management

- Find out whether the press are interested and if so, where they are getting their information.
- Talk to stakeholders and ease their fears.
- Think about a worst-case scenario and work out the likelihood that this will arise.
- Open up a communications channel and use professionals in managing the information flow – any gaps in information will lead to a vacuum that will be filled by other means.
- Bring in the contingency plans that should have been developed to deal with an assortment of major problems.
- Announce immediate action – and longer-term plans.
- Put people before profits and deal with fears before making excuses.
- Remember, it is about staying in control and not letting perceptions take over from the real situation.
- If the issue is overplayed, it may attract more attention.
- If it is underplayed, it may give out an impression that the organization does not really care about the matter.
- Give a considered response that does not make assumptions, particularly where legal advice is required – certainly do not try to assign blame at this stage.
- For bigger issues a multidisciplinary team may be used to assess the situation and develop strategies for moving forward.
- Link problems to procedures and plan reviews that will strengthen them.
- Dig into the corporate value system and remind people how the business operates.

When establishing an MII, there should be a business case for justifying the time and effort involved. An **investigation** may be designed to:

- Uncover the truth.
- Preempt an external inquiry.
- Improve systems and procedures.
- Demonstrate that the organization is serious about standards.
- Reinforce corporate values and try to look good in the eyes of stakeholders, thereby turning a negative into a positive.

Analysing stakeholder positions

In terms of assessing stakeholder positions regarding the MII, it is possible to analyse where each group stands, as in Table 7.1.

The idea is that whenever a problem occurs, management places the risks that have materialized against the relevant stakeholder perspective and the controls, or response to risk, that have been decided. Then it weighs up the effect on corporate reputation in the minds of the relevant stakeholders.

Table 7.1 Assessing stakeholder positions

A. Expectations of employees	Risks	Controls	Reputation

Factors:

1. Fair reward system
2. Safe working environment
3. Challenging work
4. Clear sense of direction
5. Positive values
6. Friendly team

B. Expectations of the board

Factors:

1. Regulations adhered to
2. Key targets met
3. Best practice achieved
4. Value of organization enhanced
5. Strategy implemented
6. Hardworking staff

C. Expectations of customers

Factors:

1. Fair price
2. Aftercare package
3. Pleasant buying experience
4. Helpful staff
5. Ethical practices
6. Trusted brand

D. Expectations – tensions between stakeholders

Factors:

1. Short v long term
2. Cost v quality
3. Dividends v growth
4. Passive v aggressive marketing
5. Good ethics v lowest costs
6. Positive brand name v fair published information

In short

Corporate reputations are hard earned and easily lost. It is about appreciating the value of a good name as a long-term issue, and spending time and money to retain, maintain and enhance it.

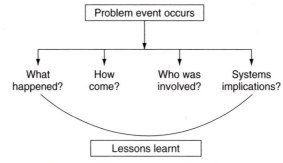

Figure 7.4   Responding to problems

Types of investigations

> **A4M 7.52** *The MII approach can be applied to routine investigations into breach of procedure, complaints, unmitigated risk and staff conduct. It is not equipped to deal with more complex issues such as major fraud, accounting irregularity and abuse by senior officials of the organization.*

We have noted that there are different types and levels of investigations. Some issues are based on unfounded gossip whereas others derive from very serious allegations. The response should fit the event – bearing in mind that a minor problem may be symptomatic of a much more serious concern resulting from poor controls. Figure 7.4 suggests one way of responding to a control failure.

The idea is to respond to each of the four questions in Figure 7.4 and solve the problem, learn lessons and work out what this means for corporate traditions and whether there is a need to revisit the way values are set.

Types of investigations

In getting a good focus in the MII into, say, a complaint from a dissatisfied customer, the manager needs to work out where the problem stands in the scheme of things. Figure 7.5 can be used to position the issue.

Using Figure 7.5, each problem can be given a classification:

- **Type 1** – less serious issues resulting from events in the past may be given a quick check to see if there is anything that needs to be done to respond to the remaining concerns about poor control and strengthen them if necessary.

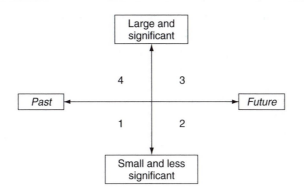

Figure 7.5   Types of investigations

Really old events may be of less interest and could have moved on from the circumstances that caused them to arise in the first place. It may not be worthwhile doing much work on type 1 issues.

- **Type 2** – again, these are less serious matters but this time affecting future plans. Revisit the risk assessment and determine whether there are any changes to controls required.
- **Type 3** – these problems are more serious. Where they have an impact on future events it may be necessary to realign existing strategy to deal with outstanding concerns. Investigations into very recent transactions and decisions will probably relate to the current control arrangements and may call for some action to reset controls.
- **Type 4** – these investigations relate to days past but are fairly significant. The focus tends to move away from controls and may involve more consideration of individuals and their conduct. The question to ask is: whatever happened then, could it happen again?

The commissioning party

A4M.99 is not about encouraging managers to start investigating anything and everything, as this detracts from work and could get out of hand. What is required is a structured way of dealing with known or alleged failings in internal control. To give such work some credence, it is an idea to establish a structured way of organizing all MIIs, including a consideration of the following matters:

- Determine which officials can be deemed a commissioning party (CP) in terms of setting up an MII. These persons may be sub-board-level executives.
- Each MII should be supported by a one-page business case that is approved by the CP before the work is started.

- The CP then owns the MII and will want to ensure that the manager, or appointed reviewer, performs a good job.
- The work should be carried out in line with a written brief that details the terms of reference, scope, objectives, boundaries and approach. This document should specify what falls within the jurisdiction of the investigating manager and which issues need to be placed before the CP for decision.
- For larger jobs that last more than one day, a budget should be approved by the CP and monitored using the organization's standard budgetary control arrangements.
- Once resources have been secured, tasks should be documented and allocated, work monitored and standards applied to the way the work is performed.
- Any changes to the terms of reference should be approved by the CP.
- Progress should be reported back to the CP on a regular basis.
- The CP should not interfere with the MII. The CP is there to ensure that the review happens properly and promotes and protects the interests of the organization in addressing control failings and taking steps to ensure the problem does not reoccur.
- The CP should review the file before the MII report is released for publication.
- On conclusion of the work, the CP may report to the board on the MII.

In terms of point 4 above, where respective decision-making roles are determined, Figure 7.6 may be of some help.

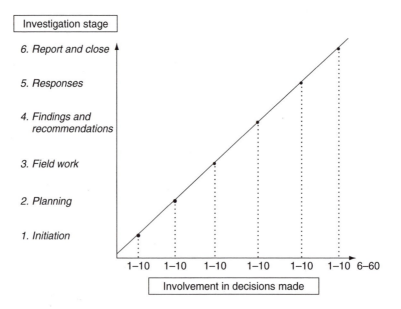

Figure 7.6 Stages of involvement

We can break the MII into defined stages and determine the type of involvement of the CP at each of stages 1 to 6. Levels of involvement may range from 1, which is no involvement other than to review the file after the report is drafted, through to level 10, which is close review of work carried out and endorsement of decisions made. It is a good idea to make these decisions before the work is started and we expect that the more serious the matter, the more involvement there will be from the CP.

Continuing with point 3 above on setting the terms of reference, there are several possible questions that may be part of the brief, including:

- What happened?
- How did it happen?
- Who did what and when?
- How long has this been going on?
- How does it affect the business?
- Should we take a tough line?
- Is this going to be a cover-up?
- What are our options?
- What do we tell people?
- How do we limit the damage?
- What messages are we sending out?
- Who can we trust?
- If we don't act, will someone step in?
- Can we turn this into a positive?
- What are our immediate and longer-term actions?

If these 15 questions are not built into the terms of reference for the MII, then people will find other ways of answering them, which could be quite dangerous. The other matters that should be considered before the work is approved cover questions such as:

- Would an investigation be effective?
- Is the matter too old to look into?
- Is it trivial, vexatious or not made in good faith?
- Is there a more appropriate forum for the investigation?

Standards

Everyone associated with the MII will need to act:

- Within the law.
- Reasonably.
- In a just and proper manner.
- To explain their decisions.

- Based on verifiable facts.
- In line with procedures.

The size and scale of the MII should be determined as early as possible and Table 7.2 is a rough guide.

In short

All investigations should be structured and organized in a sensible manner so that they have credence and meaning to all those who are interested in the results.

Finding out

> **A◀M 7.53**   *The MII approach can be applied to uncovering the reality where this is not immediately obvious. The search for the truth should involve sufficiently rigorous inquiries to address the matters set out in the formal terms of reference that is agreed with the commissioning party.*

It is possible to set out a standardized approach to carrying out MII and this is noted below:

1. **Allegation**. The problem, issue, allegation or error comes to light and the manager in question needs to respond. For example, it may involve a suspicion that overtime claims are being inflated as standard practice in one district in particular.
2. **Initial checks**. This stage is about making some basic checks to find out the scale of the matter and any implications. This may mean looking at the extent of overtime claims in the district as compared to others and working out whether the allegation has any merit. This stage should also consider how urgent and serious the matter is and whether the organization will be exposed to any ongoing criticism. Concerns such as disappearing evidence, effect on staff morale, claims of cover-up and stakeholder expectations will

Table 7.2   What size should the investigation be?

	Time	Resources	Budget	Structure
SMALL	1 day	1 person	None	Brief given
MEDIUM	Several days	1 + people	Expenses	Formal plan
LARGE	Several weeks	Team	Formal code	Project

also be addressed. For more significant issues there may be a need to issue public comments and close obvious control gaps. For a full-scale damage limitation and contingency planning exercise, a further report will be needed and specialists brought in to take over the investigation. This may happen where, for example, the overtime claims are material and have led to significant overcharging of customers.

3. **Commissioning party (CP) authorization**. The manager should prepare a brief note on the matter containing a view on whether it is necessary to launch an investigation. This will be considered by a member of the board and approved if necessary with formal terms of reference setting out the aims of the MII and the boundaries that it should stay within.

4. **Defining roles**. This stage is about working out who does what. The chosen lead officer will have to have proven ability, including integrity, drive, balance, inquisitiveness and a reputation for being fair and thorough.

5. **Determining capacity**. The regional manager may appoint a suitable member of the management team to undertake a review of the problem and detail a budget for the job, again approved by the CP. The lead officer will have to have had MII training and an understanding of the standards for conducting MII. The work will not normally require a team, since if it is serious and in need of a comprehensive inquiry, it will be handed over to specialist investigators or internal audit.

6. **Investigation plan**. The lead officer will prepare a plan setting out how the matter will be tackled and get this approved by the CP or nominated person. The theme of the work may be summed up in the phrase 'Let's pull together and sort out this mess – leave the post-mortem for later'.

7. **Evidential considerations**. That is working out where evidence fits in civil and criminal law. In our example the approach to the work will have to be well balanced. It is generally possible to use set suppositions for the work. These suppositions are what we suppose may have happened as per the given allegations or the tentative research so far. Evidence is then secured that tends to support or refute these suppositions. Our supposition is that there may be inflated overtime claims in district X and the evidence gathered may, for example, involve confirming that the overtime claiming system is lax and that there should be better controls put in place. The lead officer will have to have authorized access to records and information and will be alert to maintaining confidentiality. There may well be a need to interview employees as part of the evidence gathering stage. All work will have to be in line with set standards for this type of initial audit (e.g. Appendix C), and in particular any procedures relating to evidence gathering and storage.

8. **Tools**. It may be necessary to apply statistical sampling or automated data interrogation. For example, a manager could select a representative random sample of overtime claims comparing the target district with others. An automated data interrogation tool could then be used to extract overtime claims that fall outside a set of chosen parameters for further analysis.

9. **Interim reports**. Short reports will be drawn up periodically. In our example, the recommendation may be that operatives in the district could be told about the tighter controls and reminded that further claims will be considered a disciplinary offence and formally dealt with. Note that the organization's legal officer may wish to have sight of the reports before they are finalized. It is a good idea to prepare weekly progress reports where the work drags on for a bit. For matters that may be of interest to stakeholders, it may be an idea to provide regular briefing sessions.

10. **Further investigation**? The matter may rest there or there may be further implications. For example, it may be that a supervisor at the district has authorized inflated overtime on the basis of a kickback, and this may be seen as a more serious issue that needs to be formally investigated by, say, internal audit.

11. **Final reports**. This will contain an account of the work and any findings and recommendations. The stress should be on the state of controls and how they may be improved.

Budgets and monitoring

Managers will need to set up a monitoring system to ensure that the work stays on target. The CP authorization may cover aspects of the work including:

- **Person** – the lead officer and anyone who may need to assist the project from time to time.
- **Tasks** – and tentative dates for each one.
- **Timeframes** – from start and possible finish dates.
- **Budgets** – financial budget and expenditure codes.
- **Reports** – how results will be reported and to whom.

For bigger projects it may be necessary to secure a formal budget, which may contain various detailed elements, along with information for monitoring purposes, along the lines of Table 7.3.

Financial constraints should not normally get in the way of an investigation unless the expenditure is unreasonable or the item is not worth spending money on. But note that the more you do, the more you spend. In addition, weekly progress reports may be issued covering:

- Tasks, roles, changes.
- Evidence so far.
- Immediate action carried out.
- Interfaces with other systems and problems.
- Link to interim reports.
- Problems and solutions.
- Next week's logistics.

Table 7.3 Setting the budget

Total budget	Budget for period	Actual spend	Variance	Explanation
Training				
Offices				
Stationery				
External fees				
Staff and team				
Support services				
Equipment				
Publications				
Interviewer expenses				
Interviewee expenses				
Other, e.g. legal fees				
TOTALS	£	£	£	

It is a good idea to get the lead officer and any others who work on the MII to log times spent on the work. The actual times may be compared with the approved hours and any variances included in the interim reports issued by the lead officer back to the commissioning party. A change authorization procedure can be applied where the terms of reference, times allowed and resources may be altered if the MII takes a new direction and more work needs to be carried out. In our example, it may be that most of the districts are submitting inflated overtime and the problem may be bigger than originally thought. Any change procedure should include details of:

- Change.
- Request by.
- Reason.
- Impact.
- Approval.
- Dates.

This should be cross-referenced to the original plan, which in turn should be altered to reflect the agreed changes. At all stages of the work, consideration should be given to whether it is time to bring in the internal auditors or a team of specialist investigators.

Brainstorming

For more vexatious MIIs it is possible to pin a planning frame on the wall that shows considerations such as:

- Task.
- Must dos.
- Should like to dos.
- Assigned to.
- Dates.
- Summary results.
- Possible next steps.

Note that a simple flow diagram of the problem and people, sections and systems involved can be prepared to help focus on the key issues.

Reporting results

The MII should be fully reported. One pivotal form that helps with this task is called the summary schedule of results (SSR). The SSR lends itself to the preparation of interim and final reports and contains the summary information in Table 7.4.

Documentation file

It is essential that a file is maintained holding all the information that has been secured during the course of the MII. The file will contain material such as:

1. Terms of reference.
2. Report to commissioning party for authorization to proceed.
3. Quality assurance reviews.

Table 7.4 Suppositions and research

Issues	Supposition	Research	Evidence	Conclusions
1				
2				
3				

IMPACT ON CONTROLS:

RECOMMENDATIONS:

4. Plans for the work.
5. SSR (see Table 7.4).
6. Interview records.
7. Evidence secured.
8. Background notes and correspondence.

Blame and accountability

One issue that must be addressed in terms of the MII approach to investigations is the need to stand back and consider whether the organization is operating in a blame culture or a fair and balanced accountability culture. Most writers will argue that a blame culture causes many problems and does not promote good accountability. They maintain the view that well-established accountabilities represent the way forward. The problem lies in the fact that there are certain blurred lines. For example, good accountability frameworks mean that people become responsible for the consequences of their actions – and as such can be blamed where they fall down in their duties. When someone is blamed, others claim that this is the result of a blame culture, and therein lies the confusion. There is a link between accountability and blame and this is explained in Figure 7.7.

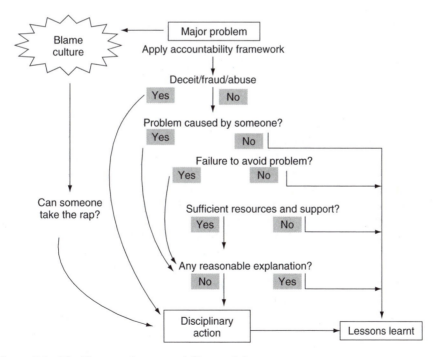

Figure 7.7   The blame and accountability model

When a major problem arises, many questions should be asked before disciplinary action is taken to sanction someone for their actions or failure to act. The blame culture on the left of Figure 7.7 goes straight into 'disciplinary action' as it is based on finding someone who can 'carry the can' when a big problem arises. The 'accountability framework' is much more sophisticated and, as we said, there is much that needs to be studied before arriving at the 'disciplinary action' box. The focus here leans much more towards the 'lessons learnt' box. The important point about Figure 7.7 is that both a blame- and an accountability-based organization may lead someone to the 'disciplinary action' box – it is just that one uses this route much more frequently than the other.

In short

A good investigation is mainly about setting standards and then ensuring we are able and prepared to meet these standards. An investigating manager needs to prove that the result is a reliable piece of work, not a whitewash.

Making sense and making good

A4M 7.54   *The MII approach should involve all efforts to make sense out of the evidence that is gathered during the course of the field work. Making sense means interpreting the findings in the context of the actual circumstances so as to be readily understandable by anyone who has authorized access to the findings.*

The main reason to study problems, past events and complaints is to learn more about the way systems work in practice. The manager's initial investigation is about making sense of the findings when reviewing these problems, past events and complaints and, as a result, making good organizational controls. Problems arise because risks have not really been addressed, and it is the controls that guard against risk that cause problems. Investigations should uncover things that are done well and things that are not and will reveal what is operating as planned and what is falling down. Moreover, we have already said that such inquiries will uncover matters relating to past events and those that feature in present operations and therefore the immediate future. Figure 7.8 uses these four dimensions of what is good/what is not good and past/future orientations to explain further.

Future successes (top right Figure 7.8) relate to strengthening strategies and innovating towards a better future. Bottom right issues present problems and call for more attention to contingency plans to minimize problems if they occur. Past failings (bottom left) should be assessed to work out how to ensure

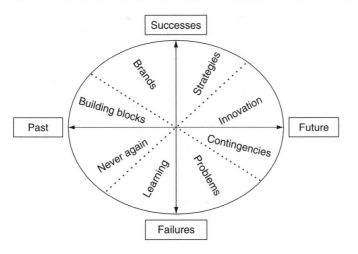

Figure 7.8   The MII focus wheel

this never happens again, as part of the corporate learning process, while past successes (top left) create a platform based on the corporate reputation and brand to build future successes.

When considering investigations in this way, using Figure 7.8, it is possible to keep the accent on forward thinking and future successes, rather than blaming people and making excuses for any known problems. There are many reasons why people do not want to get involved with an ongoing investigation, including the following:

- There are no real standards in place and this may be revealed by the investigation.
- No one cares about anyone's performance anyway, people do as they please.
- Most people turn a blind eye to abuse.
- Stakeholders would be most upset if they knew what was going on here.
- A prevailing attitude of 'you scratch my back and I'll scratch yours'.
- If the manager acts, people may rebel.
- A view that problem people can always be transferred to another section if they get really bad.
- If ignored the problem will simply go away.
- Not wanting to 'squeal' on friends.

Views on honesty

These views are not made up, they are real. One survey showed how corporate figures were rated by the public (Table 7.5).[1]

Table 7.5 People who can be trusted

	Most can be trusted %	Can't be too careful with them %
People who run small businesses	75	22
Military officers	73	24
CEOs of large corporations	23	73
Car dealers	15	81

Another survey considered employees' observations of any violation of law or company standards. 60% of employees had observed a violation of law or company standards some time in the previous 12 months, and 37% had observed misconduct that they believed could result in a significant loss of public trust if known.[2]

This is why managers cannot always rely on team workshops to brainstorm all risks, in for example the team initial auditing approach mentioned earlier, as by mutual consent there may be some aspects of risk that are not spoken about. At times management needs to carry out investigations into known problems, rather than relying on, say, the whistleblowers' hotline. Where the results of a MII concentrate on better controls, managers can arrive at process redesign to deal with problems associated with entrenched views and poor compliance with procedures. The criticism is not about the people and their personalities, but about how to deal with the problems resulting from a poor control culture. The bottom line is that where improvements are needed they must be made. Where there are problems leading to poor performance or damage to the corporate reputation, they must be addressed.

In short

An investigation is not about doing something just to get the wolves off your back. It is about responding to entrenched problems and breaking through with improvements that work.

Common mistakes

> **A4M 7.55** *MIIs that involve the consideration of specific issues under investigation should be carried out by people who are able to undertake the work with adequate competence and credibility.*

Figure 7.9 Good investigations

Scenario one

Problems can occur in even well-run organizations and they can become a cause of deep embarrassment. The key is to keep things under wraps and ensure that if there is bad news, it is played down and hopefully such negatives will be hidden from the public eye.

Scenario two

The A4M.99 process turns much of this on its head by suggesting that the scenario should change to the following:

Problems can occur in even well-run organizations and they can become a cause of deep embarrassment. The key is to clear the air, probe the problem and the underlying causes and deliver honest messages about improving controls. In this way a negative occurrence may well be turned into positive energy.

Is it that simple?

There is much that could go wrong in moving from scenario one to scenario two:

- **Managers are seen to have no role in investigating problems at work**. Where there is no delegated authority given to managers to provide an initial response to problems at work, there will be less scope to develop the MII process.

- **Much reliance is placed on specialist investigators whenever there is a problem at work that needs looking into**. Where the specialists are used for all investigations, there will be less chance to develop a skilled capacity in the workplace.
- **There is no set procedure for carrying out investigations, such as involving a commissioning party or living up to formal guidelines**. Where management inquiries and investigations follow no standard or suggested guidelines, the outcomes will tend to be hit and miss.
- **There is no set damage limitation strategy for dealing with problems that affect the corporate reputation**. Where contingency plans have not been devised for events that dent the corporate reputation, the response to a significant problem will be developed in a chaotic climate.
- **Investigations carried out with no real focus on improving controls**. Where an investigation does not address control failure, there will be no way to ensure that lessons are learnt and improvements made.
- **There is no consideration of stakeholder expectations when setting up an investigation**. Where an investigation does not recognize the impact on all those interested in the outcome, it may not be seen as valid.
- **There is no clear definition of respective roles, which means the work can be interfered with in worst-case scenarios**. Where roles are not sorted out for investigations, the problem of interference and compromise may occur.
- **Investigations are set up with no regard to resources, budgets and monitoring arrangements**. Where an investigation is not resourced at the planning stage, there is no certainty that it can be completed properly.
- **A blame culture is in place, which means all investigations are designed to remove the person who it is easiest to pin the blame on**. Where an investigation is solely based on establishing blame, there is a chance that it will be steered in a preset direction.
- **The potential scale and impact of employee breach of procedure is underestimated by management**. Where an investigation fails to address real issues on staff noncompliance, there may be gaps in the report that is issued.

Helpful models for overcoming problems

The main model for working out what is wrong with an organization and moving it forward is found in Figure 7.10.

When an organization spends a great deal of time carrying out investigations into a continuous stream of problems, this could indicate a deep-seated imbalance. It may be that people are given lots to do but impose no accountability, in which case a 'cowboy culture' develops. Or it may be the other way round, in which case a 'blame culture' is more the norm. If an organization can achieve a good balance between both aspects of corporate

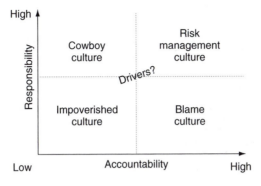

Figure 7.10   Responsibility and accountability

life, it can move towards a 'risk management culture', where controls are sound and fit the risks and these controls are seen as important to success. Professional investigations into corporate problems that look for this imbalance and can root out 'impoverished cultures' will provide much more value than quick fixes that look to blame someone or simply cover up the mess.

In short

Problems can be compounded where attempts to investigate them cause more problems to arise and so muddy the water for all sides.

Check your progress

A◀M 7.56 *MIIs should be carried out in accordance with set standards.*

One tool that can be applied to track your progress is to test the extent to which you have assimilated the key points raised in this chapter. The multi-choice questions below will check your progress and the answer guide in Appendix D is based on what is most appropriate in the context of this book. Please record your answers in the table at Appendix D. You may also record the time spent on each test and enter this information in the 'Mins' column of Appendix D.

Name ....

Start time .... **Finish time** .... **Total minutes** ....

Multi-choice quiz

1. Which is the odd one out?
For A◀M.*99*, a manager's initial investigation (or MII for short) is an inquiry
carried out (or organized) by a business manager that involves the following:

a. initiated by a commissioning party.
b. nonroutine aspect of work.
c. search for and assessment of evidence.
d. must be supported by all stakeholders.

2. Select the most appropriate sentence.
a. The principle behind A◀M.*99* is to give those most independent from an
   activity an opportunity to provide an initial response to auditing this activity,
   and this includes working out where controls have failed.
b. The principle behind A◀M.*99* is to give those most responsible for an
   activity an opportunity to provide an initial response to auditing this activity,
   and this includes working out where controls have failed.
c. The principle behind A◀M.*99* is to give those most responsible for an
   activity an opportunity to provide a definitive response to auditing this
   activity, and this includes working out where controls have failed.
d. The principle behind A◀M.*99* is to give those most responsible for performing
   investigations an opportunity to provide an initial response to auditing this
   activity, and this includes working out where controls have failed.

3. Insert the missing words.
Most people who have a dispute with a local business really only want an apology
and a response that steps have been taken to.............................

a. strengthen controls.
b. dismiss staff.
c. compensate them.
d. contact the authorities.

4. Which is the odd one out?
An investigation may be designed to:

a. uncover the truth.
b. encourage an external inquiry.
c. improve systems and procedures.
d. demonstrate that we are serious about standards.

5. Select the most appropriate sentence.

a. We have noted that most investigations are fairly similar. Some issues are based on unfounded gossip whereas others derive from very serious allegations.

b. We have noted that there are different types and levels of investigations. Some issues are based on formal assertions whereas others derive from very serious allegations.

c. We have noted that there are different types and levels of investigations. Some issues are based on unfounded gossip whereas others derive from hearsay.

d. We have noted that there are different types and levels of investigations. Some issues are based on unfounded gossip whereas others derive from very serious allegations.

6. Insert the missing words.

A4M.99 is not about encouraging managers to start investigating anything and everything, as this detracts from work and could get out of hand. What we want is a structured way of dealing with ....

a. known or alleged failings in internal control.

b. known or alleged failings in personal behaviour.

c. suspected or alleged failings in internal control.

d. known or alleged failings in internal communications.

7. Which is the odd one out?

Everyone associated with the MII will need to act:

a. within the law.

b. in a just and proper manner.

c. to explain their decisions.

d. based on evidence that is beyond all reasonable doubt.

8. Select the most appropriate sentence.

a. The theme of the work may be summed up in the phrase 'Let's pull together and sort out this mess – start with a post-mortem'.

b. The theme of the work may be summed up in the phrase 'Let's pull together and find out who caused this mess – leave the post-mortem for later'.

c. The theme of the work may be summed up in the phrase 'Let's pull together and sort out this mess – leave the post-mortem for later'.

d. The theme of the work may be summed up in the phrase 'Let's pull together and sort out this mess – what we do not need is a post-mortem'.

9. Insert the missing words.

The manager's initial investigation is about making sense of the findings when reviewing these problems, past events and complaints and, as a result, ...

a. making good our promises.

b. making good our controls.

c. stripping down our controls.
d. enforcing our controls.

10. Select the most appropriate sentence.
a. This is why we cannot always rely on team workshops to brainstorm all risks in, for example, the manager's initial auditing approach mentioned earlier, as by mutual consent there may be some aspects of risk that are not spoken about.
b. This is why we cannot always rely on team workshops to brainstorm all risks in, for example, the manager's initial investigation approach mentioned earlier, as by mutual consent there may be some aspects of risk that are not spoken about.
c. This is why we can always rely on team workshops to brainstorm all risks in, for example, the team initial auditing approach mentioned earlier, as by mutual consent there may be some aspects of risk that are not spoken about.
d. This is why we cannot always rely on team workshops to brainstorm all risks in, for example, the team initial auditing approach mentioned earlier, as by mutual consent there may be some aspects of risk that are not spoken about.

Newsflash – read all about it

There is so much behind the move towards effective governance and risk management in all walks of life, and a small selection of relevant examples is provided to illustrate this new way of thinking.

10 new dimensions

Old thinking	New dimensions	A suitable example
Our corporate reputation is very resilient bearing in mind that people have short memories.	It's a good idea to remember that one slip of the tongue could hurt an organization, sometimes fatally.	In April 1999 Gerald Ratner managed to wipe £500 million from the value of the Ratner jewellery empire by referring to his goods as 'crap' in front of an audience of 6000 business men and women.
Damage limitation is partly about getting a message out to the public quickly and with conviction.	Damage limitation is partly about getting a message out to the public quickly, while making sure this message is based on the best evidence available.	The railway engineering firm Jarvis is to issue a humiliating apology to survivors of the Potters Bar train crash for its controversial assertion that the accident was caused by sabotage . . . they finally admitted joint liability for the crash . . . The company produced photographs and analysis which it claimed amounted to evidence that a set of damaged points which caused the accident had been tampered with. Its stance was dismissed by police and caused outrage among survivors.[3]

It remains a mystery to this day.	Prepare a list of tough questions that really must be answered.	Manchester United football club was presented with a list of 99 key questions that they had to answer – most concerning transfer dealing (buying and selling players) and the use of agents.[4]
This job has lots of extras – you know, perks and such things.	Once high standards of behaviour are set, we need to ensure they are observed by everyone.	The Ritz hotel has dismissed the hotel general manager. Some felt this was due to his wife having her hair styled on a regular basis at the hotel's expense.[5]
Disciplinary action will be taken for all breaches of the code of conduct.	Disciplinary action should be blended with common sense so that it is applied in an appropriate and sensible manner.	The brain surgeon suspended in a dispute over a bowl of soup has been cleared to return to work, nine days after the suspension.[6]
If in doubt conduct a public inquiry.	It is really only worth starting a major inquiry if previous reviews were inadequate and something new may be gained from the effort.	The decision by a British coroner to investigate the death of Princess Diana was questioned by a French judge. The original French investigation involved 30 detectives, 300 witnesses and 6000 pages of evidence.[7]
Disasters happen, and the best remedy is to take time out to heal the pain.	Where a disaster is caused by the act or omission of an employee, the company in question may be fined.	One of the train companies involved in the Paddington disaster (in which 31 people died) was fined a record £2m yesterday... the train operator admitted that the newly qualified driver who was killed in the crash was not properly trained or warned about the complex signalling system outside the west London station.[8]
Official inquiries must be carried out by good people who know the business and understand the issues in question.	Official inquiries must be carried out by independent people who also know the business and understand the issues in question.	In one study US scientists found that passive smoking is less dangerous than claimed and living with a smoker did not significantly raise the risk of death from heart disease or lung cancer. But health campaigners pointed out that the research was partly funded by the tobacco industry.[9]
If you need to catch a thief at work then set up a surveillance camera.	When deciding on covert surveillance, one needs to be very careful about adhering to the regulations covering this type of activity.	A senior school teacher who caused a security alert by hiding a spy camera clock has been ticked off for breaking regulations... there are laws preventing schools from using covert video surveillance except in extraordinary circumstances, with police involvement.[10]

(Continued)

Old thinking	New dimensions	A suitable example
Where there are known problems in an organization they must be addressed.	Where known problems continue to hamper an organization they must be addressed by considering more drastic measures.	Greater Manchester police is to launch its own undercover investigation into racist police officers following last week's exposé of bigotry in the ranks. The force denounced the BBC for using an undercover reporter in the shocking documentary, which led to six racist officers quitting in disgrace. But now it is to use civilian black and Asian investigators to see if officers treat them differently from white victims of crime.[11]

The key messages

The last section of each chapter contains a short story or quote that should provide an interesting format for illustrating some of the book's key messages.

Learning lessons?

The inquiry into the Ladbroke Grove rail disaster commented:

> Accident investigations are geared to find the person to blame and not to find the unsafe act. The investigations are very superficial and hardly ever is an effort made to discover the root causes, the removal of which is the only guarantee of preventing a recurrence of the same or similar incident.[12]

Notes

1. CNN/*USA Today*/Gallup poll, July 2002.
2. KPMG LLP, based on its 2000 Organizational Integrity Survey.
3. *The Guardian*, Wednesday, April 28, 2004, News, page 3.
4. *Daily Mail*, Friday, January 30, 2004, page 93.
5. *Mail on Sunday*, Sunday, April 11, 2004, page 7.
6. *Daily Mail*, Thursday, March 25, 2004, page 21.
7. *The Times*, Wednesday, January 7, 2004, page 24c.
8. *The Independent*, Tuesday, April 6, 2004, Home News, page 7.
9. *Daily Mail*, Friday, May 16, 2003, page 43.
10. *Sunday Express*, Sunday, April 25, 2004, page 43.
11. *The Mail on Sunday*, Sunday, October 26, 2003, page 47.
12. Second Ladbroke Grove Rail Inquiry, report by Lord Cullen, 2001.

8 Successful risk management

> **A4M Statement H** *The A4M.99 approach should promote the integration of successful risk management into the way people behave at work.*

Introduction

> **A4M 8.57** *The initial audit process should be based on engaging everyone in risk management with a view to helping them perform and work smarter.*

Figure 1.1 in Chapter 1 shows how the book is put together. Chapter 8 puts together some of the ideas we have been discussing into an account of what makes successful risk management. We have said that the manager needs a good understanding of risk concepts. Moreover, the manager needs to be able to mobilize three main tools:

1. The manager's reviews of risk management and internal controls.
2. The team's review of specific risk and internal controls.
3. The manager's investigation into control failings.

In short

Three tools have been discussed in the previous three chapters of the book. What we need to do now is to put together the above and come out with a successful way of managing risk across the organization.

Building on the risk concepts

A4M 8.58 *In areas of the business where initial auditing is being introduced, existing expertise in specialist risk assessment work should be used as a foundation for rolling out the wider risk process built into initial auditing.*

The COSO ERM is a fundamental platform for getting risk management into the heart of an organization in a holistic way. COSO argues that enterprise risk management:

- Is a process – it is a means to an end, not an end in itself.
- Is affected by people – it is not merely policies, surveys and forms, but involves people at every level of an organization.
- Is applied to strategy setting.
- Is applied across the organization, at every level and unit, and includes taking an entity-level, portfolio view of risks.
- Is designed to identify events potentially affecting the entity and manage risk within its risk appetite.
- Provides reasonable assurance to an entity's management and board.
- Is geared to the achievement of objectives in one or more separate but overlapping categories.[1]

To get to successful risk management, we need to put ideas and concepts together. Figure 8.1 starts the ball rolling.

We set our objectives and plans, which translate into a series of corporate and divisional targets, section and team targets, and this falls into the performance framework. The hope is that the resultant outcomes will serve to deliver set objectives. Within this cycle sit the basic controls that must be in place relating to financial management, reporting, corporate compliance, integrity of data, employee conduct and so on. At the sharp end of every operation are the local risks and these are addressed through customized controls, designed by local managers and their teams. A review and validation process falls at the end of the cycle and this supports the performance framework described earlier. That is, the risks and controls reflect the need to perform and deliver the set outcomes. The four stages are important:

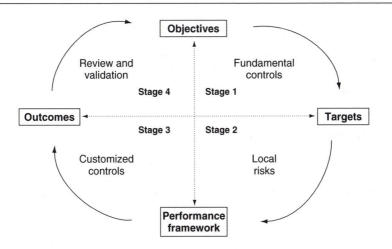

Figure 8.1   The risk management cycle

- **Stage one** – fundamental controls need to be set at a corporate level, say in terms of access controls for the customer accounts database, and observed by all.
- **Stage two** – local risks need to be properly identified and understood by those who run the local offices and operations.
- **Stage three** – additional controls need to be designed to respond to local risks.
- **Stage four** – these controls need to be reviewed and validated so that they are seen to be sound and this fact can be reported upwards.

Levels of standardization

A national retail outfit will have loads of corporate controls that must be observed. However, the local arrangements will vary, since a huge super-market in a rural middle-class area will be very different from a much smaller, high street shop in a deprived, high-density part of the country, even if these two outlets are part of the same retail chain. Each branch/unit will have its own profile and need its own risk management solutions in line with a corporate framework. This principle applies to chains of banks, estate agents, govern-ment offices, libraries, leisure centres and a whole range of businesses that need to be responsive to local factors such as the region, customers, staff availability, services provided and social conditions. So long as the local managers are given the right tools, options and guidance, they can then decide on the best approach. In terms of understanding roles and responsibilities, the local managers may be told to check that your local controls work and corporate standards are observed; get your people involved in the review process; and sort out any particular control failings – and then report back that this has been done.

In short

Risk management concepts and tools can look pretty impressive. But local managers should be allowed the scope to adapt and apply them in a way that suits their particular business circumstances.

The risk policy

A◄M 8.59 *The corporate risk policy should refer to initial auditing, or an alternative tool, and indicate the way in which this approach may be used to support the risk management process.*

This section of the book begins with a simple figure and then a more challenging one. Figure 8.2 is the simple one.

Figure 8.2 says that the organization is a series of processes that run various operations, which consist of inputs, the process and then whatever is delivered; that is, the outputs. Meanwhile there are risks that affect this dynamic, which have to be countered by controls. The board will typically formulate a risk policy stating that this model should be in place throughout the organization and that risks will be managed in line with the risk appetite set by the board.

Now for the more difficult model. Figure 8.3 takes the basic idea of a risk policy and asks whether something that has been designed for plain sailing will work in murky waters.

The problem is that boardroom mumbojumbo has to reach the various management teams, and then dive down into what we have earlier called the 'murky waters' of reality. That is, the risk policy has to be translated into everyday language for busy work teams. Some organizations run risk workshops and call them something like 'getting ahead', or 'doing business better' or 'managing for results', in an attempt to deliver risk messages in a way that can be understood and accepted.

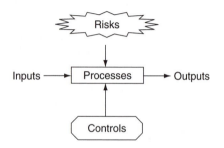

Figure 8.2   Risk and controls

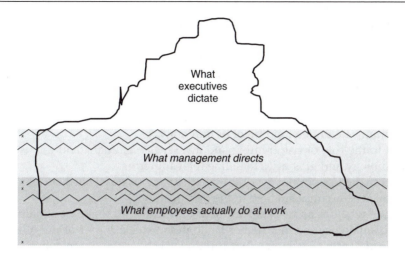

Figure 8.3 Foggy messages

Levels of maturity

Less mature organizations may see risk as that which affects, say, health and safety, insurance, fire and security people. In these circumstances, a tick-box approach may be designed primarily to bring down the costs of insurance premiums and reduce the exposure to random compensation claims. The risk policy should really be a dynamic document that contains a message from the top to get risk management understood, applied, reported on and driven down into the business. It is a good idea to set milestones for this task and review progress over the months and years. The key issue is that the board needs to have a vision of what it sees as a well-managed and controlled organization and then 'sell' this vision to the executive management team.

In implementing its risk policy, an organization will need to consider the following practical issues that affect the way risk management is applied in practice. It should:

- State that there should be an effective risk management process in place across the organization and point to some of the benefits that mean it is supported by a strong business case as well as regulatory compliance.
- Be endorsed by the board and related to a vision of embedded risk management that is part of the desired culture and management style.
- Contain clear attitudes towards different types of risk, including an attempt to categorize risks into key groupings.
- Define roles and responsibilities across the organization, along with guidance on risk ownership, and the role of the lead officer (chief risk officer), the

auditors, and any defined risk forum to share information and tools. It may be an idea to look for risk champions across the organization. Whatever the format, there should be strong messages from the top.

- Dictate that suitable actions should be taken where control failures arise.
- Suggest that risk needs to be considered at planning and performance levels.
- State that all new and existing activities be assessed for risk.
- Communicate understanding of terminology.
- Point to the role of risk training and awareness seminars, and the use of set terminology and glossaries to define relevant terms.
- Promote the use of pilot exercises where a new risk tool (such as team initial audits) is being implemented in the organization.
- Indicate whether an understanding of risk and control is part of employees' core competencies, and whether facilitation skills are part of the role of the risk lead officer. Recognize that certain aspects of the organization, say the insurance side, will have a background in risk.
- Gauge the level of understanding of the risk policy among employees by regular surveys and targeted interviews.
- Describe the risk and business controls assurance arrangements, and how key risks may be reported upwards through the organization in an accelerated reporting system. This is linked to the way risk tolerances are set and observed.
- Define the links between risk management and normal business systems and the code of ethics. The aim may be to embed risk into normal business systems and milestones for this process may be set and monitored. In the end, risk assessment should be applied to setting real priorities across the business.
- Define what is seen as a key control.
- Indicate that risk registers should be developed and subject to formal review.
- Provide guidance on how the policy and approach can be communicated to staff.
- Define the risk management process and links to internal control and assurances.
- Show how stakeholders can be involved in the process.
- Point to interdependencies, cause-and-effect relationships and the trend towards enterprise risk management, along with reference to a risk map of the organization.
- Ensure that all new projects and ventures are subject to careful risk assessments using a team approach and that risk registers record all results.
- Make sure any significant divergence in views of the relative importance of specific risks across the organization is explored through exception reporting that picks up wide spreads of perspectives between different people and teams. Voting technology and chart-based reports showing split views on risk may assist in securing this type of information.

- Show how risk may be evaluated using our four Vs model, and that the chief risk officer must approve any new tools (and software-based packages) that are acquired. Explain the use of workshops to facilitate this process.
- Relay a requirement that suitable documentation and standardized risk registers should be provided, to document all risk-related activities.
- Indicate how the risk management process is quality assured and audited and how evidence for decisions made should be based on sound standards.
- Demonstrate how contingency plans fit into the risk process for key but infrequent risks.
- Define what may be seen as a significant control weakness for reporting purposes, and how triggers can be applied to act as an early warning system.
- Describe the impact on the reputation of the organization.
- State whether a tool such as A4M.99 should be applied, including the role of values, standards, reporting tools, models and guidance.
- State how the three complementary forms of initial auditing should be applied; that is, manager's initial audit, team initial audit and manager's initial investigations.

In short

There is a lot to think about when setting a risk policy and overall strategy and it is not a good idea to use the 'risk police' to enforce standards. A brief document may be the answer, with important material on the corporate intranet, and several attractive online presentations, with short examples, are a better way of delivering the key messages.

Links to control

> **A4M 8.60**   *The initial audit process should include a consideration of ways of tackling any poor performance measures that increase the impact of risks to the achievement of business objectives.*

Good risk management means good controls. Risk management is a wide concept that encompasses all those decisions that are taken in the face of those risks that affect the business and its goals. At times, it may mean accepting a risk as something that hopefully does not happen, or if it does arise, it is responded to in the best way possible. Control is devised from a control strategy and this may mean doing nothing, in that it would simply cost too much to set up a cast-iron bunker around the business.

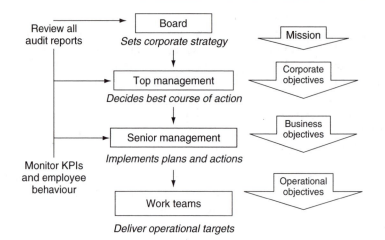

Figure 8.4   The old control model

There is also the view that a control philosophy operates within an organization and this will be different in different parts of the business. Figure 8.4 illustrates what we can call the old-fashioned control philosophy, which is based around the theme: 'Have we got enough controls over our staff?'

Ten drivers for failure

Here the mission, vision and objectives are set by the board members to enable them to deliver their promises to the marketplace. Lots of pressure is applied downwards and the business responds to the plans implemented by senior management with the hope that work teams will deliver their set targets. Meanwhile, the KPIs reveal the extent of success, complemented by detailed reviews by the auditors. This constant pressure can lead to a high-performing workforce as it tries to deliver more and more to keep the business buoyant. Control is seen as setting targets and then monitoring performance. However, this entrenched version of control can create a mechanistic workforce who may well embark on 10 drivers for failure:

1. Driven only by key performance indicators.
2. Trying to keep management's attention away from them.
3. Encouraging problems elsewhere.
4. Competing against colleagues.
5. Massaging reported figures.
6. Burying bad news.
7. Presenting a 'clean sheet' to the auditors.
8. Avoiding being 'tagged' by assigned risk ownership.

9. Seeking targets that have already been achieved.
10. Understanding and trying to 'beat the system'.

Ten drivers for success

The old version of control argues that people have their responsibilities and now they are fully accountable through loads of balanced performance indicators. However, an obsession with controls leads to the above potential risks and can result in very little real control. We need to reverse these 10 drivers for failure to create 10 new drivers for success. These new drivers are based on a supportive management that uses a completely different control philosophy, where employees:

1. Are driven by a desire to improve performance.
2. Want managers to help them work smarter.
3. View their colleagues as crucial to a successful business.
4. Work well and support their colleagues.
5. Seek to make KPIs meaningful and useful.
6. Identify and deal with problems quickly.
7. Ask auditors for help.
8. Understand that risk ownership brings pride and passion.
9. Seek targets that are challenging and interesting.
10. Understand and try to improve the system.

A new control philosophy can lead to a more modern framework, in Figure 8.5, where a changed theme is promoted along the lines of: 'Are we all in control of what really makes us successful?'

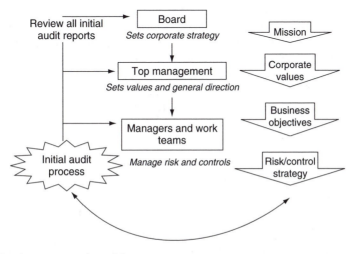

Figure 8.5   A new control model

In Figure 8.5 the board still fulfils its responsibility to set a corporate strategy, but this time senior management only sets values, a clear sense of direction, and an environment where people know about the risks to their business and become responsible for managing these risks and flagging up any concerns that need to be tackled by the executives. Audits fit in on an assurance and consulting basis where most appropriate and encourage employees continually to audit their own systems. Employees will not embrace real accountability unless they are helped to develop in an environment that encourages them to take responsibility. This becomes a new way of looking at employees, and an entirely new control philosophy.

In short

Risk management is all very well, but it is the adopted control framework that makes most impact on the way people are expected to behave at work, and the way they actually do behave. New philosophies towards controlling a business are needed to reflect the changing environment of modern organizations.

Driving and leading

> **A4M 8.61** *The board, CEO and all directors should provide a clear direction on the use of initial auditing and apply this approach to reviewing the performance of the board and other forums such as the audit committee and risk committee.*

The empowerment concept is well established in many organizations, but in different ways and for different reasons. Driving this concept to the limits is not an easy task, and when it relates to the risk and control agenda it can be even more difficult. The risk management, internal control and initial audit strategy should be driven by a board-level sponsor who is able to:

- Set the tone for effective risk management.
- Make the entire approach challenging and energizing.
- Lead the programme.
- Set standards.
- Manage (and not ignore) conflicts.

Using mistakes

One of the first things to establish is a policy where mistakes are seen as something that are not covered up but used to move forward. We can learn from them and so long as there is no deceit we can use this learning to help build a more successful organization. There will be some pain in admitting to error or substandard performance, but accepting this stance will mean that we will always ask whether, in the face of adversity, we can turn a loss into a win. To make this work we have to address several key issues, including:

- What is acceptable?
- What is normal practice?
- What fits with procedure?
- What is right?
- What is justified?
- What can be done to move forward?

In short

Empowerment can be difficult to manage as we attempt to balance giving people lots of freedom with the need to ensure that corporate standards are achieved at the same time.

Tuning into enterprise risk management

> **A4M 8.62**   *The initial audit process should be adopted throughout all parts of the organization and support moves towards enterprise-wide risk management.*

We start with the leading document in enterprise risk management (COSO ERM):

> Management considers risk from an entity-wide, or portfolio, perspective. Management may take an approach in which the manager responsible for each department, function or business unit develops a composite assessment of risk and risk responses for that unit.[2]

Figure 8.6 provides a representation of the problems we have with ERM and the gap that needs to be closed if any progress is to be made.

In Figure 8.6 the business moves onwards towards the optimum position, which means it needs to change and flex as the market shifts and customers' demands become harder to meet. Meanwhile, the board has said that all business units should establish a robust system of risk management and work on a set of key initiatives in this respect. The gap represents a belief that risk management sits away and removed from the real business pressures. If the board fails to appreciate the need to resource a 'culture shift' programme, then this credibility may remain in place.

Risk management in specialist pockets of the organization, like health and safety, is easy to implement. But to get it to reach the real heart of the business is much more difficult, since many of the front-line managers are not used to

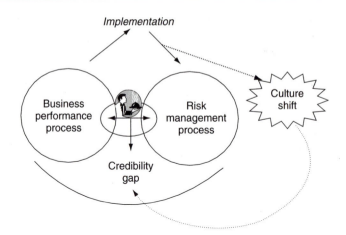

Figure 8.6   The credibility gap

seeing corporate policies as anything more than box-ticking exercises in compliance forms. The next chapter has a go at analysing culture change in the face of new developments.

Successful risk management may be seen as having three main levels:

- **Level 1**: Awareness and understanding of ERM across the organization.
- **Level 2**: Implementation of tools and techniques to promote ERM.
- **Level 3**: ERM moved into the business culture in terms of the way plans are established, resources managed and decisions made.

Embracing ERM

By moving steadily through the three levels, ERM can be embedded into a business and even change the way people work and relate to each other. Organizations will eventually get to a place where people understand that they have both individual and shared responsibilities.

One problem experienced by some organizations derives from the need to keep a focus on driving risk awareness down and through the organization. That is, the energy can trail off and people tend to switch off after a while. The vision of embedded risk management means that we are trying to change culture and this takes both time and effort. Figure 8.7 tells this story.

The energy that builds up from stage A falls off at stage B and needs to be recharged. There is a tendency for many organizations to experience false starts where they run a few *ad hoc* workshops and the entire initiative stalls because it does not attach to the real day-to-day work. There are several key questions from Figure 8.7 that will form part of the risk management implementation strategy, including:

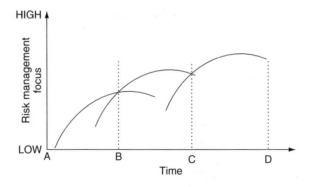

Figure 8.7   Leaps in risk management

- How do we get from A to B?
- How do we ensure B happens?
- How do we get from A to C?
- What happens when we get to C?

The COSO ERM position is noted below:

> Management is directly responsible for all activities of an entity, including ERM. Naturally, management at different levels will have different ERM responsibilities. These will differ, often considerably, depending on the entity's characteristics.[3]

In short

Enterprise risk management is an attempt to spread best practice across the organization. As in most such endeavours, we need to get people talking the same language, even if this is in a number of different dialects.

Common mistakes

A⬛M 8.63   *The board, CEO and all directors should review the reliability of the initial auditing process and the action plans and reports that are generated by this process.*

Scenario one

Many teams in an organization have a close association with risk assessment and risk management. The board can rest assured that so long as these teams are experts in their field, they will have a good, risk-smart enterprise.

Figure 8.8   Powerful messages

Scenario two

The A4M.99 process turns much of this on its head by suggesting that the scenario should change to the following:

Many teams in an organization have a close association with risk assessment and risk management. The board will need to codify and consolidate this expertise so that it becomes immersed in the way all employees work in what will become a risk-smart enterprise.

Is it that simple?

There is much that could go wrong in moving from scenario one to scenario two:

- **There is no real policy on enterprise risk management**. Where there is no real vision of ERM, there is much less chance that it will be achieved.
- **The risk management cycle is not aligned to business performance systems**. Where the risk cycle is not aligned to the performance process, there is less chance that people will see a benefit from getting involved in risk assessment and control reviews.
- **The risk policy is superficial and not very meaningful**. Where there is no real direction set from the top, there will be more chance of a silo approach to risk that is fragmented across the organization.

- **The risk management strategy is not 'bought' by the typical employee**. Where there is no real pull towards better risk management, it will be more difficult to achieve good results.
- **There is no robust staff awareness training in place covering risk management and related tools**. Where there is no clear format to spread messages on risk management, it will be hard to build a sound capacity among employees.
- **The corporate intranet does not host risk awareness presentations**. Where standard communication tools such as the intranet are not employed for risk awareness, an opportunity to consolidate the approach will have been missed.
- **No milestones are set for getting risk management in place**. Where there is no paced approach to getting risk management in place, it will be hard to measure any progress made.
- **The tools employed are cumbersome**. Where the tools to support risk management are cumbersome, there may be high levels of resistance from managers and staff.
- **There is no board-level sponsor who has a particular interest in ERM**. Where there is no senior driver for ERM, it may be seen as a low priority among staff.
- **The chief risk officer comes from a specialist background and has no consulting-based skills**. Where the risk champion has no real consulting skills it may be hard to 'sell' the underpinning ideas to everyone.

Helpful models for overcoming problems

There is one particular model that can be used to assess whether a successful risk management system is being delivered. Figure 8.9 can be employed to plot progress against several criteria.

Figure 8.9 is based on encouraging a bull's-eye, which is a score of 10 in the middle as opposed to 0 on the outside. The criteria against which to score the extent of success cover:

- Awareness of ERM and the A4M.99 statements and values.
- Good buy-in from all levels of management and workers.
- Good understanding of the tools available to support the endeavour.
- Early successes in making a difference for the business and compliance issues.
- A noticeable improvement in the time people are prepared to give to risk-based activities such as intranet sessions, risk workshops and meetings with the chief risk officer.
- And finally, extensive integration of risk management principles into normal business processes.

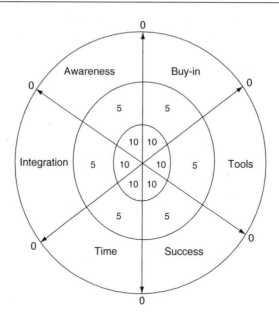

Figure 8.9 Scoring a bull's-eye

In short

Successful risk management operates on a number of fronts and it is as well to ensure that each aspect is properly recognized.

Check your progress

> **A4M 8.64** *Initial audits are based on the premise that people most involved in a business area are best able to review their risk and controls, so long as this review is competent, transparent and performed with integrity.*

One tool that can be applied to track your progress is to test the extent to which you have assimilated the key points raised in this chapter. The multi-choice questions below will check your progress and the answer guide in Appendix D is based on what is most appropriate in the context of this book. Please record your answers in the table at Appendix D. You may also record the time spent on each test and enter this information in the 'Mins' column of Appendix D.

Name ....

Start time ....   **Finish time** ....   **Total minutes** ....

Multi-choice quiz

1. Which is the odd one out?
We have said the manager needs a good understanding of risk concepts. Moreover, the manager needs to be able to mobilize several new tools:

a. Manager's reviews of risk management and internal controls.
b. The team's review of specific risk and internal controls.
c. The auditor's checks on internal control.
d. The manager's investigation into control failings.

2. Select the most appropriate sentence.
a. Risk management concepts and tools can look pretty impressive. But we really must give our local managers the scope to adapt and apply them in a way that suits their local business circumstances.
b. Risk management concepts and tools can look pretty impossible. But we really must give our local managers the scope to adapt and apply them in a way that suits their local business circumstances.
c. Risk management concepts and tools can look pretty impressive. But we cannot always give our local managers the scope to adapt and apply them in a way that suits their local business circumstances.
d. Risk management concepts and tools can look pretty impressive. But we really must give our auditors the scope to adapt and apply them in a way that suits their local business circumstances.

3. Which is the odd one out?
Some organizations run risk workshops and call them something like '........................', in an attempt to deliver the risk messages in a way that can be understood and accepted.

a. getting ahead.
b. doing business better.
c. managing risk and controls.
d. managing for results.

4. Select the most appropriate sentence.
a. The aim may be to embed risk into our normal risk systems and milestones for this process may be set and monitored. In the end, risk assessment should be applied to setting real priorities across the business.

b. The aim may be to embed risk into our normal business systems and milestones for this process may be set and monitored. In the end, risk assessment should be applied to setting real priorities across the business.

c. The aim may be to embed risk into our normal business systems and milestones for this process may be set and monitored. In the end, risk assessment should be applied to setting risk priorities across the business.

d. The aim may be to embed risk into our normal financial systems and milestones for this process may be set and monitored. In the end, risk assessment should be applied to setting real priorities across the business.

5. Insert the missing words.
Risk management is a wide concept that encompasses all those decisions that are taken in the face of those risks that affect our ....

a. people.
b. controls.
c. customers and suppliers.
d. business and our goals.

6. Which is the odd one out?
But this entrenched version of control can create a mechanistic workforce who may well embark on drivers for failure, including:

a. asking auditors for help.
b. being driven only by key performance indicators.
c. trying to keep management's attention away from them.
d. encouraging problems elsewhere.

7. Which is the odd one out?
New drivers are based on a supportive management that uses a completely different control philosophy, as follows:

a. driven by a desire to improve performance.
b. wanting managers to help them work smarter.
c. understanding and trying to 'beat the system'.
d. viewing their colleagues as crucial to a successful business.

8. Insert the missing words.
The board still fulfils its responsibility to set a corporate strategy but this time senior management only sets values, a clear sense of direction, and ...., where people who know about the risks to their business become responsible for managing these risks and flagging up any concerns that need to be tackled by the executives.

a. clear rules.
b. an environment.

c. close supervision.
d. good documentation.

9. Which is the odd one out?
There will be some pain in admitting to error or substandard performance, but accepting this stance will mean that we will always ask whether, in the face of adversity, we can turn a loss into a win. To make this work we have to address several key issues, including the need to define:

a. what punishment is applied to failure and errors.
b. what is acceptable and normal practice.
c. what fits with procedure and what is right.
d. what is justified and what can be done to move forward.

10. Insert the missing words.
Enterprise risk management is an attempt to spread best practice across the organization. As in most such endeavours, we need to get people talking the same ...., even if this is in a number of different ....

a. dialects ..... language.
b. jargon ..... language.
c. way ..... ways.
d. language ..... dialects.

Newsflash – read all about it

There is so much behind the move towards effective governance and risk management in all walks of life, and a small selection of relevant examples is provided to illustrate this new way of thinking.

10 new dimensions

Old thinking	New dimensions	A suitable example
Everyone in our hospitals tries to do their best.	Standards in our hospital are really important and if ignored this may pose an additional threat to the health of patients.	An investigation found major lapses in hospital hygiene leading to soaring rates of the MRSA superbug. One cleaner regularly touched MRSA patients in breach of hygiene regulations.[4]

(Continued)

Old thinking	New dimensions	A suitable example
Strategic takeovers ensure a company is able to move forwards.	Strategic growth must be managed carefully and not all prospective acquisitions will pay off.	British Airways is ready to write off around £40m investment in loss-making travel website, Opodo.[5]
Our contingency plan was good enough then and it is still good enough today.	Contingency plans really must be updated regularly as the nature of the risks and our knowledge of how we can best respond to them change.	If you ever wondered what to do in the event of an imminent nuclear attack, the answer is simple: Fasten your top button and put your hat on. The farcical recommendations for how to survive the fallout from an atomic bomb are part of the preparations for war outlined in a public information film from the fifties.[6]
Everyone, whether private or public sector, must abide by all applicable laws, rules and regulations.	Risk management is a funny old game. Some accept the risk of breaking specific rules.	He has been beaten up, spat on, arrested 15 times and jailed for a total of five months. But yesterday Stephen Gough finally completed his naked ramble from Land's End to John O'Groats.[7]
Social risks can be tackled through campaigns that simply warn against the risk.	Risk management ebbs and flows and one strategy can lead to unexpected results. Pilots can be used to ensure that our efforts are not actually making matters worse.	A dramatic rise in sexually transmitted diseases among teenagers is being fuelled by Government efforts aimed at reducing unwanted pregnancies, an expert has warned. The strategy has been a double disaster because not only has it had an impact on health, but it has also increased the number of pregnancies by encouraging promiscuity.[8]
As well-known companies expand they help generate more wealth in local communities.	Expansion plans should be risk assessed and it is important that all relevant stakeholders (even if they are difficult) are brought into the equation.	Wal-Mart, the discount retailing group, was regrouping yesterday after voters in Inglewood, California, threw out by a large margin arrangements that would have allowed the company to build a megastore in their midst without the normal reviews and hearings.[9]

Risks need to be tackled and if possible eradicated.

Risks need to be understood and before drastic measures are taken, it is as well to think carefully about the pros and cons of any intended action.

An enduring symbol of Christianity, the yew tree had stood in the churchyard for generations. Such historical significance, however, held little sway with the safety conscious vicar of St Thomas's. Deciding the tree was a safety hazard (it could poison children with its toxic berries, injure them if they climbed it, trip up the elderly on their way to worship, and even provide a hiding place for paedophiles) it was chopped down.[10]

We have all learned lessons from past failure when introducing new systems, and now such problems are a thing of the past.

We have all learned lessons from past failure when introducing new systems, and sadly we still need to be on our toes to ensure such problems are a thing of the past.

The bungled introduction of new tax credits, which delayed payments to hundreds of thousands of families, was condemned yesterday as 'nothing short of disastrous' by Commons spending watchdogs . . . The Inland Revenue introduced the system too quickly and has inadequate contingency plans.[11]

Risk management is about anticipation and careful planning. We are finally seeing this happen in all walks of life.

Risk management is about anticipation and careful planning. We still have a way to go to embed this concept into all walks of life.

Weather forecasters had been warning about the impending storm for days. But when it finally came, it smashed through Britain's defences as if they had not been there. Gritters and snow ploughs simply could not cope with the volume of snow tumbling from the skies yesterday.[12]

Reputational risk is an important aspect of risk management and is one of our key risk categories, along with financial, market, operational, HR and other key risks.

There are several key risk categories such as financial, market, operational, HR and other major risk areas, but they all feed into the generic concept of reputational risk, which is the most important aspect of risk management.

Anyone in marketing will tell you that trust is essential to the sales process. Trust in the quality and consistency of the product makes people willing to pay more for it, be it a tin of beans, a bottle of shampoo or a can of beer, and resolutely ignore the temptation of cheaper options alongside. Trust creates brands out of commodities. It does not come easily. It has to be won and nurtured because once lost it is almost impossible to regain.[13]

The key messages

The last section of each chapter contains a short story or quote that should provide an interesting format for illustrating some of the book's key messages.

Securing innovation

> I think the tendency for successful companies to fail to innovate is just that: a tendency. If you're too focused on your current business, it's hard to change and concentrate on innovating.[14]

Notes

1. Committee of Sponsoring Organizations, Enterprise Risk Management, Draft framework at July 2004, page 3 (www.coso.org).
2. Committee of Sponsoring Organizations, Enterprise Risk Management, Draft framework at July 2004, page 57 (www.coso.org).
3. Committee of Sponsoring Organizations, Enterprise Risk Management, Draft framework at July 2004, page 93 (www.coso.org).
4. *Evening Standard*, Wednesday, March 12, 2003, page 15.
5. *Mail on Sunday*, Sunday, March 28, 2004, Financial Mail, page 5.
6. *Daily Mail*, Thursday, April 1, 2004, page 17.
7. *Daily Mail*, Friday, January 23, 2004, page 23.
8. *Daily Mail*, Monday, April 5, 2004, page 25.
9. *The Independent*, Thursday, April 8, 2004, World news, page 28.
10. *Daily Mail*, Tuesday, January 27, 2004, page 23.
11. *The Independent*, Thursday, April 22, 2004, Politics, page 10.
12. *Daily Mail*, Thursday, January 29, 2004, page 23.
13. *Evening Standard*, Friday, September 26, 2003, page 43, Anthony Hilton.
14. Bill Gates, *The Road Ahead*, Penguin, Harmondsworth, 1995, page 276.

9 Achieving the cultural shift

To expostulate . . . why day is day, night is night, and time is time, were nothing but to waste day, night and time.

William Shakespeare, *Hamlet*, Act II, Scene 2

A◀M Statement I *The A◀M.99 approach depends on achieving a culture where initial auditing is immersed in the mindsets of all employees of an organization.*

Introduction

A◀M 9.65 *The initial audit process should be set within the cultueral context of each part of the business, but should seek to influence this culture so as to promote better management of risk and corporate accountability.*

Figure 1.1 in Chapter 1 shows how the book is put together. Chapter 9 discusses how to shift corporate cultures to get people to be much more risk smart. We start Chapter 9 by revisiting our COSO ERM guidance:

> Individual business units, functions and departments will have slightly different risk cultures. Managers of some are prepared to take more risk, while others are more conservative, and these different cultures sometimes work at cross-purposes.[1]

What is culture?

Culture is defined by many as a commonly held set of beliefs. A◢M.*99* is about establishing a new way of looking at the audit process and changing attitudes so that people will respond to this new challenge to be risk aware, because they have adopted a new way of looking at the audit process. Much depends on how much they know about auditing and whether it makes sense in their view. There is little to be gained from paying lip service to A◢M.*99* and what we are looking for is for people to internalize new ways of thinking about risk, control and auditing.

In short

It is a good idea to understand the different cultures that are in place within an organization when trying to achieve a shift in these cultures.

Starting from zero

A◢M 9.66   *Staff surveys should be carried out at regular intervals whenever representative information is required to assess the state of awareness of risk management and controls in an organization.*

Auditing is a process that is about involving people in recognizing risk and managing controls to promote a successful organization. In a healthy corporate culture people will feel valued, trusted, empowered, supported and motivated. If these are the official messages mouthed from the top, the informal culture is much more about the way things are actually done at work. The reality will either be removed from or fit well with official soundbites. On the whole, people will support measures that make sense to them. Figure 9.1 contains the main arguments for A◢M.*99* and may be put forward in developing any new approach.

Risk management appreciation tends to be high among auditors and specialist support staff in an organization. Here there is generally a good understanding of risk, risk management and internal controls reporting. However, the front-line people who have the most direct impact on customers understand their service delivery priorities but have traditionally had much less contact with the risk and control agenda. In this way, familiarity with the risk, control and audit process tends to be removed from front-line services as it is seen as a specialist area not related to business delivery.

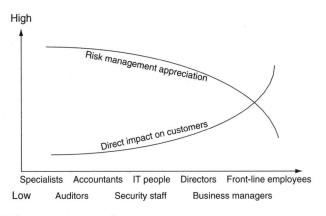

High

Risk management appreciation

Direct impact on customers

Specialists   Accountants   IT people   Directors   Front-line employees

Low   Auditors   Security staff   Business managers

Figure 9.1 Risk management and customers

What results do we hope to achieve?

As managers develop a strategy to get A◄M.*99* into the front line, they will need to set a clear agenda that considers:

1. Resources for the project.
2. Behaviours and how they need to be changed.
3. Measuring changes – how do we know when we have succeeded?

External help

To make initial auditing work as per A◄M.*99*, organizations may need to bring in an outsider to help drive the approach. This person will have some expertise in risk management and auditing and may facilitate the project so that people can progress and learn to accept new ways of working. The old culture of submitting themselves to checks and balances is replaced by a new culture of employees performing these checks themselves and holding out this initial attempt for review. As has been said by many before: 'No one size fits all!' The success of many programmes depends on the culture in place and whether this is good communication, people involvement in decision making, a move away from a blame culture and good listening skills all round.

There are several signs of failure that should be avoided where something along the line of an A◄M.*99* project is being launched, including:

- Overconfident consultants who do not appreciate the difficulty of the task.
- No training given to employees.
- No expertise in risk management in the organization.
- No insights or vision as to what the final picture should look like.

Governance frameworks

In some organizations risk management is done intuitively, where there is some good work being done in pockets of the organization but there is often a risk-averse stance that has developed over the years. Managers need to develop the governance and accountability frameworks and good risk management as part of the prevailing culture. Mature organizations may have developed some risk management capacity but may be less open to new ideas. In newer organizations that are developing a capacity, there may be more eagerness to learn and being open to new ideas. The worst-case scenario is where the entity has run out of ideas and tends to rubber stamp everything. Here new initiatives are mainly seen as developing new forms and then getting someone to sign them each year.

Many private-sector companies are constrained by the short-term search for profits that can drive them as a sole concern. Public-sector organizations may suffer from unclear objectives, or public expectations do not match what can reasonably be delivered with the shrinking resources that have been provided.

External consultants can kick-start the A4M.99 project but, although they will have excellent communication skills, they can arrive with a packaged solution that may be inappropriate. The packaged solution, often a software tool, may be too basic for a large and complex organization or too complex for those smaller entities that need a straightforward approach. Relying on in-house staff to drive the project can mean that a best-fit solution is developed, but this person may have a limited interpretation of the wider possibilities that could have been learnt from looking at what others in the industry are doing. Moreover, while they will have the best interests of the business in mind, the internal resource may not have good selling skills to energize and keep the project moving forward. One interesting approach is to bring in an experienced outsider and get them to work alongside an in-house lead person, who will eventually take over the project.

In short

It is tremendously difficult to get a new idea off the ground and running. Expertise, knowledge, high levels of energy and a clear focus are all noteworthy attributes – but it is the ability to 'sell' a product that you believe in that can make all the difference.

Why culture changes

> **A4M 9.67**   *All new employees should be given a suitable outline of the initial audit process in their induction programmes.*

An organization's culture should be changed only if it really needs to be changed. It is generally better to take a new idea, such as the initial audit concept, and set it out in a way that people will understand within the existing culture. A simple risk map of the organization that is kept up to date can be a good platform to start from. In one sense, the preparation of a risk map of responsibilities, accountabilities and categories of risk, and where they fall in the entity, starts to place the risk, control and initial audit agenda into the mindset of employees.

However, culture change has to be carefully planned as, if steps are taken to encourage more open communications, it could result in people lounging around in corridors. If organizations promote stretched targets they may end with people who see little of their family and become out of balance and stressed. But what exactly is it that we are trying to change? Figure 9.2 illustrates where the 'old manager' and the 'new manager' sit on our radar.

Moving towards the new manager

We start with the old-school manager in Figure 9.2, who gets the job done but is risk naive. That is, there is no considered approach to understanding and managing risk – it just happens through a mix of good luck and good instincts. This person needs to be moved to understanding risk (**risk aware**). But the first thing that happens is that they perceive that there are hundreds of risks out there and at first become **risk averse**. Many managers think that risk training is about making them less reckless, and so they bunker down and hold 10 meetings

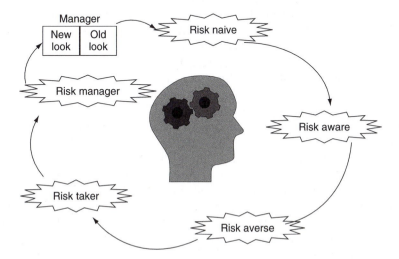

Figure 9.2   The new-look manager

before they make a simple decision. This becomes boring and counterproductive and they are told by their executives to 'get something going and stop coming to me for approval'. Oftentimes, the **risk taker** mentality comes to the fore as the new mantra 'all mistakes will be forgiven' sets in. The new manager eventually emerges after a few false starts as the **risk manager** and this person has a balanced and considered view of risk in line with the corporate risk appetite and locally set risk tolerance levels.

Culture change is about moving people through this cycle, without too much damage along the way. The progressive manager may once again become **risk naive**, but this time because risk is so immersed in business practices it is not referred to as a distinct issue. That is far removed from our original definition of risk naive. There are a few other points to be made in terms of changing culture from the risk naive to the risk manager:

- Achieve a balanced approach to new skills involving training and facilitation for employees.
- Tell people about the process and new ideas but let them get on with it without interference from the leader/facilitator.
- Set levels of awareness (say levels 1, 2, 3 and 4) and assess how people are moving up through the levels.
- Develop the new ideas and sell them by explaining the benefits and the process through which they are applied, along with several examples.
- Introduce new terms such as 'red risks' and 'risk portfolios' and get the board to appreciate their significance – for example, red risks will be reported to them and monitored.
- Give incentives along the lines that good initial auditing means fewer visits from inspectors and auditors.
- Issue head office guidance and a helpline.
- Use a dialogue and examples in a way that suits the business and work teams. Refer to what stops you achieving your goals as 'risks', and what helps you tackle these risks as 'controls'.
- Develop good induction training, even for newly appointed senior people, and use the chief risk officer to deliver key messages to new staff.
- Develop a one-page briefing paper for new executives and nonexecutives.
- Make it clear that everyone needs to live up to their responsibility to develop statements on internal control and needs a capacity to meet this challenge.
- Do not play up the conformance line – make it something that helps to deliver since the organization is not running a risk management business, it is running a business using risk management to help it.
- Simply get people thinking about risk.
- Win over the group, as 'groupthink' means there is always some pressure not to deviate from the group's norms.
- Finally, risk assess and risk manage the A4M.99 programme – in this way you can practise what you preach.

In short

Changing attitudes means working with what we have and moving on.

Change and the systems perspectives

> **A4M 9.68** *Initial audits that are carried out should consider the way that any resultant actions affect the overall balance of the existing system of internal control and should ensure that the overall results are acceptable.*

One way of considering the cultural shift is to examine the impact of initial audits as part of the change system. Figure 9.3 comes to our aid in explaining how this works.

The thinking behind Figure 9.3 is that in addressing problems and issues within an organization it is vital to consider the implications for the system of internal control. Nearly everything that happens or fails to happen can be related back to the way controls are designed and actioned. Remember, the vision of controls is that they are all mechanisms designed to promote the achievement of objectives. Problems interfere with the ability to succeed, and therefore mean they have not been controlled properly or that a new control needs to swing into place to deal with each newly identified problem. Figure 9.3 suggests that poor controls allow problems to get in our way because there is a lack of controls, inappropriate controls or a breach of what would otherwise

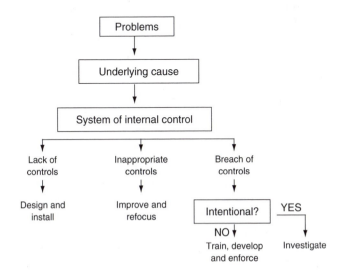

Figure 9.3 Problems and controls

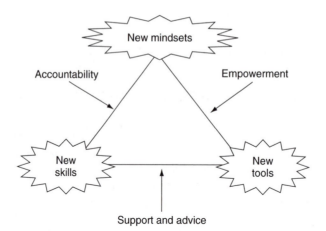

Figure 9.4   Supporting the new manager

be a good control. The second level of the figure suggests several different responses depending on which of the three reasons for control failure is being dealt with. Note that an investigation will ensue where there is an intentional breach of controls.

Linking problems to controls is empowering, as it implies that people can do something about each problem they experience and also set longer-term mechanisms in place to ensure a better future. This is an important new mindset required of all managers and staff and is explored further in Figure 9.4.

The new mindset sees employees being empowered to audit their risks and design their local controls to meet all known challenges. A◀M.99 and the various figures in this book can be applied as new tools in driving home the initial audit agenda across the organization. New skills result from new mindsets and good tools and this is set firmly within a fresh view of the accountability and empowerment concept. The bottom line on Figure 9.4 is that help and support are needed to support this model and make it work.

Clarity of objectives

The next issue to address relates to driving clear objectives through the business. People become involved in programmes that help them deliver their objectives. Each part of the organization will have a different view of what it is trying to achieve and it is a good idea to spend time clarifying aims, goals, targets and performance standards to ensure everyone is pulling in the same direction. The divisional director, office manager, team leader, back-office support, project manager, work team and the individual employee will all have their different perspectives on what they are trying to achieve. Figure 9.5 develops this theme further.

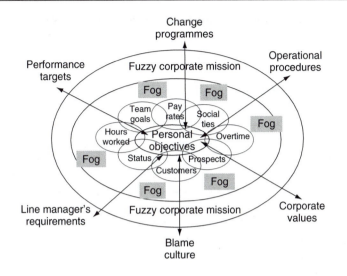

Figure 9.5 Fog gets everywhere

Many change strategies flounder because there is an assumption that everyone has clear objectives that eventually feed into the corporate whole. Figure 9.5 argues that personal objectives are influenced by many powerful forces that affect the day-to-day life of the company worker (or public-sector employee). The corporate mission sits on the outside of the circle, but there is often a great deal of '**fog**' that sits between the big picture and how people see things at ground level.

This scenario is further complicated by the many high-level factors that influence an organization around the edge of the circle. It is an idea to set out each of these factors and analyse what the organization needs to get an empowered/accountable culture in place through a new initial audit regime. Then have a go at analysing the fog that means messages from the top do not always get down into the real day-to-day business.

The final issue that pops up in this situation relates to the dual aspect of the manager's role. That is that the empowerment aspect means being allowed to take local decisions to add value to the business, while the accountability aspect takes a wider view and considers the need to ensure good compliance, proper financial reporting, reliable information systems, safeguarding assets and achieving value for money: quite a challenge.

In short

Getting employees to focus on good controls, embracing accountability and believing that this is actually their responsibility shifts us closer to the A◀M.99 concept. It is almost an ideal to promote better accountability using tools that also create a better business.

Creative work teams

> A4M 9.69   *The initial audit process should not be designed in such a way as to discourage creativity from employees. As such, audit reviews should focus on key risks and seek to curtail any controls that are not needed or are overly bureaucratic.*

All organizations need to push into the future by anticipating new trends, or even by creating new trends with new or improved products. The product life cycle is well known. It suggests that new products take a lead on the market and develop a good market share until other producers catch up and offer improved or cheaper versions, which means the original product eventually slips down the market share index. It is the constant search for this market share that drives businesses forward, as they search for better solutions and more attractive offers. The public sector is similar in that there is an ongoing search for better ways of using scarce resources to deliver public services. Meanwhile, central and local government manifestos tend to promise more and more in terms of better delivery with less funding. The not-for-profit sector cannot be left out of the creativity dynamic, in finding new ways of getting their messages and services to the right place.

It has happened before and it will happen again – people sitting around in risk workshops with a fixed agenda to see whether they can come up with any more controls. Risk management is seen as a way of bolting things down and responding to a series of scare stories that, if taken literally, would mean people would be too frightened to get out of bed, as there are hidden dangers lurking everywhere. This is the opposite to what we really want from our auditing for managers initiative. We want people to discard controls where they serve no real purpose.

Your team

The other side to getting new initiatives in place is to make a positive impact on work teams. If we tell people that the A4M.99 programme will help their business, then it is only right that they should look for positive impacts. If, on the other hand, it is just about more accountability and regulatory compliance, then this should be made clear at the outset. People do not mind doing new things or filling out more forms, so long as they are

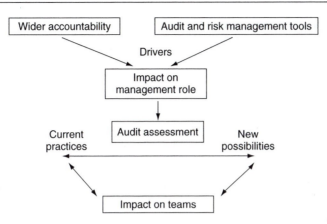

Figure 9.6   A wider view of accountability

told why and not given vague promises of value-add benefits. Figure 9.6 addresses the impact on the team.

There is a wider view of accountability and disclosure requirements in Figure 9.6 that cannot simply be ignored. There are also new tools available for reviewing risks and controls and helping to discharge this wider accountability. These two factors affect the manager's role and each manager has delegated authority to push ahead with their version of auditing for managers. The key to this model is the ability to compare current working practices with new ideas and then get them into the team. The 'it's always been done this way' one-liner delivered with a shrug of the shoulders is no longer heard at work. Nor is 'change it if you want, I don't really care so long as the auditors don't complain': an equally bad view. The new attitude is more along the lines of: 'let's work on these ideas in next week's initial audit workshop and if they pass the test, we can recommend some changes to the management team'.

This change in direction needs to be supported by an open mindset among staff and a view that A4M.99 can lead to real changes, where ideas are evaluated and there are sound criteria for making positive change. Much can depend on the use of self-directed work teams that are allowed to set their own standards, give feedback on performance to their members and even identify any training and development needs. All this should be set within the overall organization's performance management framework. Where empowered teams are in place, there is a much better chance that team initial audits will result in redesigning local controls as a way of promoting the ability of local teams to manage their business. The line manager still has a pivotal role in monitoring performance and giving lots of feedback to the team as well as the individuals. In the end, it is the manager who endorses any changes to controls that the team believes are required.

Table 9.1   Different types of management

Attribute	Type of manager		
	Monster	**Manager**	**Joker**
Theme	Order	Understanding	Fun
Approach	Victimize	Inform	Social events
Style	Shouts	Listens	Gossips
Values	Negative	Encouraging	Friendship
Information	Assumes	Finds out	Relies on friends
Discipline	Abusive	Firmness	Cover-ups
Change	Too inflexible	Balanced	Too flexible
Controls	Rigidity	Risk based	Lax
Compliance	Demanded	Encouraged	Allows breaches
Creativity	None	Criteria for new ideas	Anything goes

The new manager

Auditing for managers is based around a new vision of management control. This calls for a new approach to managing people that fits the modern organization. Some argue that the manager is now more of a coach, while others see the need to have some sense of discipline where policies such as anti-bullying or stringent health and safety rules need clear and enforced rules in place.

We can set out two types of manager in response to this dilemma: **the monster**, who sees management as a matter of enforcing rules, and **the joker**, who sees managers as making life as comfortable as possible for their staff. These versions represent each side of two extremes and a middle ground forms the basis for auditing for managers: that is, **the manager**, full stop (see Table 9.1).

Unfortunately, a firm platform is needed for auditing for managers to work and lead to real changes in work cultures. If the starting place is inappropriate such new ideas will not always work.

In short

Auditing for managers devolves the audit role to the front-line business, at least in terms of allowing front-line people to have a go at reviewing their risks and controls. But it takes a certain kind of manager to work well in this environment, and a lot depends on the way managers are trained and developed to assume a modern approach to managing people and resources.

The ultimate in risk management: auditing for all

> A4M 9.70   *All employees should have a good appreciation of the initial auditing process, which includes the importance of corporate governance, risk, risk management and internal controls.*

'Where do I sign?' may be the question posed by the chair of the board of directors when presented with the statement of internal control, recommended by the risk management or audit committee. The board will publish its process for establishing risk management and reviewing its internal controls, but how can its members be sure that what they say is happening is actually happening? By asking the internal and external auditors? By asking the audit committee to ask the auditors? By asking the CEO to go out and make sure everything is okay?

Auditing for managers suggests that if organizations need to make sure something is happening, then those who are responsible should supply the information. A4M.99 says that each manager should get to grips with 10 basic principles:

1. Establish good risk management practices.
2. Review the way controls are working in response to risk assessments.
3. Ask their teams to review their controls and report any concerns.
4. Investigate anything that implies there is a weakness in controls, and make right that weakness.
5. Get all employees to understand and buy into this initial audit concept.
6. Follow set standards in performing the above.
7. Ask the internal auditor for advice on making this process robust and reliable.
8. Provide good documentation.
9. Issue regular reports that support the above.
10. Ensure that this process makes for a better business and better results.

New competencies

We ask that all staff demonstrate a new set of competencies, including that they:

- Understand the audit concept.
- Understand the A4M.99 processes.
- Have an awareness of the underpinning tools.
- Know and accept their roles and responsibilities.
- Appreciate the governance, risk management and internal control agenda.
- Know how disclosures are prepared and reported.

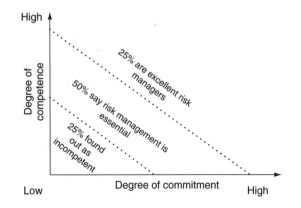

Figure 9.7   Good and poor managers

Some argue that excellent managers are really good risk managers, and there is some value in this view. In fact, we can extend this well-known viewpoint by considering Figure 9.7.

Managers who are highly competent and highly committed will have an excellent chance of being successful as they tend to understand their risks. The 25% that fall on the other side of this equation should really be developed or managed out of organizations with any sort of quality standard in place. The remaining 50% can benefit greatly from a formalized process for identifying and dealing with risk to their business areas. Organizational culture should be shifted towards the top right of Figure 9.7. Meanwhile, instil an assurance regime that means people are happy to report upwards on their internal controls and issue reports that complement the auditors' work.

In short

If managers and staff are competent and committed to A◀M.99, then we can start thinking about using it as the ultimate risk management tool.

Common mistakes

A◀M 9.71   *The initial audit process should be part of employees' basic training and development programmes, which should also incorporate an awareness of risk, controls and formal disclosures.*

Figure 9.8 The light at the end of the tunnel

Scenario one

The initial audit concept should be applied to organizations that would benefit from using a set of principles to focus their efforts to manage risk and review their controls.

Scenario two

The A4M.99 process turns much of this on its head by suggesting that the scenario should change to the following:

The initial audit concept should be applied to organizations that wish to instil a culture that promotes the effective management of risk and internal controls.

Is it that simple?

There is much that could go wrong in moving from scenario one to scenario two:

- **The risk, control and audit initiatives are dressed in a language that has little meaning to most employees**. Where the jargon attached to the audit initiative is foreign to most people and with no good explanations, its impact may be mainly lost.
- **The people who can make most difference in an organization are those least interested in the A4M.99 programme**. Where the really powerful people are not concerned about the audit initiative, it will be hard to make any real changes in the short term.
- **Excessive reliance on external consultants means that there is little expertise in audit and risk management within the organization**. Where the initial

audit programme is driven by external consultants, there will be less chance to develop the right competencies within the organization.

- **The initiative is not seen as part of a positive culture change process**. Where the initial audit programme sits outside of the wider change programmes, it will be seen as having no bearing on the real issues at work.
- **There is no appreciation of the new skills managers may need to tackle future challenges**. Where there is no strategy to develop key audit skills in business managers, there will be less chance to build a mature initial audit programme.
- **A systems view of controls is not taken, which means problems are not related back to control failings**. Where there is no loop that relates problems to controls, there will be less value from auditing by managers and teams.
- **A focus on new skills and new tools is not matched by a view on new mindsets that need to complement this development**. Where the change in perspectives among managers and teams is not seen as part of the initial audit programme, there will be less real belief in the concept.
- **Rather than having good managers in place the organization lives with a mix of monsters and jokers**. Where there are no good management competencies in place in the organization, the initial audit process is less likely to be successful.
- **No attempt is made to gauge the level of risk, control and audit understanding among employees**. Where there is no effort to survey employees on risk and control awareness, there will be less scope to measure progress in initial auditing.
- **The board still places more trust in audit assurances than in what it is told by its front-line people**. Where there is no real confidence in reports from the front-line, initial auditing will not deliver much value to the organization.

Helpful models for overcoming problems

The main model for getting the necessary changes to happen and become fixed in the organization is found in Figure 9.9.

Moving from old to new-look organizations

Figure 9.9 implies that we simply set this diagram in front of our employees and suggest the need to move from an 'old-look' to a 'new-look' organization. The old version emphasizes the audit, compliance, inspection, supervision and checks over front-line people, much like the image where one person does the work and another stands over their shoulder and inspects what's being done. The new-look organization is based much more on front-line staff operating an initial audit process that suits them and is supported by their management.

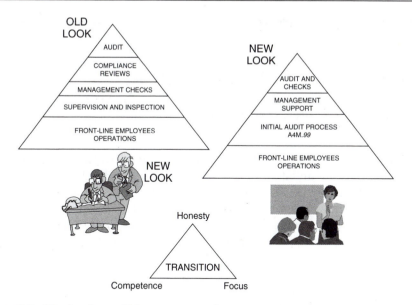

Figure 9.9 Moving from old to new approaches

The auditors simply check that this system is reliable. But this can only happen where three key components are in place:

1. Employees are **competent**, in their job and understanding of risk, control and auditing.
2. Employees are fully **focused** on clear objectives that they are committed to and able to work towards.
3. The final component is the most difficult to envision. It is **honesty**: honesty in the way people work and honesty in the way they apply A4M.99. Having said this, there will always be a need for a quick check by the auditors to make sure that initial reviews are being done in a reliable way.

The idea is to look for a strategy that builds the transition from the old- to new-look organization and ensures the new culture is promoted and embedded in the workforce and their activities.

In short

We need to aspire towards the new-look organization that achieves reliable assurances on controls through competent, committed and honest employees – with a little help from the auditors.

Check your progress

> **A✚M 9.72** *Competencies relating to the initial audit process should be assessed during staff recruitment and performance appraisal and supported by suitable training and development for all employees.*

One tool that can be applied to track your progress is to test the extent to which you have assimilated the key points raised in this chapter. The multi-choice questions below will check your progress and the answer guide in Appendix D is based on what is most appropriate in the context of this book. Please record your answers in the table at Appendix D. You may also record the time spent on each test and enter this information in the 'Mins' column of Appendix D.

Name ....

Start time .... **Finish time** .... **Total minutes** ....

Multi-choice quiz

1. Insert the missing words.
Culture is defined by many as a commonly held set of ......

a. risks.
b. goals.
c. beliefs.
d. controls.

2. Select the most appropriate sentence.
a. Risk management appreciation tends to be high among managers and general staff in an organization.
b. Risk management appreciation tends to be low among auditors and specialist support staff in an organization.
c. Risk management appreciation tends to be high among auditors and non-specialist support staff in an organization.
d. Risk management appreciation tends to be high among auditors and specialist support staff in an organization.

3. Insert the missing words.
In some organizations risk management is done intuitively, where there is some good work being done in pockets of the organization but there is often a .... stance that has developed over the years.

a. risky.
b. risk-averse.
c. formal.
d. standardized.

4. Select the most appropriate sentence.
a. The new manager eventually emerges after a few false starts as the risk manager and this person has a balanced and considered view of risk in line with the corporate risk appetite and locally set risk tolerance levels.
b. The new manager eventually emerges after a few false starts as the risk manager and this person has an aggressive view of risk in line with the corporate risk appetite and locally set risk tolerance levels.
c. The new manager eventually emerges after a few false starts as the risk manager and this person has a balanced and considered view of risk in line with the local risk appetite and locally set risk tolerance levels.
d. The new manager eventually emerges after a few false starts as the risk taking manager and this person has a balanced and considered view of risk in line with the corporate risk appetite and locally set risk tolerance levels.

5. Which is the odd one out?
a. Achieve a balanced approach to new skills involving training and facilitation for employees.
b. Tell people about the process and new ideas, but make sure they employ a full-time leader/facilitator in the team.
c. Set levels of awareness (say levels 1, 2, 3 and 4) and assess how people are moving up through the levels.
d. Develop the new ideas and sell them by explaining the benefits and the process through which they are applied – along with several examples.

6. Insert the missing words.
Remember, our vision of controls is that they are all mechanisms designed to
....

a. promote the achievement of objectives.
b. assist in delivering good performance.
c. promote the good conduct of team members.
d. promote compliance with procedure.

7. Insert the missing words.
Each part of the organization will have .... on what they are trying to achieve and it is a good idea to spend time clarifying aims, goals, targets and performance standards to ensure we are pulling in the same direction.

a. similar views.
b. conflicting views.

c. a different view.
d. high-risk views.

8. Select the most appropriate sentence.
a. The 'it's always been done this way' one-liner delivered with a shrug of the shoulders is no longer heard at work. Nor is 'change it if you want, so long as we have carried out a proper risk assessment': an equally bad view.
b. The 'it's always been done this way' one-liner delivered with a shrug of the shoulders is no longer heard at work. Nor is 'change it if you want, I don't really care so long as the auditors don't complain': an equally bad view.
c. The 'we need to ensure an initial audit is done' one-liner delivered with a shrug of the shoulders is no longer heard at work. Nor is 'change it if you want, I don't really care so long as the auditors don't complain': an equally bad view.
d. The 'it's always been done this way' one-liner delivered with a shrug of the shoulders is no longer heard at work. Nor is 'change it if you want, I don't really care so long as the auditors don't complain': an equally good view.

9. Insert the missing words.
The '...........' sees management as a matter of enforcing rules and the '...........' sees managers as making life as comfortable as possible for their staff. These versions represent each side of two extremes.

a. monster ..... animal.
b. joker .... monster joker.
c. monster .... joker.
d. animal .... monster.

10. Which is the odd one out?
A4M.99 says that each manager should get to grips with basic principles, including the following:

a. establish good risk management practices.
b. ask their teams to decide which procedures should be complied with.
c. review the way controls are working in response to risk assessments.
d. investigate anything that implies there is a weakness in controls, and make right that weakness.

Newsflash – read all about it

There is so much behind the move towards effective governance and risk management in all walks of life, and a small selection of relevant examples is provided to illustrate this new way of thinking.

10 new dimensions

Old thinking	New dimensions	A suitable example
People prefer to buy their products over the Internet.	Not all services are best explained over the phone or Internet.	British banks are investing over 100m on their branches as research finds people prefer to buy their products face to face.[2]
New products are the lifeblood of business and it's a good idea to have a go even if they fail.	New business lines (and production short-cuts) mean new risks may arise, and these risks need to be assessed for a better chance of success.	You have to have a heart of stone not to laugh at the latest and surely the final blow to the heart of Dasani, the Coca-Cola company branded water. The launch was very swiftly followed by the revelation that the source of this marvellous stuff was tap-water in Sidcup, Kent, bottled and flogged at a mark-up of several thousand per cent. The brand was eventually withdrawn when it appeared to contain high levels of a chemical linked to cancer.[3]
Our people may be a bit expensive, but they get the job done.	We will search the world for people who can get the job done at the right price.	Many companies like HSBC and Standard Life have been outsourcing their call centres to countries like India.[4]
Once a service has been outsourced, it's up to the external provider to manage their affairs.	Just because a service has been externalized, this doesn't mean the client is not responsible for making sure things are done properly.	An undercover reporter worked as a customer services advisor at Capita (who administer the London congestion charge system) and found that operators sometimes hung up on difficult customers, their advice was frequently wrong, new recruits were told not to file complaints and the computer system collapsed on a regular basis.[5]
I can't imagine anyone trying to claim compensation against a well-run company like ours.	The possibility of compensation claims represents a real risk for all corporate bodies.	They have been part of the summer fetes for years – but now home-made cakes have been banned by a school. Parents were stunned to receive a newsletter saying children's favourites such as fairy cakes and Victoria sponges will no longer be acceptable in case the school is sued over food poisoning.[6]

(Continued)

Old thinking	New dimensions	A suitable example
Just because a system doesn't work well all the time, you can't keep asking for the Minister concerned to resign.	Government is based on accountability and if any Minister fails to deal with a major problem that is brought before them, they must put their hands up and take personal responsibility for the fallout.	The Government's Immigration Minister resigned in April 2004 after it emerged that she was warned about a visa scam in Romania and Bulgaria by a fellow minister over a year ago. In her resignation speech the Minister in question made it clear that '... I believe strongly that on an issue as sensitive as immigration – one so open to misunderstanding – there is an obligation on me as minister to set the highest standards, not only of my personal integrity, but also of the policies we are pursuing.'[7]
Organizations have moved forward to a workplace culture that is inclusive and brings out the best in people.	While progress is being made, there are still too many negative practices going on in the workplace.	Harassment is rife in the City according to a survey which has revealed that more than half of brokers, traders and analysts have experienced or witnessed it in the workplace. The City of London is one of the most brutal places to work, if the findings of the survey are to be believed. It reveals that there is a culture of intimidation within the Square Mile.[8]
Innovation, research and development and new ideas are what good business is all about.	It is about doing the everyday simple things better and making small incremental improvements. But doing so on a continuous basis is what delivers real benefits.	Too many managements can avoid tough decisions, settle for modest performance and still survive.[9]
All businesses now respond positively to feedback from their customers to ensure that the risk of losing their market share is minimized.	All businesses should respond positively to feedback from their customers, but some do not always understand the link between customer satisfaction and minimizing the risk of losing their market share.	When a guest wrote to complain about being charged for a glass of water, the managing director of the three-star hotel in Newquay replied as follows: 'I feel the need to enlighten you about the workings of the modern world. I buy the water from the South West Water Company. I buy the glasses that the water is served in.

| | | I buy the ice that goes in the water and I buy the labour to serve the water. I provide the luxury surroundings for the water to be drunk in and again pay for the labour and washing materials to wash the glass after you have used it, and you think I provide all of this free. As regards your comments about not returning to the Hotel – customers who only drink water and complain about paying for it I can certainly do without.'[10] |
| A new corporate killing law would have a negative impact on British business as it would make companies more risk averse. | Corporate bodies have to bear full responsibility for what they do or fail to do, and this means the people who run them being truly accountable. | Imagine there were no laws prohibiting manslaughter by individuals, or causing death by dangerous driving, and, in order to stem the mayhem, someone proposed a law against recklessly causing death. Can you imagine anyone opposing that by arguing that such a new law would have a negative impact on 'British life' or that it be undesirable because it would 'make British people more risk-averse'?[11] |

The key messages

The last section of each chapter contains a short story or quote that should provide an interesting format for illustrating some of the book's key messages.

Culture change strategies

I had travelled to the harbour of Polperro, set deep on Cornwall's south coast, to find a little peace and quiet. The small fishing community consists of dozens of cottages dotted around the harbour, many of them located up in the hills. At low tide the habour becomes dry and it slowly fills up as the sea stretches inwards as the evening progresses. I sat on a large boulder with my face turned towards the sea and watched the small fishing boats bobbing around as they moved in towards the safety of this inlet. One boat came towards me and I could see a group of people waving and taking pictures as they returned from their boat trip. The boat came in and the skipper secured it to an old wooden jetty. He then helped each of the excited passengers step up to dry land and looked at his watch.

Through the shafts of sunshine that glowed around the boat I could see him waving to me and as I strained to hear I could see he wanted me to come over to the boat. As I got closer I could see he was your typical old sea dog, with weathered face, wispy beard and an old cap pulled down firmly over his white hair.

'Come on, step up,' he grumbled in a low voice as he scratched his beard. 'Take the last boat trip for the day. Half an hour round trip and you'll see the coastline of Polperro.'

I shook my head but without conviction and he could see that I would not take much persuasion.

'Half an hour. Time well spent,' he went on.

I shrugged and stepped on board. The engine spluttered into life and chugged away as the boat swung out of the harbour towards open sea.

The old man surveyed the sky and muttered something about rain tonight and started a low humming sound of a unfamiliar tune. The boat continued to slop along and dip softly from side to side.

'You have a weight on your mind, son?' the old man asked as he continued to hum his song.

I found my voice, realizing that I had not spoken to anyone since I left my hotel earlier that morning. 'Just work. The usual problems,' I heard myself saying.

The old man continued his song and I recognized this one, an old tune about love lost or some such theme. I realized that he was waiting for more from me. I trailed my hand into the water and obliged.

'I'm at a work conference and this is our day off. My colleagues are going into St Austell to the covered market, looking for bargains. I wanted to see Polperro. You see, I've got to make a presentation tonight and I thought I could take a bit of time off to think it through.'

'Very good,' the old man suggested as if congratulating me, 'but all is not well. Is that so?' he asked.

'Not really. I'm trying to get people to take responsibility for their work and ensure they are handling things that are thrown at them. And it's not easy.'

I trailed my hand over the side of the boat again and felt the trickle of cold salt water. 'It's not easy. I've told all the business managers what is needed and they don't seem too interested. I think my presentation is a bit boring and I'm not sure it'll make any impact tonight.'

The old man pulled out a pipe and managed to light it while still keeping the boat steady. He hummed a new tune and I thought about my slides, some 50 presentation slides, and whether I could get through all of them in an hour. I wished I could stay on the boat and just float away. I did not realize that I had dropped off to sleep for a few minutes and as the boat gently rocked from side to side I opened my eyes to see the hills around the coastline and, in the distance, the cliffs that jutted out above the harbour.

The old man was pulling on his pipe and as he looked left towards the sun, I could see the creases along his forehead and around his eyes. He started humming a new tune.

After a few minutes he turned around to look at me and said, 'Forget the slides. Why don't you draw them a picture of a tree?'

I thought I had misheard and so did not answer. He continued, 'Why don't you draw a tree and tell them what it represents? Look yonder. That old oak tree over there. The leaves are pretty little things that attract the sun and rain. The dressing. The huge trunk reaches far up to the sky while this is all we see.'

He went off into a deep humming, which was interrupted by an occasional word or two from another song in his repertoire.

We approached the harbour and I had to admire his skills as he turned the boat into the jetty and threw a rope to secure it alongside a spot that I could safety jump onto.

'Thanks. That was really relaxing,' I said, as I realized that he had not asked for any money or told me anything about the places we had seen on our tour.

I turned to walk away and he held up his hand in a sort of salute. As I moved away he shouted, 'The trunk does not hold up the tree. It's the huge root system that ensures the tree stands up and thrives, but most people ignore them because they are underground. They are kept in the dark. Feed the roots and the tree will prosper. Starve them and it will die.'

I stopped walking and faced the boat. But before I could ask him what he meant he waved, turned the boat and headed back out to open sea.

Notes

1. Committee of Sponsoring Organizations, Enterprise Risk Management, Draft framework at July 2004, page 21 (www.coso.org).
2. *The Times*, Monday, April 12, 2004, Business, page 1.
3. *The Independent*, Friday, March 26, 2004, page 33, Philip Hensher.
4. *The Mail on Sunday*, Sunday, April 11, 2004, Financial Mail, page 2.
5. *Evening Standard*, Monday, November 24, 2003, page 8.
6. *Daily Express*, Saturday, June 5, 2004, page 7.
7. *The Independent*, Friday, April 2, 2004, page 4.
8. *Evening Standard*, Thursday, October 23, 2003, page 15.
9. *Evening Standard*, Tuesday, March 16, 2004, page 33, all quotes from column by Anthony Hilton.
10. *The Times*, Friday, February 6, 2004, News, page 27.
11. *The Times*, Tuesday, March 16, 2004, Law, page 3, Gary Slapper, professor of law and director of the Centre of Law at the Open University.

10 Reporting results

> 'Tis better to be brief than tedious.
>
> William Shakespeare, *Richard III*, Act 1, Scene 4

A4M Statement J *The results (and underlying evidence) of A4M.99 activities should be reported and made available to support published disclosures on risk management and internal controls.*

Introduction

A4M 10.73 *All senior employees should be in a position to report on the state of the system of internal control in place in their areas of responsibility.*

Figure 1.1 in Chapter 1 shows how the book is put together. Chapter 10 describes the reporting arrangements that may be established to underpin the statement on internal control. We turn now to reporting on A4M.99. It is important that all initial auditing measures are documented and that summary reports are made to the appropriate director each quarter. The theory is simple. The board members need reports from their management teams that let them know that:

- Effective risk management is in place.
- Significant risks (e.g. red risks) and action plans to address them are reported to them for monitoring purposes.
- Each manager is involved in reviewing their internal controls.

- Internal controls are sound.
- The auditors are happy with these arrangements.
- The board can publish a reliable statement based on the above.

As we have said, the theory is simple, but getting the above in place poses more of a problem.

In short

It's easy for the regulators to ask organizations to report on their controls, but the reality can be quite difficult to achieve as people need to learn a whole new language and a new way of looking at their duties at work.

Public disclosures

> **A4M 10.74**   *All employees should be able to give a formal assurance to their line manager regarding the extent to which existing and potential risks are being managed.*

All substantial organizations in all sectors have to publish their financial results. In addition, there are bound to be codes, regulations, laws or directives that mean each organization has to disclose set pieces of information, or explain how they met certain principles – or explain why they chose not to. This is called the 'comply or explain' theory, where good governance arrangements are encouraged but not enforced. The principle is that investors will take a dim view of organizations that fail to live up to defined standards and may reassess the risk to their investment. Similarly, public-sector organizations will come under tremendous pressure where they fail to meet published standards.

National Health Service

For example, National Health Service (NHS) trusts and bodies since 2003/2004 have disclosed:

- Their scope of responsibilities.
- The accountable officer.
- The purpose of the statement on internal control.
- Their capacity to handle risk.
- The risk and control framework.

- Their review of effectiveness of internal control and the assurance framework such as internal and external audit, the audit committee (or risk committee) and the manager's assurances.

Accountable officers have to make clear that they are responsible for maintaining a sound system of internal control that supports the achievement of the organization's policies, aims and objectives. They are also responsible for safeguarding the public funds and the NHS assets for which they are personally accountable.

Central government

Central government organizations are covered by standards issued by the Treasury, who require the accounting officer to state that the effectiveness of their system of internal control has been reviewed. The published information covers items such as:

- Comments on the role of internal control.
- The role of the board and audit committee and any risk committee.
- Responsibilities of the accounting officer.
- Capacity to handle risk and the risk and control framework.
- Risk managers, and methodologies for obtaining control assurance across the organization.
- Risk improvement managers appointed to the large government departments.
- Internal audit.
- Other independent review teams and assurance mechanisms.
- Actions to take care of significant control problems.
- How staff are trained and equipped to manage risk appropriate to their authority and duties, including guidance given to them.

Local government

Local authorities are covered by the Accounts and Audit Regulations 2003, which says that there should be a sound system of internal control in place that is reviewed at least once a year. The official guidance suggests that directors assigned with ownership of risks should routinely monitor and review related internal controls as part of the risk management process and should report on internal control to the corporate management team. Each local authority needs to:

- Establish principal statutory obligations and organizational objectives.
- Identify principal risks to achievement of objectives.
- Obtain assurances on effectiveness of key controls.
- Evaluate assurances and identify gaps in controls/assurances.

- Develop action plans to address weaknesses and ensure continuous improvement to the system of internal control.
- Issue a statement on internal control.

Listed companies

The UK's 2003 Combined Code for companies listed on the London Stock Exchange requires companies to publish certain disclosures. Accordingly:

- The board should maintain a sound system of internal control to safeguard shareholders' investment and the company assets.
- The board should at least annually conduct a review of the effectiveness of the group's systems of internal control and should report to shareholders that they have done so. The review should cover all material controls, including financial, operational and compliance controls and risk management systems.
- Managers should implement board policies on risk and control.
- All employees have some responsibility for internal control as part of their accountability for achieving objectives.
- Management report to the board with a balanced assessment of significant risks to the effectiveness of controls in managing these risks in their areas of responsibility.

Operating financial review

Meanwhile there is growing interest in the operating financial review (OFR) and it is becoming increasingly significant as stakeholders are looking for better published corporate information on past performance, future prospects and policies on the environment, employees and suppliers. Corporate boards decide what information they will feature in their published annual report, although in most developed countries there is a growing trend towards legislation requiring more nonfinancial information to be formally published to present a clearer picture to shareholders and prospective investors.

The USA

In the USA the Securities Exchange Council has approved new rules, via the Sarbanes-Oxley Act 2002, Section 404, including that executives have to certify that their companies have adequate controls to prevent and detect accounting violations and fraud. These new rules were adopted by federal securities regulators mainly to combat the various corporate frauds of 2002/2003. Company management will have to evaluate and report at the end of each quarter any substantial change in internal controls and company executives are now accountable for deterring, although not necessarily eliminating, fraud. Section 404 now means that companies have to:

- Assess controls against a suitable control framework.
- Document how controls are assessed and deficiencies corrected.
- Test that controls actually work.
- Report on the above.

We could go on and extend our comments to housing associations, the charity sector, universities and colleges, professional bodies and so on. But all these bodies, companies and corporate entities will be covered by pretty similar requirements to report formally on their controls. There are a number of matters that arise from the current position:

- There needs to be an ongoing process to monitor internal control and risk management that is embedded in the business.
- Senior management needs to be aware of key risks and develop systems to keep up to date, as well as auditing its work areas.
- Managers, auditors and other review teams need to prepare regular reports on the organization's internal controls.

In short

Published disclosures are becoming increasingly relevant as we move away from prescribed wording and ask that organizations explain the way in which they have been able to meet a set of basic principles.

Professionalism and credibility

> **A4M 10.75**   *All managers should be required to furnish quarterly reports on the adequacy and effectiveness of systems of internal control in areas that they are responsible for and should consider using the initial auditing process to help them discharge this responsibility.*

The COSO ERM has something to say on this matter:

> A CE normally would want to be apprised, for example, of serious infractions of policies and procedures. He or she also would want supporting information on matters that could have significant financial implications or strategic implications or that could affect the entity's reputation.[1]

The internal auditor and the external auditor spend a great deal of their time developing and implementing professional standards. Each profession trains its members over an extended period and budding auditors undergo formal examinations in audit, accounting, review, consulting and other related topics. There is also a robust monitoring process in place to ensure members are able to live up to these high standards and meet the expectations of their stakeholders and clients. When the auditor issues an opinion on the state of internal controls, it is against this background of credibility and professionalism. This means the reports are taken seriously by management, the board, the audit committee and the regulators.

There is no similar process in place that covers the way managers review their internal controls. There is generally no set of standards and detailed training programme that enables managers, teams and workers to say they have carried out a review of their internal controls to set standards that can form the basis of published disclosures in the annual report. Figure 10.1 highlights what is needed to give initial audits some credibility.

The primary factors in Figure 10.1 that may give credence to the initial audit process are:

- **Goals**. The aim of initial auditing, say along the A4M.99 lines, needs to be set out quite clearly and also the benefits that derive from people reviewing their own controls.
- **Standards**. There needs to be some form of written guidance or standards, including those relating to good documentation, that form the basis for the initial audit process. The appendices contain one example. The idea is that so long as the reviews have been performed in line with these standards, they can be deemed professional and reliable.
- **Plans**. Each manager should publish their intended reviews for the year in question.
- **Performance**. The various initial audits, MIA, TIA and MII, should be completed throughout the year.
- **Review**. The initial audit process should undergo some form of quality assurance or external review by, say, the internal auditors, who can assess whether it is robust and reliable.

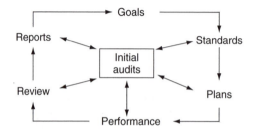

Figure 10.1   Initial auditing credibility

- **Reports**. The process should result in formal reported assurances on internal control and action plans to address any areas of over- or undercontrol.

Quality assurance

The quality assurance that attaches to initial auditing methods may involve a sign-off of various factors that should be taken on board when reporting on the way initial audit has operated during a period. A standard form may be used to sign off the following:

- All enquiries made.
- All tasks completed.
- Standards achieved.
- All work reviewed.
- Files held and backed up.
- Report cleared.

A good initial audit process achieves the following:

- Objective.
- Respected by stakeholders.
- Addresses tough questions.
- Deals with any problems identified.
- Fair and balanced.
- Makes good business sense.
- Completed in good time.
- Helps the organization.
- Points to ways forward.
- Does not aim at perfection.

A bad process is the opposite of the above. It compounds the problem and spreads negativity and distrust and worse – it suggests that there is something in place that in reality is not reliable.

Professionalism

Professionalism starts with people having an honest belief in the value and competence of a process or procedure. Organizations should ensure that their people are fully engaged in the initial audit process and that they see how it helps them and their stakeholders. Figure 10.2 addresses this matter.

This sharing, caring model in Figure 10.2 looks at four main factors and how they relate to the three shared cornerstones of myself, stakeholders and the organization. The four factors are that each employee:

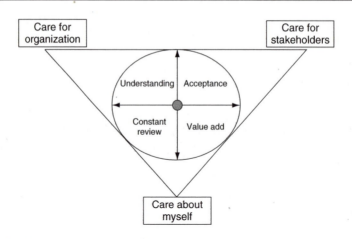

Figure 10.2   The sharing, caring model

1. Understands the concepts of A◀M.99.
2. Accepts that it should be applied.
3. Is able to see the business value of initial auditing.
4. Uses it to keep controls under continuous review.

The idea is to balance these four ideals and achieve for all components at the requisite level of accomplishment:

- **Level one** – good understanding.
- **Level two** – full acceptance.
- **Level three** – adding value to the business.
- **Level four** – constantly updating and reviewing the model.

There are those who see the value proposition as the ability to conform with all regulations, laws and procedures, while there are others who emphasize the enhanced performance value from smarter controls. These two thoughts go hand in hand and we can consider each of these two aspects in Table 10.1.

In short

There is no hiding place when relying on an initial audit process. Top executives cannot delegate controls certification down to the most junior staff – they have to establish and implement a sound process and then make sure the results are reported and make sense.

Table 10.1 Performance/conformance

1. Performance argument	Conformance argument
The performance stance makes for a good selling point	Some start with 'you have to do it anyway' stance
Initiatives may be driven by better business solutions	Senior people respond to tough regulations
Encourages ownership and commitment from everyone	Less senior people have less appreciation of regulations
Makes commercial sense on a day-to-day basis	The issue of personal responsibilities needs to be pushed
Clear focus on the business and efficient operations	There is no hiding from compliance issues

Evidential base

> **A4M 10.76** *All initial audit reports should result in a view on the adequacy of internal controls that is based on reliable evidence. This evidence should be documented and made available for review by authorized third parties such as internal and external audit.*

We can set up dozens of standards, procedures and values to support the initial audit process, but one question will always come back to haunt the board: 'Is there good evidence that supports our review of internal control?'

The questions then are: what is good evidence and how do we present it? If a manager has submitted a report that says the system of internal control has been reviewed and has made the board aware of any significant control weaknesses, there must be an acceptable basis to support this opinion. The board and the auditors are entitled to look at this evidence before signing their high-level statement. This viewpoint is supported by COSO ERM:

> Where management intends to make a statement to external parties regarding ERM effectiveness, it should consider developing and retaining documentation to support the statement. Such documentation may be useful if the statement is subsequently challenged.[2]

Evidential chain

We need to establish a evidential chain that makes sense and is firmly located in reality. When team members sit around and engage in an open-ended discussion

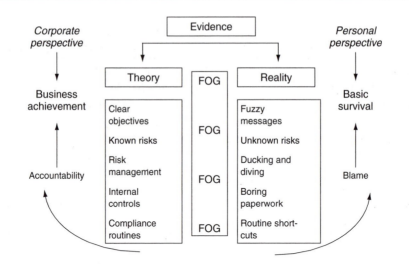

Figure 10.3   Moving from theory to reality

about their controls and whether they are a match to all risks that have been identified and assessed, they may come up with many ideas. They will discuss issues that are uppermost in their minds and have a go at drafting a list of 'top 10 risks' – and this list will be as reliable as the efforts made on the day. The concept of personal perspectives affects the results of risk workshops and control review exercises, as suggested by Figure 10.3.

The **theory** behind reliable evidence sits on the left of Figure 10.3 and is straightforward. It is based on clear objectives and the risk assessment process that results in a firm view on the reliability of internal control and whether compliance is an issue or not. This feeds into the performance process and is reported upwards in terms of the manager and team view of internal control. The **reality** sits on the right of the model and we can have staff with very fuzzy objectives, loads of unknown risks and a climate where people try to duck out of taking responsibility for difficult issues. Where the initial audit is seen as a boring paper exercise that is manipulated to get rid of controls, such as cumbersome authorization procedures that staff simply dislike, an organization may arrive at a completely inappropriate output from the initial audit review. In this scenario, there is a danger that people will try to blame each other to survive and work towards their own personal perspectives, rather than the corporate perspective on the left of the model. The **fog** in the middle of Figure 10.3 may make it hard to reconcile the theory with the reality and it is here that training, good standards and professionalism become really important.

Standards of evidence

Nevertheless, we need not go over the top. We need not assume that all control reviews must meet sky-high standards of evidence to be accepted by all. Figure 10.4 throws some light on this matter.

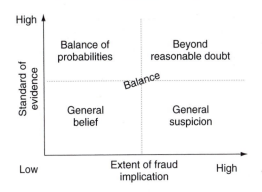

Figure 10.4   Standards of evidence

Full-blown fraud investigations need to work to evidential standards that would support a conclusion that is beyond reasonable doubt – and these standards are very demanding. Our top left control reviews that do not entail fraud implications work to a much less demanding balance of probabilities, which means what is reasonable in the circumstances.

The nature of evidence

Evidence is anything that moves one closer to unravelling the true nature of the matter being reviewed. One interesting model that can help assess the value of evidence is in Figure 10.5.

Evidence needs to be relevant, sufficient and balanced and needs to support or refute the suppositions that have been developed. A structured approach to arriving at good evidence to support an opinion is normally appreciated by

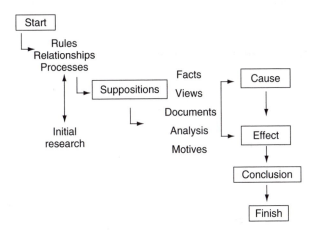

Figure 10.5   Exploring cause and effect

executives, who can take some comfort that control reviews feeding up to them are trustworthy. When developing and considering suppositions we will want to establish a clear link between the evidence and the supposition that has been examined and tested by asking:

- Does it relate to our inquiry?
- Does it have an impact on the supposition?
- Does it stand up to rigorous examination?
- Does what is on paper really happen?
- Is there anything that refutes it?
- How may our sources be confirmed?
- Are there any other factors that have been overlooked?

How much is enough?

When evidence has been developed from a reliable process, the next question to ask is whether it is sufficient. Sufficiency relates to having enough to satisfy those who are relying on the evidence either to make a decision or to know that they need not make a decision on the matter in question. Good controls make for a good business and reports that say controls have been reviewed and are sound suggest that there is a better chance of delivering business objectives.

Where, for example, there is an issue about the significant level of first-class flights, hotels and other expenses claimed by top executives, it is vital to test whether there are adequate controls over the expense claim system. As well as reviewing this system, we may look at a sample of claims to see whether they have been processed in line with the set rules, and consider a sufficient number to make the conclusions valid. Figure 10.6 shows the months of claims that are available for examination and the number of transactions on the left column that could be selected.

Transaction	MONTH 1	MONTH 2	MONTH 3	MONTH 4 ETC.
1				
2		POINT		
3	OFF			
4	CUT-			
5				
6				
etc.				

Figure 10.6   Testing cut-off periods

The cut-off point is selected so that a number of claims over several months are selected for review and are seen as sufficient for the purposes. It is generally better to take fewer items over a short timeframe than lots of items that start to get old, in that they were processed some time ago, unless it is a special investigation into a particular problem at a particular time. When selecting a sample there are several considerations, including:

- How far to go?
- Do we have a reasonable amount?
- Does every new item add value?
- What about practicalities?
- Is older material less reliable?
- Does older material show a different view?
- How much time do we have?
- Is the matter controversial?

Where there is a large database that runs into many hundreds, if not thousands, then statistical sampling may be used to ensure the sample that is selected is representative of the entire population, within set limits. Look-up tables can be used to give the sample size where the level of confidence required from the selected sample has been decided in advance. The greater the need to ensure that the sample reflects the population, the greater the confidence levels required, and therefore the bigger the sample required. Where samples are selected at random from a known population, it is possible to predict the scale of a problem having secured and analysed a representative sample. If a sample indicates that some 5% of children at a particular school with 1000 pupils have been wrongly graded, it is possible to suggest that around 50 (5% of 1000) pupils may have the wrong grade assigned to their work.

Striking a balance

Evidence on the functioning of controls needs to be balanced. So, for example, if examining the size of shoes left outside a gym to get an average shoe size, this may be misleading. It will depend on the balance between male and female or whether the class is for adults or children. The results obtained from this exercise will not be balanced without some additional information. If, for example, a survey into staff morale were conducted and only recently promoted managers were questioned, researchers will get a different view than if they had questioned long-serving junior managers who had not been recently promoted. Where evidence is relevant and sufficient it may be poor if not well balanced. This means when designing audit work ask:

- Are there different sides to the agreement?
- Have we had access to all areas?

- Has there been any material that was thrust at us?
- Have some people or records not been available?
- Is there the need to pursue other lines of inquiry?
- Are there any complaints that have been ignored?
- Has the work been discreetly manipulated at all?
- Are there inconsistencies to follow up?

In one hotel it was standard practice to show the representative from the tour operator a magnificent bedroom that was specially set aside for this review, while many of the other rooms were pretty substandard. This practice resulted in the hotel receiving rave reviews from the tour operator in its brochures. What the representative should have done is examine several rooms selected at random for a more balanced view of the hotel's standards.

In short

Evidence is important to support an opinion on internal control, and this tends to fall down in team workshops where most findings are based on the personal views of team members and the bias of groupthink.

Using the risk register

> **A4M 10.77**   *Relevant aspects of the initial audit process should be used to compile or update the risk register for the area in question.*

The risk register may be seen as a pivotal aspect of the initial audit process. This is because it is a document, or record, that captures the main ingredients of the review of internal control. This in turn supports the controls assurance and reporting process that is eventually reviewed by the audit committee before arriving at the board for its statement on internal control. Where risk registers are prepared using good standards and where they are part of a formal controls reporting infrastructure, they can enable great progress.

We have referred to risk registers throughout the book and they can take a number of different formats. One possible version is in Table 10.2.

A   This is about risk identification and steps taken to note all those risks that affect the business objectives.

B   This stage records the impact (I) of the risk and likelihood (%) that it will materialize if there are no controls put in place. A top 10 (or 12) set of key risks may be provided by each part of the business.

Table 10.2   The risk register

Objective...						
List of risks	Score impact+likelihood	Mitigation controls	Extent of compliance	Evidence obtained	Opinion on controls	Action plan
A	B	C	D	E	F	G

C   This is about risk management and the controls that are put in place to mitigate the effects of the risks from column A.

D   Assesses the extent to which controls from column C are adhered to on the basis that those that are ignored cannot really be taken seriously as part of the overall risk management strategy.

E   Records all the evidence obtained to support the comments in the previous columns.

F   This contains the formal opinion on internal control that is the basis for assurances that are given upwards through the line, as part of the overall corporate review and statement on internal control.

G   Action to remedy control weakness, noncompliance or reduce redundant controls is here, along with risk owners, target dates, review process and links into the business planning, decision-making and performance management systems.

The risk register records the control review process in a nutshell. In terms of A4M.99 the following should be noted:

- **The manager's initial audit** will review the way risk registers are put together and whether aspects of control solutions are in place and perform as well as they should. More fundamental reviews will reconsider the way risks have been compiled and whether the current response is adequate in getting residual risk to fit the corporate risk appetite. The manager's initial audit will also address new risks that have appeared and need immediate action. The focus is on the way columns A through to G have been developed and whether they reflect the business reality – but an extra effort will be made on securing evidence for column E to support all the findings.

- **The team's initial audits** will be designed to prepare the risk register in the first place and to update it on a routine basis or where new developments change the risk portfolio facing the business. This is about working through columns A to G, but there will tend to be a very low standard of evidence for column E, as this is based mainly on the general views and feelings of team members.

- **The manager's initial investigation** will be an attempt to review control failings and assess which part of the risk register needs amending in terms of improved controls. This will tend to focus on columns C and D and it may well result in further action to improve controls (C) or the level of compliance with existing controls (D).

Risk and reporting

Where the organization has a robust set of risk registers in place that result from the A4M.99 process, it can apply the controls reporting infrastructure in Figure 10.7. Figure 10.7 takes a little explaining and the best way to do this is to list some of its features:

- The board, on advice from the audit committee, needs to publish disclosures on its system of internal control.
- The chief risk officer coordinates the process for arriving at this statement.
- Meanwhile the board issues a corporate strategy that meets stakeholders' expectations and results in divisional objectives and plans.

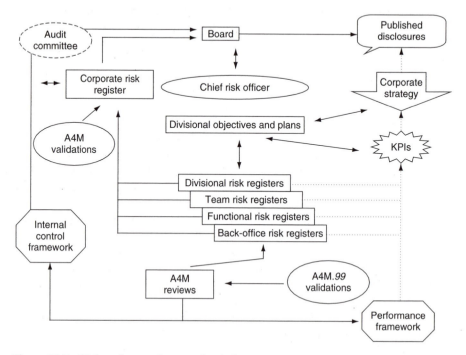

Figure 10.7   Risk and controls reporting infrastructure

- These plans are linked to KPIs, which suggest that in meeting set targets the organization will be able to deliver the plans and achieve corporate objectives.
- The business plans are supported by a series of risk registers, which record a strategy for dealing with risks that affect the ability to deliver the plan.
- These risk registers operate in divisional, functional, back-office and other areas that reach across the organization.
- Moreover, these are divisional, departmental, section and team-based registers that cascade downwards in terms of more and more detailed objectives.
- These risk registers are compiled by using the A4M.99 process and key risks and controls are aggregated upwards until key or red risks feature in a corporate risk register.
- The process derives from a control framework that has been adopted by the organization to drive the risk and control review process. This contains elements such as integrity standards and competence in risk management.
- The A4M.99 process is validated by the internal auditors for business systems and also by the external auditors for financial systems that feed into the main financial accounts reporting system.
- The cycle is closed by a link from the risk register to the performance management system and the knock-on to the KPIs.
- This entire risk and controls reporting system is coordinated by the chief risk officer and the audit committee, but it is owned by the board.
- The main activity that generates transactions for the system is based in the three types of A4M.99 reviews (MIA, TIA and MII).
- The entire process revolves around the risk registers.

Good systems ensure that red risks are reported to board and audit committee and there is an action orientation where, armed with information on risk and controls, managers try to make a difference. All actions should be owned by someone and they feed into and from a credible system of high-level risk registers. This is because all actions and decisions made from the risk auditing and reporting system should be able to be tracked back to their origin, via an audit trail.

In short

It takes a bit of time and effort to get good risk management in place, but there is little to be gained from running loads of risk workshops without establishing an integrated reporting structure.

Good reporting

> **A4M 10.78**   *Aggregate divisional action plans and details of severe unmitigated risks should be available to the board and audit committee.*

Figure 10.8   Reporting components

The reports that go up through the line in an organization using good risk management and initial audit reviews will help move the business towards its goals. Auditing for managers is an attempt to bring together three key aspects of management and accountability, as shown in Figure 10.8.

Here published reports are concerned with informing stakeholders about the risk management process and whether it is reliable or not. The reports are also concerned with the shape and direction of the business and its performance. They are there to fulfil disclosure requirements by commenting on all those matters set out in the regulator's code, including a formal statement on internal control (SIC). Organizations need to cover all three bases and ensure that their review processes address performance and compliance and also explain how it is done – and convince users that it is being done properly. Reports are prepared to:

- Provide information.
- Show how the review work has been done.
- Indicate that action has been taken.
- Document findings.
- Provide recommendations where appropriate.
- Provide a formal record for external parties.
- Demonstrate commitment to action.
- Show how specific problems have been dealt with.
- Promote transparency.
- Make sure there is no cover-up.
- Draw a line under the period in question.

Whatever the approach, it is necessary to report the results of control reviews back to the team, the management, the director and if necessary the board. As we move up through the organization the report findings become more and more aggregated until they end up as a one-page briefing document that sets out the key items of information needed by the forum in question. A management report on internal control may contain the following details:

- Objectives.
- Scope.
- Findings (any red risks).
- Supporting evidence.
- Significant control weaknesses.
- Formal assurances on controls.
- Recommendations.
- Action plans (changes to risk register).

The report should make it clear that whatever is wrong with specific controls has either been identified outright or is in the process of being corrected. As such, reports only comment on the past as a way of helping an organization move into the future. There is a lot of fog that can get in the way of delivering some basic messages and it is necessary to secure understanding and acceptance of the actions that are needed or endorsed as a result of the work that has been carried out. Good reports should try to be:

- Clear.
- Concise.
- Accurate.
- Readable.
- Useful.
- Insightful.
- Timely.
- Not too long.
- Logical.
- Cross-referenced.
- Without gaps.
- Structured.
- Consistent.
- Positive.
- Focused on key issues.
- Focused on priorities.

They should indicate what happened, why, what has been done, what needs to be done, and by when.

Executive summary

The executive summary is in reality the report. People do not have the time nor inclination to delve into more detail than necessary and in the age of the PC screen it is very hard to get people to scroll down at all. The reports on internal control should elicit appropriate information, show key decision points and input into the decision-making cycle, taking us from risks to issues to action and decisions. The best type of report is in fact a high-level risk register that highlights all the information needed to manage risk and maintain control over the business. Each register could be aggregated upwards, so that red risks appear in the higher-level summary registers until the board gets a helicopter position that maps risk across the business and helps set an agenda for change, progress and even success, as well as forming a basic disclosure reporting framework.

It is possible to deliver the messages by using the following flows of responsibility:

- **CEO and board** sign financial statements and hold personal responsibility. The board is responsible for what people do at work.
- **Disclosures committee (or audit committee)** makes sure disclosures are done and make sense and decides what should be released to investors.
- **System of internal control** is developed and reviewed so that deficiencies are corrected.
- **Ongoing review of internal controls** is conducted by business managers through initial audits supported by the internal auditors.

Using this approach, management can design an entire controls reporting process in a way that makes sense at every level of the business. An organization may also use our four V model as the four components against which to derive objectives and then measure risks to the achievement of these objectives, as in Figure 10.9.

This approach draws on one developed by the British Ministry of Defence, which applied its version of the balanced scorecard to drive objectives along four

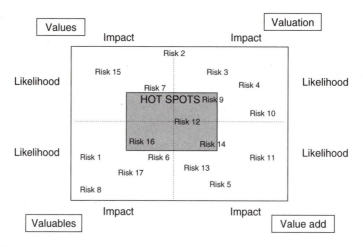

Figure 10.9 Four V risk hot spots

main fronts. It then applied risk assessment to this performance framework to comprise a fully embedded risk management approach. Our four objectives may appear along the following lines:

- **Values** – realistic, reflect mission, focused on stakeholders, drive conduct.
- **Value add** – value for money and improved quality of operations and systems.
- **Valuables** – protected, sustained, people and resources fully utilized.
- **Valuations** – accurate, fair, thoroughly audited, appropriate accounting policies and full disclosures.

Risk 16 in Figure 10.9 may be that our buildings are vulnerable and there is poor security and an inadequate contingency plan in the event of a disaster, while risk 1 may relate to the availability of specialist key staff that would affect the business. However, there are good human resource planning processes that are aimed at ensuring this risk does not materialize. Risk 9 may relate to a significant new accounting policy that has not been agreed with the auditors. Meanwhile, the board and top management will want regular reports on what is happening with hot spots risks that fall within the inner shaded box.

In short

Loads of reports, excessive paperwork and other such nonsense: when will it all end? That is how most executives view their lot. It will end when we stop sending out reports that do not feed into the strategic decision-making priorities of the people who receive them.

Common mistakes

> **A4M 10.79** *Reports that result from the initial audit process should be brief and to the point. They should highlight key aspects of the review of risk management arrangements and typically consist of a one-page summary with accompanying graphics, such as four V risk hot spots.*

Scenario one

Executives want information on the state of their controls so that they may report in turn on their system of internal control. The more information that addresses this basic need, the better, so that in time a complete picture is available covering the entire organization.

Figure 10.10   As I was saying

Scenario two

The A⁴M.*99* process turns much of this on its head by suggesting that the scenario should change to the following:

Executives want information on the state of their controls so that they may report in turn on their system of internal control. They need a carefully designed reporting system that accelerates key information upwards in an aggregate way that results in concise executive briefings that actually cover the entire organization.

Is it that simple?

There is much that could go wrong in moving from scenario one to scenario two:

- **No good understanding of current disclosure requirements for the sector in question**. Where the disclosure needs are not properly understood by employees, the link between initial audits and good published reports will be missed.
- **Policy of using control reports from consultants in an effort to save time and trouble**. Where there is no attempt to develop unique reporting systems, there will be less scope for developing a unique corporate message.
- **Little appreciation of standards that should be applied to techniques for reviewing internal controls**. Where there is no real knowledge of audit standards, the initial audit work will be less than professional.
- **Lack of documentation covering efforts to review controls**. Where the documentation produced by the initial audit activity does not impress the internal and external auditors, it will be less than professional.

- **Little effort is paid to providing reliable reasoning in support of control evaluation**. Where there is little attempt to ensure that outputs from initial auditing have resulted from a robust and valid consideration of all available information, there will be less credibility gained from the efforts made.
- **Excessive amounts of paperwork produced from risk and control evaluation exercises**. Where the degree of paperwork from risk management exercises is not aggregated into meaningful reports, there will be less interest from and benefits to the organization's executives.
- **No quality assurance process attached to reports on internal control**. Where reports that result from initial auditing are not examined for accuracy and balance, they will have less impact on the organization.
- **Failure to see the risk register as a pivotal component of business control assurance reporting**. Where the risk and control audits do not use the risk register as a key document, they will have less of an effect on the risk management process.
- **A view that risk and control assessment can be done by anyone with no expertise at all**. Where there is no appreciation of the scope to perform substandard initial audits, there will be less effort made to ensure this does not happen.
- **No real integrated risk and controls reporting infrastructure in place**. Where there is no careful thought given to the entire risk and control reporting structure, including appropriate software, there will be more chance that the results will be poor.

Helpful models for overcoming problems

The model that is used for this section of the book comes in two parts, an old format and a new one. The old format is in Figure 10.11.

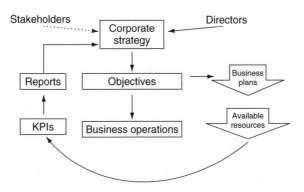

Figure 10.11 Old-fashioned reporting

This is a straightforward reporting system that is based around set plans and the associated performance management process. The new format changes this position, as in Figure 10.12.

Here we have an updated version, where we set an assessment of risk and resulting controls within the business planning process to ensure more successful results and good disclosures. Underpinning this is the idea that values are also important. The corporate entity provides a mandate to deliver along with a clear accountability framework of roles and responsibilities. Once objectives have been set, the business can push on and think about its risk management strategy. Risk and control appear again at the top right of the model, where business plans are formulated only after having considered key internal and external risks. In this way disclosure reports have much more value to an entity as controls are seen as part of the business rather than a series of add-ons.

In short

Disclosure reports can be formula based or meaningful, depending on how far the reporting arrangements derive from the actual working practices in place rather than being a separate element.

Check your progress

> **A4M 10.80** *The initial audit process should not result in excessively detailed reports that have no real value or meaning to business managers.*

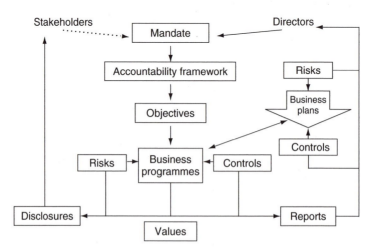

Figure 10.12 New-style reporting

One tool that can be applied to track your progress is to test the extent to which you have assimilated the key points raised in this chapter. The multi-choice questions below will check your progress and the answer guide in Appendix D is based on what is most appropriate in the context of this book. Please record your answers in the table at Appendix D. You may also record the time spent on each test and enter this information in the 'Mins' column of Appendix D.

Name ....

Start time .... **Finish time** .... **Total minutes** ....

Multi-choice quiz

1. Select the most appropriate sentence.
a. It is easy for the stakeholders to ask regulators to report on their controls, but the reality can be quite difficult to achieve as people need to learn a whole new language and a new way of looking at their duties at work.
b. It is easy for the regulators to ask organizations to report on their controls, but the reality can be quite difficult to achieve as regulators need to learn a whole new language and a new way of looking at their duties at work.
c. It is easy for the regulators to ask organizations to report on their controls, but the reality can be quite difficult to achieve as people need to learn a whole new language and a new way of looking at their duties at work.
d. It is easy for the regulators to ask organizations to report on their controls, but the reality can be quite difficult to achieve so long as people need not learn a whole new language and a new way of looking at their duties at work.

2. Insert the missing words.
In the USA the Securities Exchange Council has approved new rules (via ....) whereby executives have to certify that their companies have adequate controls to prevent and detect accounting violations and fraud.

a. Sarbanes-Oxley 2002, Section 404.
b. Sarbanes-Oxley 2004, Section 202.
c. Oxley-Sarbanes 2002, Section 404.
d. Sarbanes-Oxley 2004, Section 404.

3. Insert the missing words.
There is no set of standards and detailed training programme that enables managers, teams and workers to say they have carried out a .... to set standards and this can form the basis of published disclosures in the annual report.

a. review of their disciplinary records.
b. assessment of risk-averse practices.
c. review of their external controls.
d. review of their internal controls.

4. Select the most appropriate sentence.
a. The initial audit process should undergo some form of quality assurance or external review by, say, the security staff, who can assess whether it is robust and reliable.
b. The initial audit process should undergo some form of quality assurance or external review by, say, the internal auditors, who can assess whether it is robust and reliable.
c. The internal audit process should undergo some form of quality assurance or external review by, say, the business unit managers, who can assess whether it is robust and reliable.
d. The external audit process should undergo some form of quality assurance or external review by, say, the director of operations, who can assess whether it is robust and reliable.

5. Which is the odd one out?
The quality assurance that attaches to initial auditing methods may involve a sign-off of various factors that should be taken on board when reporting on the way the initial audit has operated during a period. A standard form may be used to sign off that:

a. all inquiries have been made.
b. most tasks have been completed.
c. standards have been achieved.
d. all work has been reviewed.

6. Which is the odd one out?
A good initial audit process achieves the following, in that it:

a. Aims at perfection.
b. Is objective.
c. Is respected by stakeholders.
d. Addresses tough questions.

7. Select the most appropriate sentence.
We can set up dozens of standards, procedures and values to support the initial audit process, but one question will always come back to haunt the board:

a. 'Is there any evidence to support our review of internal control?'
b. 'Is there good news to support our review of internal control?'
c. 'Is there good evidence to support our compliance with internal controls?'
d. 'Is there good evidence to support our review of internal control?'

8. Select the most appropriate sentence.
a. Documentation is anything that moves one closer to unravelling the true nature of the matter being reviewed.

b. Evidence is anything that moves one closer to unravelling the true nature of the matter being reviewed.

c. Evidence is legal material that moves one closer to unravelling the true nature of the matter being reviewed.

d. Evidence is anything that moves one closer to unravelling the possible nature of the matter being reviewed.

9. Insert the missing words.

The .... may be seen as a pivotal aspect of the initial audit process. This is because it is the document (or record) that captures the main ingredients of the review of internal control.

a. risk register.

b. control register.

c. interview records.

d. risk workshop.

10. Select the most appropriate sentence.

a. The executive summary is in reality only part of the report.

b. The executive summary invites the reader to ask for the whole report.

c. The executive summary may be requested in lieu of the full report.

d. The executive summary is in reality the report.

Newsflash – read all about it

There is so much behind the move towards effective governance and risk management in all walks of life, and a small selection of relevant examples is provided to illustrate this new way of thinking.

10 new dimensions

Old thinking	New dimensions	A suitable example
Really big companies now know that they have to behave well, as they have too much to lose from a newsworthy scandal.	Corporate scandals tend to arise whenever the marketplace has unrealistic expectations of an industry. So long as expectations are unrealistic, there is a temptation to publish information that is much the same.	Shell shocked investors in 2004 when it revealed that its oil and natural gas reserves had been overstated by a fifth. The chairman and several executive directors had to resign over the issue.

(Continued)

Old thinking	New dimensions	A suitable example
Publish and be damned.	Make sure of your facts before going to print.	The editor of the *New York Times* resigned after a scandal where a journalist had allegedly been involved in plagiarism, deception and inaccuracies. The journalist went on to suggest that there was a culture of drugs and suicides at the newspaper.[3]
Walt Disney is sheer paradise.	There can be trouble, even in paradise.	There was blood on the magic carpet at the Walt Disney annual general meeting in Philadelphia – where a band of angry shareholders called for the Chief Executive's resignation.[4]
You must give people the benefit of the doubt.	Many people put self-interest over and above legitimate behaviour.	Some argue that 60% of the population has engaged in illegal practices, such as paying cash for goods to avoid Value Added Tax. One report details how A Level students are buying essays guaranteed to achieve A or B grades over the Internet.[5]
Information is fundamental to control: the more information the better the feeling of control.	We need to be careful about the provision of information to enhance controls, as too much data can be just as bad as too little.	A study found that modern jet planes can contain computerized control systems that are so complex that they create the risk of wrong decisions that could lead to disaster. There is often an overload of technical information.[6]
Unlike the private sector, public services do not have a profit motive and therefore need lots of targets to ensure good performance.	Accepting that the public sector does not in general have profit incentives, there is a need to apply a suitable range of carefully selected targets that make sense and lead to better services.	Many parts of the public service face 'excessive' numbers of government targets and performance measures, the Treasury admitted as it revealed for the first time the scale of controls imposed on front-line staff.[7]

Communicating is a key aspect of risk and the new generation of younger managers have a lot to offer in this respect.

Communicating is a key aspect of risk management and the new generation of managers should be helped to engage in a meaningful dialogue where this may not be happening.

Communication skills will be tested at school for the first time to eradicate the monosyllabic grunts used by many teenagers. Experts fear young Britain has become a generation of Kevin the Teenager created by comedian Harry Enfield who would only talk to his parents in one-word snorts.[8]

Computers make our lives easier in a multitude of ways and can safeguard our liberty.

Computers make our lives easier in a multitude of ways but can never safeguard our liberty.

This was starkly demonstrated by the technology failure at the Criminal Records Bureau. The CRB was set up in March 2002, and enables employers to check whether an applicant for a job has a criminal background. It was designed specifically to prevent paedophiles from being given jobs supervising children. The applicant's details are fed into the Police National Computer and the results, positive or negative, are forwarded to both the employer and the applicant. The Home Office has revealed that 193 people have been wrongly accused of having a criminal past since the system came into effect.[9]

It may be possible to develop a common standard to measure risk and so help restore trust in the financial services industry.

Unforeseen events do occur, and that is when blood gets spattered over the walls. Risk measurement will never remove uncertainty – and uncertainty is every bit as fatal as risk.

Comments extracted from an article by City columnist Anthony Hilton.[10]

(Continued)

Old thinking	New dimensions	A suitable example
Internal controls (and therefore the chances of successfully achieving one's objectives) are operated by people and are affected by the way that people behave and respond to different situations. Investors should find out about an organization's controls before they make investment decisions.	Internal controls (and therefore the chances of successfully achieving one's objectives) are essentially about the way people behave and respond to different situations. Investors should find out about an organization's people before they make investment decisions.	The difference between the good, the bad, the successful and the unsuccessful, the innovative or the dull, the living and the dead, is almost always the quality of the people working in the business and the way they are managed and motivated. It is much more than money. Yet attempts to express this are greeted with either hoots or indifference.[11]

The key messages

The last section of each chapter contains a short story or quote that should provide an interesting format for illustrating some of the book's key messages.

Reporting on internal controls

The director of operations bumped into his production manager in the corridor and asked: 'How are your internal controls? Are they okay?'
    'Yup. They're fine.'
    'I have to report to the board on our internal controls. Do you review them?'
    'Yup. Pretty much I do.'
    'And does your review say they're okay?'
    'Yup.'
    'Great. I'll tell them that at tomorrow's board meeting. Many thanks, Jack.'
    'No problemmo.'

Notes

1. Committee of Sponsoring Organizations, Enterprise Risk Management, Draft framework at July 2004, page 86 (www.coso.org).
2. Committee of Sponsoring Organizations, Enterprise Risk Management, Draft framework at July 2004, page 83 (www.coso.org).

3. *The Guardian*, Friday, June 6, 2003, page 3.
4. *The Independent*, Thursday, March 18, 2004, page 28.
5. *Evening Standard*, Thursday, September 11, 2003, page 9.
6. *The Times*, Wednesday, January 7, 2004, Politics, page 24.
7. *The Independent*, Thursday, March 18, 2004, Budgets Special, page 11.
8. *Daily Mail*, Saturday, February 14, 2004, page 47.
9. *The Independent*, Saturday, April 17, 2004, page 36.
10. *Evening Standard*, Tuesday, February 24, 2004, page 33.
11. *Evening Standard*, Monday, November 3, 2003, page 33, Anthony Hilton.

11   So, why auditing?

The common curse of mankind, folly and ignorance.
William Shakespeare, *Troilus and Cressida*, Act II, Scene 3

A4M Statement K   *The A4M.99 concept, if properly applied, ensures everyone is empowered, equipped and fully motivated to audit their own areas of responsibility.*

Introduction

A4M 11.81   *The initial audit process should be an integrated part of the normal business processes relating to planning, decision making and performance management.*

Figure 1.1 in Chapter 1 shows how the book is put together. Chapter 11 takes us full circle and sets out to answer the question: why auditing? Our final chapter represents a brief jog through some of the ideas we have developed so far. We are asking that managers and for that matter all employees:

1. Understand the risk management process and actively apply the policies and practices in question.
2. Identify all existing and potential risks that have an impact on their objectives.
3. Know whether or not their controls are robust, reliable and make good sense.
4. Ensure they are able to provide regular updates on the state of their systems of audit, risk management and control.

There are many reasons why the above needs to happen in modern organizations, and there are many factors that work against this ideal. What needs to happen is that all organizations should develop a strategy that seeks to achieve the above four outcomes, reinforces drivers that help this happen and tackles anything that holds it back.

In short

The local hospital, national newspaper, the city university, the dairy, the local town hall, the small high street retail business, the leisure centre, library services, the huge out-of-town supermarket, the bank and many other organizations have aims, risks, people managing these risks as they meet their aims and others who have a stake in whether the entity is successful or not. All these people and corporate bodies will benefit from getting their controls right and being able to demonstrate that they have done this.

Why auditing?

> **A4M 11.82**   *The initial audit process should be seen as an attempt to equip people throughout the organization with the necessary support to review their controls.*

We said that auditing has developed in response to a society that is increasingly less likely to tolerate scandals, misselling, corporate crashes, public-sector waste and abuse and all those problems that continue to plague both private and public-sector organizations. Auditing is and will continue to be a very important part of corporate life. What we have also said is that the temptation to employ an army of auditors is creating a two-tier economy: those who deliver the goods and those who check that those in the first group are doing their job properly. To move towards a one-to-one relationship is ridiculous.

What is starting to happen is that the people who check others (the auditors) are starting to explain what they feel should happen and are helping those who deliver to do so and also check whether it is going well or not. In other words, people are performing an initial audit that is an attempt to assess whether they have got it right. This means the auditors can decide whether to rely on the results before launching into their checks.

Sticking to the approach applied throughout the book, we turn to various models to describe the changes that form the main theme of our viewpoint. Figure 11.1 describes the stresses and challenges facing the typical busy manager where we insist that the new risk and control initiative is implemented.

The typical manager has a demanding workload (top of Figure 11.1) and is under constant pressure to keep up with these demands. The standard response

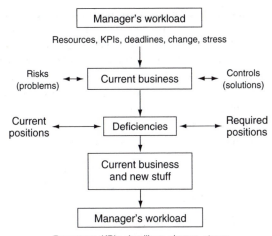

Figure 11.1   Adding to the manager's workload

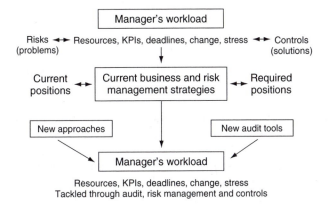

Figure 11.2   Helping managers deal with their workload

to getting risk management in place is that senior executives will instruct that risk assessment be carried out and controls developed according to these assessments and that all deficiencies form part of an action plan. Our manager then has to deliver the current business and also attend the risk management workshops and events, which simply adds to an already full workload. This may well result in some negative perceptions of the initiative, including a temptation to cover up weaknesses and control gaps to avoid taking on new work that any additional action plans would require. The entire process can lead to increased levels of stress among managers and their staff. A better way of implementing the risk and control agenda is set out in Figure 11.2.

We start once more with the manager's workload, but this time link the concept of risk and controls into the stresses, problems and issues that face most managers trying to deliver increasingly more demanding targets. The analysis of control gaps is set against the current strategies and not located in an action plan that falls outside the real business. The way this comes about is to focus on new approaches and new tools to audit the current strategy. The result affects the manager's workload and the aim is to help the manager and work teams to deliver this workload by prioritizing high-risk matters and getting strategies and controls in place to address the problems that spin off from inherent risks. The simple idea is to use A4M.99 to help the manager deliver and perform, and not make it seem like just another piece of work that adds to the workload.

In short

Managers and their workforce do not really need more initiatives – they need help in meeting demanding challenges at work, and this means better approaches and better tools rather than more approaches and more tools.

External auditing

> **A4M 11.83**   *The external auditors should be asked to provide ongoing support to the initial audit process, particularly relating to financial reporting systems.*

The external auditor has had a hard time of late. The mix of consulting work and pure audit work has, in the past, led to highly competent auditors being developed by firms, while the pressure is on to stick to basic audit work so as not to impair professional independence. The accountancy profession, where the external auditors come from, has responded to the new risk-managed business context by itself developing a risk-based approach to its work. Its members have also moved outside of fixed financial systems and dipped their toes in the governance arrangements of the organizations they audit. So an organization's managers will describe their corporate governance, risk management and control arrangements and the external auditor will confirm that what they say is true. In the US, the external auditors have a more defined role, where they have to attest in the annual report that company officials consider the internal controls over financial reporting to be adequate.

The external auditor is quite happy to work with organizations that have developed good risk management practices and will help promote this theme. They will also review the managers' efforts to review their internal controls and take a view on whether this enhances the chances that controls are reliable, particularly where these controls affect the financial accounting systems and are part of the anti-fraud and compliance arrangements.

The external auditor has much to offer in supporting an organization that is driving initial auditing into the way it works. The old approach was to turn up after year end to perform exhaustive tests of financial transactions to verify that the entire accounting system is sound. Nowadays, the external auditor is quite prepared to meet with management and talk about their efforts to ensure the accounting records, financial systems and resulting financial statements are fair and accurate, including any control reviews that are being planned. In this way, the external auditor is seen more as an ally in the fight to get things right, rather than just a checker.

There will always be the need to perform some basic testing and ask questions about the preparation of the accounts and accounting policies used, but the change in emphasis can be marked. The old days where external auditors worked pretty much to their own clandestine agenda are pretty much gone. The auditor will not come in and check that employees are complying with financial regulations, but is more likely to ask: 'Are your arrangements for ensuring compliance with financial regulations working?' They then go on to confirm that these arrangements are doing the job and even help management improve them if required. In terms of governance, risk management and internal control, the external auditor has an important role that is greatly helped if an organization carries out its initial audits in accordance with in-house standards and maintains good documentation.

In short

The old version of external audit, where auditors turned up and moved in very mysterious ways, is long gone. It has been replaced by a new, forward-looking approach that recognizes and supports the risk management arrangements in place to support good governance and sound internal controls.

Internal auditing

> **A4M 11.84**   *The internal auditors should be asked to provide ongoing support to the initial process, particularly relating to enterprise risk management arrangements.*

Like external auditors, internal auditors have moved on tremendously over the years. They now have a great focus on risk management. In fact, internal audit is the only professional body that has 'risk management, control and governance processes' built firmly into the definition of its role. The internal auditor has a dual role in providing consulting advice and help to the business and also providing objective assurances across the organization. The consulting help is given to managers on request, or as spin-off from a previous audit, and there will be a clear criteria to approving all requests for help. The internal audit can help with, for example:

- Developing risk management arrangements.
- Internal control awareness training.
- Facilitating risk workshops.
- Establishing control reporting structures.
- Implementing compliance checks and supporting management's compliance teams.
- Understanding the new governance agenda.
- Developing good audit committee resources.
- Reviewing and updating procedures.
- Developing control frameworks.
- Assessing the level of control awareness among staff.
- And a whole assortment of other related projects.

In getting risk management and formal internal control reporting in place in an organization, the internal auditor may be the first person to visit for help and advice. The tools, techniques, approaches and competencies described in this book are all well known to the internal auditor, who is brought up on risk management and controls at a strategic and detailed operational level.

Assurance work

The other side of the coin relates to the assurance role of internal audit. Many people in big organizations 'agree to agree' in an attempt not to rock the boat. This is all very well, but where control design is wrong, misdirected, misapplied, abused or simply not quite right, employees need to know about it and act. Having people sit round a table to agree with each other over everything they do and decide leads to harmony but little real improvement. Consultants tend to agree with their clients, as they earn fees from doing what they have been told, and while a small amount of debate may occur, on the whole they are not always independent from the people they have been called in to help.

The internal auditor is one of the few and perhaps the only person in the organization whose professional standards say that they must be objective, independent and work for and on behalf of the best interests of the organization. This assurance role is very powerful. It means that what the internal auditor says about the state of controls is more likely to be true and reliable than what someone with a vested interest says about their controls. A good way of employing the internal auditor's highly developed skills is to ask them to give advice on the way A4M.99, or whatever alternative version, is established in the organization and even help with some of the underpinning work that is required. They can then be asked in their assurance role to judge whether specific initial audit activities are adequate. The internal auditor will review all such efforts as part of their formal audit assurance work. The internal auditor's reports will go to the business manager in question, and the executive summary to the appropriate director, but the auditor's work will also be summarized for the audit committee and board.

In effect, the internal audits can be used as a form of quality assurance over the initial audit process. We have called self-audits initial auditing as this conjures up the view that management and team audits are a first attempt and the internal auditor can come in and tell us whether they are okay or not, and even help refocus them to work better. The auditor will also tackle systems that get left out of the business's initial audit work, such as a review of managing staff absences and levels of staff morale. The internal auditor will be able to tell the audit committee and board whether the process behind the compilation of risk registers across the business is reliable. There is much at stake, since the internal auditor is a crucial source of assurances on governance, risk management and internal control – and their words and opinions are extremely important.

Why internal audit?

All governance codes either require an internal audit cover or at a minimum encourage it. Internal audit can quality assure the initial audit process and will be able to audit less explicit corporate systems, such as ethics awareness among employees and the extent to which the adopted control framework is in place. Moreover, any good internal auditor will start their work by considering the way in which risk registers have been put together by the business line and let the board members know whether they can place reliance on the results of the initial audit process.

In short

Acquaintances engage in small talk, while friends tell you what you want to hear. Best friends, however, tell you the truth even if some of it hurts. Bearing this in mind, the internal auditor can be a manager's best friend in helping to get good systems of risk management and internal control in place.

Compliance auditing

> **A4M 11.85** *The initial audit process should equip people throughout the organization with the necessary tools for reviewing the extent to which defined controls are being adhered to.*

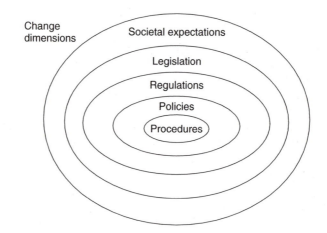

Figure 11.3 Society and procedures capsule

The compliance debate has moved on and it is also part of the initial audit process that we have featured in this book. Most organizations respond to growing compliance requirements by setting up small compliance teams to ensure that the myriad of detailed rules and regulations are properly addressed. This has to be handled very carefully, as there is a need to strike a careful balance between an enforcement and encouragement approach to compliance.

One complementary response is to establish a compliance capsule, as shown in Figure 11.3. This attempts to translate what society needs organizations to do through several layers until the vision is set within the business procedures. The hope then is that these procedures become the actual working practices. Meanwhile, the capsule is dynamic in that it responds to changes in societal expectations and whether we move towards a high-risk growth stance or a low-risk, measured approach to corporate and personal investments.

Is compliance important?

Figure 11.3 suggests that organizations can bring stakeholder expectations inside the business through its procedures, or more properly the way it works. It is by using the initial audit process built into A4M.99 that managers can ensure they reflect all relevant issues. One further point to note: when working on risk identification, managers must bring home compliance issues as potential risks to the business. This means the facilitation of team initial audit exercises needs to include compliance issues, say relating to rules against money laundering, data protection issues, or health and safety matters.

All employees need to understand the compliance process and build this into their work and efforts; that is, they should know that compliance is about the need to:

1. Establish the set criteria against which compliance is measured.
2. Make sure operational procedures meet this criteria.
3. Implement such procedures.
4. Look out for emerging issues – and make changes to the criteria where required.
5. Think about what can go wrong and how to tackle such problems.
6. Determine what should be versus what is – and make changes as required.
7. Train staff and make sure they understand the reason why certain work practices are included in their routines.
8. Make sure compliance is action oriented.
9. Check that people adhere to procedures and set a culture where they are seen as important. A whistleblower's hotline may also be considered.
10. Be prepared to issue reports on compliance arrangements.

The A4M.99 vision of compliance

The A4M.99 vision of compliance suggests that compliance issues are built into the initial audit process in two ways. First, make sure initial audits cater for the risk of failing to observe external laws and regulations and also make sure such risks are assessed with a full understanding of regulations and consequences of falling short.

The second level of compliance is when controls guard against the risks that have been deemed significant. When these controls have been designed, endorsed or changed, think about ways of ensuring they are observed. That is, compliance aspects should be built into the control itself so that, for example, as well as a control that says all remote access to the corporate database should be subject to call-back to check it is from an authorized source, make sure there is an way of telling if this control is working well, and report on its reliability if necessary. Likewise, if a supermarket issues bargain buys on a regular basis, it needs a strong set of controls to ensure all goods are accurately priced up and reflect the latest offers. The risks are great if people think some supermarkets are inflating their prices above published offers – many people will not complain, they simply do not return and tell others how unfair the shop is.

Compliance needs to be built into the way an organization works by ensuring its people understand the need to comply and take all reasonable steps to manage this matter.

In short

A corporate strategy that turns a 'have to' compliance culture into a 'want to' one will reap great benefits, far beyond those organizations that simply employ an army of compliance inspectors.

Fundamental components

> **A4M 11.86**   *The initial audit process consists of 88 values and 11 statements, which should be considered by each manager in terms of how they should be employed in their respective area of responsibility.*

We need to put together a final portfolio of models that summarizes the A4M.*99* process. Many organizations have made great strides in getting their workforce to self-assess their controls. There are many different approaches and tools in use that support and promote various interpretations of initial auditing. What we are saying here is that the move depends on a major shift in attitude and perception for a new approach to replace old styles of command-and-control cultures.

Chapter 1 described an old approach to risk, audit and control (Figure 1.7), while we have now arrived at a new approach in Figure 11.4.

In Figure 11.4 we know we need to address the three challenges of good **performance**, high levels of corporate **integrity** and full and published **disclosures**. Delivering these challenges is founded in the KPIs and we go down through the factors that end with a strong ethical base to support them. On the right we have the standard audit validations and along the left we have the initial audit process. These together ensure that risk assessments and control arrangements work well.

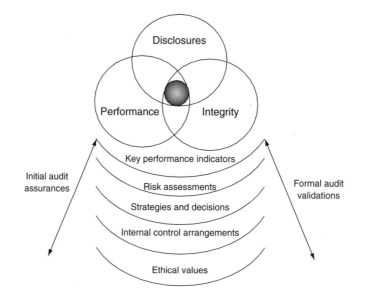

Figure 11.4   New approach to audit and accountability

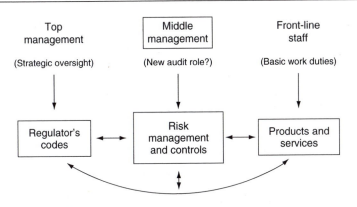

Figure 11.5   Roles and responsibilities

Roles and responsibilities

The next issue we need to address is the need to define new respective responsibilities between executives, management and front-line employees. Figure 11.5 develops this theme.

Top executives are in tune with the regulator's codes and principles and their job is to translate these into standard business practices, while the management needs to work with the new initial auditing role and sell this to people. The front-line staff are involved in day-to-day work duties. We can use the middle box of Figure 11.6, the system of risk management and controls, to merge these positions and bring the regulator's vision into the way the organization delivers its various products and services. This is because the risk assessment process includes the key risk of not living up to the regulator's expectations and principles.

Implementation

Turning now to implementation, there are several ways of getting initial auditing or a version of A4M.99 in place. Figure 11.6 takes up the challenge.

The y-axis assesses the extent to which organizations set up fixed approaches and methods for implementing initial auditing. A high level suggests a fairly mechanical method that all staff would be trained in. The x-axis relates to an organic approach where organizations simply build initial auditing into the way people talk, work and relate to each other in an organic fashion. Here, senior executives could say to each business manager: get something along the lines of initial auditing in place any way you like. The four dimensions could then be:

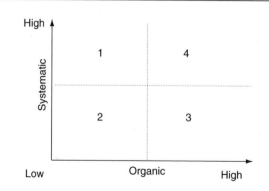

Figure 11.6   Growing the initial auditing agenda

1. **Imposed**. Systematic approaches rely on people doing what they are told and learning a whole new set of risk and control terminology.
2. **Hit or miss**. This position has nothing to it at all. There is no method and no attempt to meet the business context.
3. **Silo based**. The wholly organic approach means different parts of the business will apply initial auditing in a way that suits them. It is useful in that people will take to it quite quickly, but it can result in a silo approach that does not fit with enterprise risk management and a structured approach of business controls reporting.
4. **High impact**. This is what we are aiming for in this book. It means that a set of general principles is applied to encourage the organic style, along with a fairly general set of professional standards that aims at encouraging a systematic and well-documented initial audit process.

Management competence

The Chartered Management Institute has developed a defined set of chartered management skills that include the following:

1. Leading people.
2. Managing change.
3. Meeting customer needs.
4. Managing information and knowledge.
5. Managing activities and resources.
6. Managing yourself.

To make any form of initial auditing work, we suggest an additional competence along the lines of:

7. Managing business assurance, audit and accountability, which may include elements such as:

- Understanding appropriate initial audit processes.
- Identifying and managing risks to business objectives.
- Demonstrating good accountability for decisions made.
- Promoting compliance with established policies and standards.
- Disclosing the company position on internal control and action to enhance the control environment.
- Involving individuals and team members in the above.

Dealing with resistance

The final issue that needs to be considered is the possibility of employees resisting moves to establish initial auditing. The implementation process should follow the same format as other change initiatives that are being adopted by the organization. To help with getting things off the ground, it is possible to use the change analysis matrix in Table 11.1 to gauge how managers and staff might respond and possible ways of dealing with any negative fallout.

Table 11.1   Dealing with resistance

Problem	Possible cause	Strategy
1. Negativity	View that this is about more work with fewer resources	Communicate the business case
2. Apathy	Too much going on at the same time	Demonstrate how it can help lessen the workload
3. Cynicism	Has seen other initiatives fail	Show top management support and good commitment
4. Aggression	Feels exposed by trying to learn new tools	Make clear that new approach is simple and not complicated
5. Dominance	Feels that the balance of power will change	Emphasize that responsibility and accountability will be clarified
6. Factions	Different groups have been told different things about it	Develop a corporate position and emphasize team building
7. No commitment	Cannot see any real reason for it	Score early benefits and tell people about them
8. Personal agenda	Feel that some will gain and others will lose	Link it to corporate values and respect for all employees
9. Hostility	Perception that there will be many personal disadvantages	Make clear impact of it on performance management and incentives scheme
10. Extreme emotions	Belief that there is a hidden agenda	Confront personal fears by finding out about them and clarifying issues

Table 11.1 (Continued)

Problem	Possible cause	Strategy
11. Distractions	Agenda is overloaded by day-to-day matters	Find ways of resourcing the change and make clear that this has been considered by top management
12. Flippancy	Belief that it will not work and it will become just another laughable management fad	Send powerful messages from the regulators making it clear that this is a serious development
13. Confusion	Misunderstanding of what is involved	Create a corporate message that is consistent and communicated in start-up seminars
14. Play acting	Fear of the unknown	Spell out what is involved and how the changes will come into play over the coming months and years

To arrive at a shared vision of what is involved and a clear strategy to get the necessary changes in place, organizations should commission someone who understands the governance, audit, risk and control agenda and how hard it is to get the envisioned structures built. More than anything, each organization needs someone who is able to sell and persuade people of the benefits of this approach.

In short

As with most change programmes, A4M.99 will work if the people with most influence want it to work and are happy to invest the time and effort to make it happen.

Common mistakes

> **A4M 11.87** *The initial audit values and standards should be implemented by each manager in a way that best suits the local circumstances in question.*

Scenario one

A initial audit programme is important in getting risk management in place and if we tell staff what to do, the hope is that they will take the baton and run with it.

Figure 11.7   We're all auditors now

Scenario two

The A4M.99 process turns much of this on its head by suggesting that the scenario should change to the following:

An initial audit programme is important in getting risk management and controls reporting in place and if we are serious about it, after much hard work we may well persuade our people to take the baton and run with it.

Is it that simple?

There are several things that could go wrong in moving from scenario one to scenario two:

- **Leader does not convince everyone of the real belief in A4M.99.** Where the risk champion does not take all necessary steps to convince people about the need for some sort of standard on initial audits and control reporting, there will be less chance that employees will rally round this venture.
- **Old-fashioned risk manager with security background.** Where careful thought is not given to the risk champion and the need to expand into areas covering more than just security, we may not arrive at successful risk management.
- **One person doing everything in the organization.** Where the corporate response to initial audit is to ask one person to do everything, we may find there are only small well-developed pockets rather than an entire risk-smart workforce.

- **Mixing leaders and facilitators**. Where there is a misunderstanding of the difference between those who lead the risk, control and audit programme and those who facilitate events, it may result in an inappropriate mix of each type of skill.
- **Trying to hold 30 workshops per month**. Where there are set targets for resource-intensive events such as risk workshops, this may result in an exhausted workforce who resist all subsequent efforts to get good risk management in place.
- **Viewing initial audits as an annual or quarterly event to meet reporting requirements**. Where audits are not seen as part of the business that responds to events and developments, a mechanical approach may develop and become stagnant.
- **Narrow view not related to the big picture**. Where initial audits are seen to address small, isolated parts of the business, with no integration, many high-risk aspects of the current strategic direction may be missed out altogether.
- **People not really getting involved willingly**. Where people are not really engaged in the initial audit process, it may be seen as a fad that is enforced by the risk police, as opposed to an important business tool.
- **Focus on anonymous voting technology**. Where the audits revolve around fancy voting technology, the initial interest may wane over time.
- **Employees not willing and able to make it work**. Where there are no incentives to getting involved in A4M.99, or an equivalent approach to reviewing internal controls, there may be some difficulty in getting people to want it to work.

Helpful models for overcoming problems

There are two main models for getting A4M.99 into your organization. The first is in Figure 11.8.

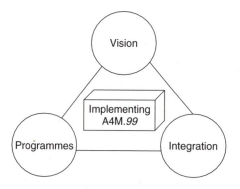

Figure 11.8 Promoting change

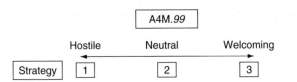

Figure 11.9   Dealing with resistance

Figure 11.8 suggests that there are three main considerations in getting something similar to A4M.*99* in place:

- **Vision** – of what we want to see from a fully developed initial auditing system across the enterprise.
- **Programmes** – tools, techniques, standard documentation, models and training events should be the main part of a strategy to implement the system.
- **Integration** – this last part is the most difficult in that it requires careful consideration of the way initial auditing fits in with the business processes already in place.

The other model is found in Figure 11.9.

By assessing the level of resistance to A4M.*99* we can develop a three-pronged approach:

1. **Hostile** – confronting problems of resistance by making an example of really bad cases.
2. **Neutral** – encouraging and explaining the concepts.
3. **Welcoming** – using the really good players as role models.

All organizations implementing initial auditing should report the results of their efforts and benefits, including:

- Firm grounding in controls assurance.
- Ability to produce a risk assessment and strategy.
- Improved communication between business units.
- Better connection between teams geographically.
- Risk management seen as important to the organization.

Many progress reports on risk management provide no information on the business or whether it is better, more successful or less onerous – which is unhelpful. All A4M.*99* work should have an impact on the way an organization manages its:

- Values.
- Valuables.
- Value add.
- Valuations.

In this way, the three A4M.99 audits (MIA, TIA and MII) are designed to help promote a better governed and, hopefully, more successful organization.

In short

There are many reasons why people do not buy into the empowerment concept, mainly because their goodwill was abused in the past where empowerment simply meant more work for no more reward or recognition. If used properly, **auditing for managers,** *or a version based on these values, could become the* **ultimate risk management tool** *in your organization.*

Check your perceptions

> **A4M 11.88** *Regular initial audits should be an integrated part of the way people in the organization discharge their obligation to manage their business.*

The following short survey can be given to colleagues and fellow team members to assess where they stand in the development of initial auditing:

Perceptions of initial auditing   **Tick**
Tick the most appropriate box: **A or B**

1. a. Audit is a mystery to me.
   b. Audit brings real benefits that I know about.
2. a. New audit skills? We are close to initiative overload.
   b. Managers should learn new audit skills.
3. a. Risk reviews should be left to the experts.
   b. Risk is everyone's business.
4. a. If it ain't broke don't fix it.
   b. Systems need to be retuned regularly.
5. a. Teams look to their management to solve their problems.
   b. Teams can solve their own problems.
6. a. Unfortunately, fate governs most things.
   b. All errors can be traced back to an underling cause.
7. a. When mistakes are made we need to find someone to blame.
   b. Most mistakes can be traced back to problems with systems.
8. a. It's best to keep one step ahead of the auditors.
   b. We can get help and advice from our auditors. ·

9. a. Never own up to a failure.
   b. Transparency and accountability are paramount.
10. a. Everyone has their own hidden agenda.
    b. Success means getting everyone working to the same agenda.

All 'A' answers score 0 points, while 'B' answers score 1 point. The total score will fall between 0 and 10. We need to develop a strategy that encourages 'level 10' teams to make A◄M.99 work in practice. Level 10 teams should be encouraged as without the right perspectives, initial auditing will not really happen. Note that a bank of questions can be found in Appendix E to support the use of general staff surveys.

Newsflash – read all about it

There is so much behind the move towards effective governance and risk management in all walks of life, and a small selection of relevant examples is provided to illustrate this new way of thinking.

10 new dimensions

Old thinking	New dimensions	A suitable example
Men and women in sharp suits can be trusted.	Sharp suits can mean sharp business practices that let everyone down.	Some estate agents have come under severe criticism for paying lip service to the truth in a bid to sell their products. One estate agent failed to warn potential buyers about problems with damp in one property that would cost over £12000 to rectify. Some of the other tricks of the trade include telling lies about other offers in order to bump up bids, selling property at knock-down prices to associates, favouring buyers who take out mortgages and insurance with the agent, operating cartels to push up agency fees, flouting a law against calling overgrown swamps 'cottage gardens' or shabby lean-tos 'conservatories'.[1]

(Continued)

Old thinking	New dimensions	A suitable example
Risk management is good management and, although representing a theoretical approach to corporate life, should be implemented as quickly as possible.	Risk management is partly about good management – but it is more akin to a perception that control is important and there are tools and techniques that can be applied to make corporate life easier to understand and handle.	'Good management practice' must be reinterpreted to imply being able to recognize and work with good practice tensions, rather than solve them.[2]
Risk management comes to the fore when corporate responsibility means that organizations will have to show how they managed personal risks that can be related back to their business.	Risk management is based on good sense and reasonableness, and corporate responsibility is balanced by the need to ensure we all understand the concept of shared personal responsibility.	Trapeze artists appearing in Britain with the Moscow State Circus have been warned that unless they wear hard hats for performances they could lose their insurance cover . . . It is really about the mad culture of blame and liability . . . unless politicians and judges are willing to call a halt, with our support, within a generation we shall have destroyed the concept of personal responsibility, which is at the root of a civilized society . . . The government must get to grips with the Health and Safety Executive, which is responsible for bringing some of the most grotesque prosecutions. I would send its entire directors to climb the Matterhorn without the benefit of ropes. Those who survived might return with a more realistic vision of school playgrounds or, for that matter, trapezes.[3]
Jailing corporate wrongdoers sends out strong messages to executives and this will end the long stream of corporate scandals.	Jailing corporate wrongdoers is a start, but the fixed link between company performance and executive pay (and bonuses) creates a potential hotbed of conflicts that at times breaks out as a new scandal.	If bonus arrangements put irresistible temptation on executives to fiddle the books, would it not make sense to redesign the schemes to remove the perverse incentives rather than pretend that this time it will be different?[4]

Corporate boards need space and freedom to get on with their business without constantly having to look over their shoulders.

Corporate boards need to ensure they tackle both the current and future risks to the business. Unlike days of old there is nowhere to hide where this is not really happening.

Phil Angelides is a name that strikes fear into America's toughest boardrooms. As head of the two giant pension funds, Calpers and Calsters . . . his plan was not only to maximise shareholder returns during tough times, but also to use his clout to bring about changes in the boardroom, in the hope that better corporate governance would foster better returns.[5]

There is only so much we can do to protect the corporate resource. This is why we have to pass onto our customers any extra costs caused by fraud.

We need to take all reasonable steps to protect the corporate resource. Its not fair to simply pass onto our customers extra costs caused by fraud.

It used to be simple. If you needed a few extra pounds, you just inflated the price of that camera or designer outfit you had recently lost and, magically, the cheque was in the post from a compliant insurance company. Times are changing. In the past few months most major British insurance companies, aware of our temptation to defraud them, have installed lie detector machines that can tell, from the inflections in our voices, when we are lying.[6]

In society the onus is on each person to check out the goods or services before buying based on the 'buyer beware' principle.

In society the 'buyer beware' principle is starting to change in the face of growing regulation to protect consumers and force industries to live up to some sort of standard of care.

Millions of homeowners are falling victim to cowboy builders, a new report shows. Being ripped off by rogue tradesman is now the UK's number one consumer complaint and there are calls for tougher action to combat the problem.[7]

Service standards, once set, should be observed to ensure we meet our targets.

Service standards are all very well, but we need to ensure staff are competent, honest and properly motivated before we can really move forwards.

An undercover reporter spent five months as a postman in several London sorting offices and described how 'I witnessed the casual criminal acts, the working practices scams, the ineffectual bosses, the appalling carelessness of sorters that is bringing this vital service – once a source of national pride – to its knees.'[8]

(Continued)

Old thinking	New dimensions	A suitable example
Each organization needs to consider its people, processes and practices if it is to become and stay successful.	No company has fully thought through the implication of extending the enterprise to include the customer. What I am describing is not best practice, it is next practice.	Quote from business professor CK Prahalad.[9]
Shareholders may attend the annual general meetings and get involved in approving the various proposals that are put forward by the board.	Shareholders are becoming increasingly involved in their companies and the big investors can have a great impact on the board and even who stays and goes.	Those tranquil days (shareholder apathy) became history last summer in the wave of shareholder rebellions that crashed through the AGMs of some of the biggest corporate names. At the first opportunity, after Government gave shareholders the right to hold an advisory vote on companies' remuneration policies, such giants as GlaxoSmithKline, Reuters, HSBC and Corus found themselves staring down the wrong end of large disapproving votes from shareholders. It was the biggest rebellion in British corporate history, and the message from investors was that it wouldn't be the last.[10]

The key messages

The last section of each chapter contains a short story or quote that should provide an interesting format for illustrating some of the book's key messages.

The strange affair of the goldfish

As promised, the two boys' grandmother came back with their goldfish and tank the weekend after she had removed it. After it was placed on a firm coffee table in the front lounge, Grandma said to the boys, 'I took this away because you let the water get so dirty that one of the fish I bought for your birthday died. If you only clean the tank when you know I am coming round to check, this type of thing will always happen.'

The boys stared at their fish and seemed to be listening.

'You two need to smarten up,' she continued. 'I realize now that you relied on my checks to prompt you to clean the tank. You don't really understand why water quality is important to a fish and why you need to take some responsibility.'

Sensing they were in for a bit of a speech, the boys sat cross-legged on the floor in front of their grandma.

'Let's play a game. You know, a quiz. Okay? Let me ask you a few questions. Why do you think I bought you two goldfish?'

Luke's hand shot up. 'So we can have a bit of fun watching them swimming around and playing in the water.'

'Good. Anything else?

Daniel took his turn. 'Because they were on sale, and you could afford them.'

'Good answer. But more than that. I bought you them so that you could learn about being responsible, looking after things and taking care of them. When you look after goldfish, what could go wrong?'

As if taking turns to answer, Luke said. 'They might die, like our one did.'

Daniel added, 'They might not get on and fight each other.'

Giving them a small hug, Grandma said, 'Good, both of you. But look at why I bought the fish. They are nice to look at and you learn about taking care of them. So a dirty tank, unhealthy fish and you two not looking after them properly mean the reasons I bought them for you fall down. It's my fault for making myself responsible for checking on them, when this should have been your responsibility.'

Daniel leapt to her defence. 'You did okay. It's just that you had to go away on holiday.'

'No, Daniel. I should have made sure you two were able to deal with them without me having to be constantly checking up on you.'

'Can we keep the fish?' asked Luke, with a wistful look.

'I think so. But let's sort out a few things. If we want healthy fish, what do we need to avoid?'

Daniel's right hand shot up. 'Poor water maintenance.'

'Excellent. And now you, Luke. What leads to poor water?'

Luke reached for the short fish care book and found the relevant page. 'Overfeeding, not changing the water and poor water filtration, it says here.'

'What happens if there is poor water?'

'The fish might die. Like what happened to the first one,' Daniel suggested.

'Right. Let's take the first cause of poor water, overfeeding. What do we need to do to ensure this doesn't happen?'

'Feed them once a week,' Daniel pronounced.

Luke's hand shot up. 'No, once a month only.'

'Hang on, boys. What does the book say?'

After much shuffling of pages, it seemed that the book offered sound guidance on feeding regimes to ensure that foodstuff was consumed in small amounts and not left to decay in the water.

'Now,' Grandma went on, observing that the two boys were still sitting cross-legged in front of her in eager anticipation. 'What about the second point, failing to change the water?'

Luke shouted out in full schoolchild mode, 'Miss, we need to take out half the water and add new stuff once a week...and...'

Daniel butted in, 'And we need to keep an eye on the water and change it when it looks cloudy.'

'Excellent, both of you. Well done. Now the final point, poor filtration.'

This prompted a bout of frantic frowning before Daniel asked, 'What does that mean, Grandma?'

'Oh, right. It means that the water is not filtered, say by a pump, to get rid of small bits of debris. You know, rubbish from the tank. You then clean out the filter say every week or so.'

'Do we need a pump then?' asked Luke.

'The more you do about fish care, the better the chance of the fish remaining healthy. So it depends on whether you guys would be really upset if they died. Would you?'

'Yes,' the boys said in harmony.

'Then you will need to save up your pocket money and buy a pump. They're not too expensive.'

'Grandma, it says in the fish book that we should use a gravel vacuum as well. What's that?'

A brief review of the book showed that a small device can be used to suck up small particles of debris from the gravel at the bottom of the tank.

Grandma studied the notes and pursed her lips. 'What we're doing is not finding everything possible to help the fish stay healthy. We are just doing enough without going entirely over the top. Sometimes you can try too hard and the effort is not worth the value you get from having something enjoyable in the first place.'

'Does that mean we need the vacuum?' asked Luke.

'Not really. We'll give that a miss and see how things go. Right now you have everything you need. I'm off home.'

Daniel smiled. 'When are you going to check the water next, Grandma?'

'You know, I really don't need to do that any more. You two need to feed the fish a few flakes twice a day. Morning and last thing in the evening. And change the water and clean the filter every weekend. All you need to do is make a note of these tasks in your diary. Remember I bought you diaries last Christmas?'

'Will you need to check our diaries?' shouted out Daniel, as their grandmother walked towards her husband who was waiting at the front door.

'Not really. You're both good boys and I trust you'll do a good job,' she answered as she waved goodbye.

'But then again, if the mood takes me, I might just have a peep now and again...' she added, as she got into the car and shut the door, before it drove off through the gates.

A final word

Initial auditing needs to start with a sense of purpose, a set of principles and some clear standards that can be translated into actual working practices. A4M.99 can help, but only as a start to a much broader process.

Notes

1. *Daily Mail*, Tuesday, March 23, 2004, page 4.
2. Chris Huxham and Nic Beech, 'Turn theory into practice', *People Management*, 12 February 2004, pages 46–47.
3. *Daily Mail*, Thursday, July 24, 2003, page 12, Max Hastings.
4. *Evening Standard*, Wednesday, January 21, 2004, page 35, Anthony Hilton.
5. *The Times*, Wednesday, April 14, 2004, Business News, page 45, James Doran, Wall Street correspondent.
6. *The Times*, Tuesday, April 20, 2004, page T2/9.
7. *Sunday Express*, Sunday, April 25, 2004, Property section, page 1.
8. *Daily Mail*, Wednesday, April 28, 2004, pages 40–41.
9. *Financial Times*, Friday, December 13, 2002, page 14, Professor CK Prahalad.
10. *Accounting and Business Journal*, April 2004, page 19, Richard Brass.

Appendix A
Manager's initial audits standards and guidance

MIA 1 – Strategic direction

A manager's initial audit (MIA) is a review commissioned by a manager to assess the adequacy and effectiveness of internal controls in their area of responsibility. The objective is to secure and assess relevant evidence regarding the extent to which controls are able to manage risks to the business objectives in question, and work out where improvements to these controls can be made.

The results of such a review should be reported through the business so that they contribute to the overall review of internal control by senior management or the board. The results will also be available to internal and external audit, the audit committee and any other authorized persons.

Where possible, the impact of the work on the way values, value add, valuables and valuations are managed should be reported to the appropriate person.

MIA 2 – Terms of reference

All MIAs should be conducted in line with set terms of reference, which could include:

- Determining the objectives of the system under review.
- Determining the scope of the system in question.
- Assessing the adequacy of the current risk identification and risk assessment arrangements.

- Assessing whether internal controls are able to mitigate risk to an acceptable level of exposure in line with the defined risk tolerances.
- Judging whether there is a culture that promotes compliance with controls and whether good compliance is generally happening.
- Determining whether current action plans need amending to reflect the results of the review.
- Documenting the review and reporting the results up through the business line with any recommendations that are appropriate.

The MIA should be carried out in a professional manner. The results and conclusions reached should be able to satisfy any formal scrutiny by internal and external auditors or specialist investigators with an interest in the area that is audited. Note that the MIA is not aimed at commenting on any person's behaviour or activities. If there are any concerns regarding the conduct of any persons as a result of the audit work, these should be reported to the director for the area in question and should not be investigated by the person carrying out the audit.

MIA 3 – Planning and preparation

All MIAs should be properly planned to ensure:

- The terms of reference are fully addressed.
- The field work is conducted in a professional manner.
- The audit work is timely and efficient.
- Progress is monitored on a regular basis.
- The overall programme of audits can be reported in an efficient manner.

MIA 4 – Leader

A named individual should be in charge of an MIA and this person should ensure:

- Work schedules are documented and provided for the key tasks.
- All those involved in the audit are fully competent, briefed and kept informed.
- Progress is reported where appropriate.
- The work is balanced, fair and focused.

This will normally be a person who works for the manager in question and who is able to stand back from the operation in as objective a manner as possible. The manager may themselves carry out the MIA if this is appropriate. The following matters should be noted:

- Competencies for performing MIAs include analytical skills, determination, objectivity and reliability.

- The criteria for performing MIAs include the need to find out the truth, stand up to pressure and ensure there are no excessive conflicts of interest, that all concerns are addressed, and that there are sufficient resources to perform a professional job.

MIA 5 – Field work

The main part of the MIA involves the field work, which is designed to achieve the set terms of reference and implement the tasks designed in the planning stage of the audit. Field work should cover:

- The delivery of all planned tasks.
- Securing and analysing relevant evidence.
- Assessing the impact of the evidence on the adequacy and effectiveness of internal controls.
- Ensuring the evidence is reliable, relevant, adequate and helps achieve the terms of reference.

All work carried out should be documented in a way that is clear and reliable. The records should provide a defensible account of the audit, conclusions, report and actions taken. Note that the standards of evidence are less onerous than those that apply to investigations (see Appendix C), and so long as the evidence is reasonable, it can be used to support the work.

MIA 6 – Future direction

The MIA comprises mainly of assessing the state of internal controls and the evidence that this generates. After the completion of the field work and before a formal report is issued, an assessment should be made of:

- Whether internal controls are sound and make good business sense.
- Whether there are any significant risks identified by the audit that are not being adequately addressed.
- Updating the current risk register where this is appropriate.
- The nature of the action required to remedy weakness in controls.

The above should be supported by suitable evidence and logical argument and should form the basis of the recommendations arising from the work carried out.

MIA 7 – Reporting

The results of the MIA should be communicated by the manager. The report should be available in the form of a formal written document that covers:

- The terms of reference for the audit, including the system under review.
- Name and designation of the reviewer.
- The approach applied and whether it falls in line with these standards.
- Findings and their implications, including any significant control weaknesses.
- Formal assurances on the adequacy and effectiveness of the systems of internal control and the reliability of the current risk register.
- Any recommendations and action plans.

The first, fourth, fifth and sixth items should be summarized in an executive summary as a standalone document along with any action plans that have been agreed by the relevant parties. The report should be brief, to the point, user friendly, clear and contain all findings relevant to the set terms of reference. The distribution of the executive summary should be to:

- The manager commissioning the review.
- The manager's line manager.
- The director for the area in question.
- The board.
- The audit committee.
- The internal auditor.
- The external auditor.

MIA 8 – Value add

All MIAs should add value to the organization and should:

- Be part of the process for reporting on internal control.
- Add value to the way risks are being identified, assessed and managed.
- Seek to be as objective as possible with no obvious conflicts of interest.
- Satisfy external bodies that have a legitimate interest in the results.
- Be conducted in an efficient and timely fashion with all significant sources of evidence addressed whenever possible.
- Be conducted in a professional manner that can be examined by third parties.

MIA 9 – Conducted in line with standards

In short, all MIAs should be conducted in line with the above standards to contribute to the good governance, effective risk management and sound systems of internal control in the area under review.

If these professional standards are being applied the organization should ensure that:

- The standards are incorporated into the corporate standards of the organization.
- The manager commissioning the audit is aware of these standards and is able to judge whether their work meets these requirements.
- The person carrying out the audit understands the standards and has received training where appropriate.
- The standards are reviewed and kept up to date to ensure they make good business sense and lead to improved internal controls.

MIA 10 – Local working practices

The business unit manager may wish to adapt these standards to reflect any local working practices, so long as professionalism is retained.

Note: The MIAs should be used in conjunction with the TIAs (Appendix B) and MIIs (Appendix C).

Appendix B
Team initial audits standards and guidance

TIA 1 – Strategic direction

Team initial audits (TIA) are a series of reviews organized by work teams and representative groups to review the adequacy and effectiveness of internal controls in their area of responsibility. The objective is to secure and assess relevant evidence regarding the extent to which controls are able to manage risks to the business objectives in question and work out where improvements can be made.

The results of such reviews should be reported to the business management so that they contribute to the overall review of internal control by senior management and the board. The results will also be available to internal and external audit, the audit committee and any other authorized persons.

Where possible, the impact of the work on the way values, value add, valuables and valuations are managed should be reported to the appropriate person.

TIA 2 – Terms of reference

All TIA exercises should be conducted in line with a methodology that may include:

- Determining the objectives of the activity in question and ensuring that these objectives reflect a realistic position for the activity in question.
- Determining the context of these objectives in terms of the expectations of stakeholders, line management's priorities, change programmes that are underway and performance targets for the activities (and people) in question.

- Selecting a suitable control framework such as COSO or CoCo to ensure the level of awareness and commitment to good control are taken on board.
- Ensuring that the team members are able to identify risks to the achievement of their set objectives and that all participants are able to contribute in a full and meaningful manner.
- Ensuring that all participants have an clear understanding of the risk appetite established by senior management for the activity in question.
- Engaging everyone in a process of rating the risks identified in terms of their importance and the likelihood of these risks arising if appropriate action is not taken to mitigate their effects.
- Enabling all participants to gauge whether the current risk management strategy and specific internal controls are able to mitigate significant risk so that they fall in line with the defined risk appetite.
- Preparing a risk register to reflect the process outlined above, or update the existing risk register in the light of any changes identified by this process.
- Determining whether current action plans need amending to reflect the results of the review.
- Documenting the review and reporting the results up through the business line with any recommendations that are appropriate, and appending a copy of the revised risk register.

The TIA process should be carried out in a professional manner and the results and conclusions reached should be able to satisfy any formal scrutiny by internal and external auditors or specialist investigators who have an interest in the area that is reviewed. Note that the TIA is not aimed at commenting on any person's behaviour or activities. If there are any concerns regarding the conduct of any persons as a result of the process, these should be reported to the appropriate manager for the area in question.

TIA 3 – Planning and preparation

All TIA programmes should be properly planned to ensure:

- The benefits that have been identified from the process are fully accomplished.
- The exercise is conducted in a professional manner.
- All relevant parties are encouraged to contribute in a positive fashion.
- The results contribute to enhanced performance, compliance and disclosure reporting.
- The annual programme of audits can be reported in an efficient manner.

TIA 4 – Leader

A named individual should be in charge of the TIA programme and this person should ensure:

- The most appropriate programme of events is applied to delivering the TIA programme across the organization.
- The events are facilitated in an efficient and effective way.
- Everyone is able to fulfil their responsibilities properly.
- Outcomes can be reported in a way that contributes to formal disclosure requirements.
- The TIA programme has a commercial value and is seen as worthwhile and constructive.
- Efforts may be organized throughout the business in a way that promotes enterprise risk management.

This will normally be a person or small team who is appointed by a board-level sponsor to promote TIA across the organization. Teams may carry out their own TIA events with guidance from the TIA coordinator, sometimes called the risk manager or chief risk officer (or this role may be supported by the internal auditor).

TIA 5 – The TIA process

TIA programmes may be delivered through employee surveys, interviews, staff meetings and/or specially organized workshops. The main focus is on engaging people (normally work teams) in developing smarter, risk-based internal controls as part of their official responsibilities and accountabilities in the organization. Whatever the chosen format, the programme should aim to:

- Deliver the set goals of the programme.
- Secure and analyse relevant evidence.
- Promote better business decisions and strategies.
- Provide an assessment of internal controls by those closest to the operation.
- Help inform the board's statement on internal control.

The above can be achieved by:

- Surveys of employees regarding their appreciation of controls and the extent to which key controls are in place and work. This is useful for obtaining information on levels of risk and control awareness across the organization and views on the current risk register where they are compiled centrally.
- Interviews with key employees to get their input into compilation and maintenance of risk registers. Such interviews may involve one or more people whose views are being solicited by the person coordinating the TIA activity. Moreover, this approach is useful to obtain views on risks for a particular area and the types of controls that should be in place, as well as endorsing current risk registers where these have been prepared centrally.

- Staff meetings with key people most responsible for a particular activity. This is useful for endorsing a particular risk register or soliciting views on corporate procedures.
- Workshops of teams and representative groups to develop, update or approve appropriate risk registers. This is particularly useful where risk registers are being developed by teams and groups.

Note that the above techniques may be applied in an integrated manner where surveys, interviews and workshops are used in conjunction with each other in a way that best promotes the team's review of internal controls.

TIA 6 – Competence

The TIA requires a degree of competence across the organization, which means:

- All employees should be provided with an understanding of the TIA process and how it may help them at work.
- Where workshops are applied, the TIA facilitator should possess all those skills that underpin professional facilitation, along with a good understanding of the TIA process and the corporate risk policy of the organization.
- Evidence should be competent and the standards of evidence are less onerous than both MIAs and MIIs, as the evidence used in TIA events tends to be based more on the personal perceptions of team members.

TIA 7 – Workshops

In most TIA programmes, workshops are used to engage employees around the risk and control agenda and empower them to contribute as far as possible. When workshops are employed in TIA, the following principles should be applied unless there is good reason not to:

- Workshops are resource intensive and should only be used where they are supported by a sound business case.
- Workshops should not take excessive amounts of time and should run for the minimum time possible to achieve the set objectives.
- Workshops should be properly planned to ensure that the right people attend, that they are prepared to commit to an intensive period of risk and control assessment, and that each participant has been contacted before the event and given a chance to ask questions and receive relevant information.
- Workshops should be run in a positive and unthreatening manner to encourage good participation and open communication from those involved.
- Workshops should follow the format in TIA 2 (see above terms of reference) unless there is a good reason not to.

- A decision should be made on the role of business management for the area in question, and whether they should attend the workshop or appear at, say, the start and end, or not attend at all. Any arrangement should take on board both the need to encourage all participants to communicate openly, and the need to make sure the authority of the line manager is not undermined.
- Clear roles should be defined for all those involved in the workshops, including the organizer, the facilitator, the note taker and the participants. The facilitator should be prepared to provide the occasional presentation on internal control models, the corporate risk policy and topics such as risk registers and the role of the internal and external auditors.
- The workshop should focus on promoting consensus between participants, but should at the same time be challenging in that all significant issues are addressed even where they are difficult to manage. Consideration should be given to corporate issues such as financial reporting, security, fraud and abuse, compliance, whistleblowing and published disclosures, so that these issues may be seen as part of the risk portfolio as well as operational risks in specific parts of the organization.
- Workshops should be recorded and no promises should be made to participants that their comments will not be revealed to any authorized third parties.
- Workshops should adhere to corporate standards on conduct, including whistleblowing, equal opportunities, and set values dealing with bullying, using inappropriate language, respecting others and similar issues.
- Consideration should be given to the use of electronic voting technology to record personal views, particularly where the team is assessing which risks are material and likely to arise. Voting may be facilitated through discussion, ticking flipcharts, or a simple show of hands. Post-it notes and other simple devices can be used to retain anonymity. Investment in electronic voting software should be subject to a business case and the pros and cons weighed up to judge whether it should be applied. Note that anonymous voting is useful where there are clear propositions or larger groups with mixed grades and members who may be reluctant to publicize their views.

TIA 8 – Future direction

The TIA process consists of attempts by those closest to the business activity to assess the state of internal controls. Formal reports should be issued that contain an assessment of:

- Whether internal controls are sound and make good business sense.
- Whether there are any significant risks identified by the TIA process that are not being adequately addressed.
- Updating the current risk register where this is appropriate.
- The nature of this action required to remedy weakness in controls.

The above should be supported by suitable risk registers and logical argument and should form the basis of the action plans arising from the work carried out.

TIA 9 – Reporting

The results of TIA activity should be communicated by the manager for the area in question. The report should be available in the form of a formal written document that covers:

- How the TIA process is applied.
- Details of the overall outcomes.
- The new or revised risk registers resulting from the process.
- Formal assurances on the adequacy and effectiveness of the systems of internal control.
- Any recommendations and action plans.

The last three items should be summarized in an executive summary as a standalone document along with any action plans that have been agreed by the relevant parties. The report should be brief, to the point, user friendly, clear and contain all findings relevant to the set terms of reference. The distribution of the executive summary should be to:

- The team members in question.
- The line manager.
- The director for the area in question.
- The board.
- The audit committee.
- The internal auditor.
- The external auditor.

TIA 10 – Value add

The TIA process and exercises should add value to the organization and should:

- Be part of the process for reporting on internal control.
- Add value to the way risks are being identified, assessed and managed.
- Involve those closest to the operation, project or process in question.
- Satisfy external bodies that have a legitimate interest in the results.
- Be conducted in a professional manner that can be examined by third parties.

TIA 11 – Conducted in line with standards

All TIA activity should be conducted in line with the above standards to contribute to the good governance, effective risk management and sound systems of internal control in the area under review.

If these professional standards are being applied the organization should ensure that:

- The standards are incorporated into the corporate standards of the organization.
- All employees are aware of these standards and able to judge whether their efforts meet these requirements.
- The person facilitating TIA activity understands the standards and has received training where appropriate.
- The standards applied in TIAs should be quality assured by the business manager and kept up to date to ensure they make good business sense and lead to improved internal controls.

TIA 12 – Local working practices

The business unit manager may wish to adapt these standards to reflect any local working practices, so long as credibility is retained.

Note: The TIA should be used in conjunction with the MIAs (Appendix A) and MIIs (Appendix C).

Appendix C
Manager's initial investigations standards and guidance

MII 1 – Strategic direction

A manager's initial investigation (MII) is an inquiry in line with formal terms of reference set by the commissioning party (CP). The objective is to secure and assess relevant evidence regarding a specific concern, establish the facts and make reasonable recommendations back to the CP.

It should assist the strategic direction of the organization and be set within the context of the existing strategies.

Where possible, the impact of the work on the way values, value add, valuables and valuations are managed should be reported to the appropriate person.

MII 2 – Terms of reference

All MIIs should be conducted in line with set terms of reference, which should include:

- Defining the objectives of the investigation.
- Determining the scope of the work.
- Indicating the current priorities.
- Linking the work to the strategic direction of the organization.
- Indicating the role and position of the commissioning party.

- Making clear any interests of external bodies.
- Documentation that supports professionalism and objectivity.

The CP should not have a conflict of interests resulting from the implications of the MII that would unduly affect their independence. The investigator should likewise be in a position to carry out an objective investigation. No incentives should be offered to anyone involved in or cooperating with the inquiry. Note that management investigations should not be applied to sensitive and material matters that are more properly referred to specialist investigators and should follow the corporate standards for more serious inquiries.

MII 3 – Planning and preparation

All MIIs should be properly planned to ensure:

- The terms of reference are fully addressed.
- The field work is conducted in a professional manner.
- The investigator's work is timely and efficient.
- Progress is monitored on a regular basis.
- The results can be reported in an efficient manner.

MII 4 – Leader

A named individual should be in charge of the investigation and this person should ensure:

- Work schedules are documented and provided for the key tasks.
- All those involved in the investigation are fully competent, briefed and kept informed.
- Progress is reported to the CP on a regular basis.
- The investigation is focused, in line with any legal requirements, transparent and fair.

MII 5 – Field work

The main part of the MII involves the field work, which is designed to achieve the set terms of reference and implement the tasks designed in the planning stage of the investigation. Field work should cover:

- The delivery of all planned tasks.
- Securing and analysing relevant evidence.

- Assessing the impact of the evidence on the matter being investigated.
- Ensuring that evidence secured is reliable, relevant, adequate and helps achieve the terms of reference.

MII 6 – Evidence

All evidence should be documented in a way that is clear and precise. The records should provide a defensible account of the investigation, conclusions, report and actions taken. Note that the standard of evidence for MIIs is higher than that for MIAs. Evidence should be compelling and, where appropriate, legally admissible in support of the work carried out during the investigation. Note that:

- Employees have an expectation of a right to privacy and there are rules as to what may be searched, for example lockers, desks, rest areas, and also rules relating to e-mail, phone calls and the use of CCTV.
- These expectations should be documented in the employee handbook.
- Legal advice should be sought where applicable.

The lead officer should maintain a formal diary of daily events and decisions made that should record the following considerations:

- Important issues, work done, information received and delivered, along with timings.
- Time spent on various tasks.
- Reconciliation of times with plans.
- Loose ends from inquiries and outstanding issues.
- Where items are on file and held on corporate information systems, that is cross-referenced to the formal investigation file and kept in a safe place.
- Copies made and retained.

Note that the record of the investigation may become public knowledge and any records made should support any comments and conclusions and they should not be used in an unauthorized or defamatory manner.

MII 7 – Future direction

The MII comprises mainly field work and the evidence that this generates. After the completion of the field work and before a formal report is issued, an assessment should be made of:

- Whether there are any risks identified by the investigation that are not being adequately addressed.

- Ways in which these risks may be managed, including any appropriate controls.
- Whether any people should be dealt with under the normal disciplinary procedures.

The above should be supported by suitable evidence and logical argument and should form the basis of the recommendations arising from the work carried out.

MII 8 – Reporting

The results of the MII should be communicated by the CP. The report should be available in the form of a formal written document that covers:

- The reason for the investigation.
- Details of the CP.
- The terms of reference.
- Details of the investigation's approach.
- Work carried out and evidence secured.
- Findings.
- Impact of the findings.
- Any recommendations.

The third and last two items should be summarized in an executive summary as a standalone document along with any action plans that have been agreed by the relevant parties. The report should be brief, to the point, user friendly, clear and contain all findings relevant to the set terms of reference. The distribution should be defined by the CP.

MII 9 – Value add

All MIIs should add value to the organization and should:

- Be worth spending time and money on.
- Avoid interference from parties with an interest in the results. Any attempts should be reported to the CP and any restrictions placed on the investigators should be duly noted in the report along with the implications.
- Comprise an objective review of the matters being investigated.
- Satisfy external bodies who have a legitimate interest in the results.
- Be conducted in an efficient and timely fashion with all significant sources of evidence addressed whenever possible.
- Be conducted in a professional manner that falls, where appropriate, entirely in line with legal provisions (including the Regulation of Investigatory Powers Legislation) and in a manner that is verifiable.

MII 10 – Conducted in line with standards

In short, all MIIs should be conducted in line with the above standards and an ongoing review of all work carried out should be organized by the CP to ensure that this is the case. If these professional standards are being applied the organization should ensure that:

- The standards are incorporated in the corporate standards of the organization.
- The CP is aware of these standards and is able to judge whether the investigation meets these set requirements.
- The investigators understand the standards and have received training where appropriate.
- The standards are implemented for investigations where this is deemed appropriate, based on scale, seriousness and potential impact of the investigation on the organization.

MII 11 – Local working practices

The organization may wish to adapt these standards to reflect any local working practices, so long as approval is obtained by the corporate legal officer.

Note: The MII should be used in conjunction with the MIAs (Appendix A) and TIAs (Appendix B).

Appendix D
Checking your progress – your score

Your score matrix

Please record your answers by ticking the appropriate box overleaf. When you have done this, check the answer guide and add up the number of correct answers you scored for each chapter and write your score in the final column. Then add up each chapter score to arrive at a total score. You may also record the minutes spent on each test and record this in the 'Mins' column. Place both total time and total correct answers for all chapters in the 'Grade box' of the enclosed certificate. Your line manager should monitor the scoring process and if satisfied may be asked to sign the A4M.99 certificate.

Name ....   Date ....

Line manager ....   Date ....

Chapter	Your answers to multi-choice questions											
	Q1	Q2	Q3	Q4	Q5	Q6	Q7	Q8	Q9	Q10	Mins	Score out of 10
1												
2												
3												
4												
5												
6												
7												
8												
9												
10												
Total time (in minutes) and scores for all chapters												

Answer guide – most appropriate response to multi-choice questions

Chapter	Q1	Q2	Q3	Q4	Q5	Q6	Q7	Q8	Q9	Q10
1	c	b	d	a	d	c	b	b	d	a
2	a	d	a	a	d	b	c	a	b	d
3	b	d	b	c	a	d	a	c	b	d
4	b	d	a	c	b	a	c	a	b	d
5	b	a	d	a	b	c	d	b	d	a
6	a	c	d	b	a	c	d	b	a	c
7	d	b	a	b	d	a	d	c	b	d
8	c	a	c	b	d	a	c	b	a	d
9	c	d	b	a	b	a	c	b	c	b
10	c	a	d	b	b	a	d	b	a	d

John Wiley & Sons Ltd

Initial Auditing Certificate

This certificate is awarded to

For successful completion of the A4M.99
initial auditing development programme

MARK: %

Signature.................................
(Staff Member)

Signature.................................
(Line Manager)

Date...............

Date...............

Appendix E
Staff surveys

It is possible to select a sample of survey questions from the list of 100 suggestions given below and prepare a questionnaire that tests the extent to which employees appreciate and support the initial audit process. If this survey is repeated each year, you can start to log the success of any initial audit programme and whether is it being internalized across the organization. Note that you are looking for a high score for the first 50 and a low score for the second 50, and that the order in which the selected questions are listed should be changed to promote less distortion in given responses.

Employee survey

For each of the questions below, indicate where you fall on a scale of 1–4 using the following scale:

1. Not at all true.
2. Barely true.
3. Moderately true.
4. Exactly true.

Please mark your score for each of the following questions	1	2	3	4
1. If our procedures can be improved then we have a duty to make such improvements.				
2. My team is able to take full responsibility for our work.				
3. Operational problems need not always be referred up to line management for resolution.				
4. Auditing is a generic concept that should be shared with everyone.				

(Continued)

Please mark your score for each of the following questions	1	2	3	4

5. Internal and external auditors are seen as useful sources of advice.
6. Compliance is mainly about clear explanations and encouragement.
7. Most problems arise in an organization due to a failing in internal controls.
8. People like to see positive examples of the impact of good risk management.
9. A risk-managed culture means clear and improved procedures.
10. All significant risks need to be managed.
11. It is quite difficult to identify all risks.
12. Good risk management provides more certainty.
13. Even with good risk management, there is always some room for doubt.
14. Reviewing current events is about supporting a better future.
15. A manager should be allowed to audit their own domain.
16. We can learn a lot from considering the past.
17. Audit work should be tailored to the circumstances.
18. All audits should be carried out in a systematic manner.
19. Audits should be challenging.
20. Significant risks should be accelerated upwards to the board level.
21. Risk appetites mean different things to different people.
22. All those closest to the business can contribute to the risk register.
23. The risk register is about recording decisions.
24. The risk register should be available to internal auditors.
25. Risks should really be recorded.
26. The audit process is dependent on securing good evidence.
27. Auditing can be rewarding.
28. Auditing involves working with people.
29. Facilitation is about listening and not dominating the action.
30. People need a reason to get involved in reviewing risks and controls.
31. In TIAs the manager should take a back seat.
32. The TIA workshops should be documented.
33. Hold TIA workshops as and when required.
34. Most investigations are concerned with discovering the truth.
35. Give each manager a chance to review their position before external resources are applied.
36. Noncompliance may indicate that controls are unreliable.
37. Risk management supports a successful business.
38. Risk management can be hard work but it is worthwhile.
39. We need to exploit risk where possible.
40. Initial auditing does not work well in a blame culture.
41. People need to understand the audit concept to perform initial audits.
42. Initial auditing depends mainly on people taking full responsibility for their work.

43. Risk should be part of our common language.
44. Initial auditing is about good communications.
45. Initial audit reports should be shared with all those affected.
46. The best initial audit reports contain pertinent highlights.
47. Presentations are good for delivering key issues.
48. The risk register is the key aspect of the initial audit report.
49. Procedures should be designed to meet key risks.
50. Better results are possible where teams are accountable for their outputs.
51 All investigations should be carried out by external specialists.
52. If auditors do not check up on staff on a regular basis errors and abuse are bound to occur.
53. The work of internal audit and other review teams is a complete mystery to me.
54. Auditing should be left to the experts.
55. Both internal and external auditors should be kept at a distance.
56. Compliance is mainly to do with enforcement.
57. Success is pretty well to do with luck and fate.
58. Only a small amount of misfortune results from poor preparation.
59. The little guy has no real influence over events in his place of work.
60. People closest to the business are often the last ones to be consulted over the business.
61. Risk management teaches you to keep your head below the parapet.
62. Risk management means that people stop taking chances.
63. Most risks have no risk owner and so cannot be addressed.
64. Risk management eradicates failure.
65. All risks need to be avoided.
66. It is easy to identify all risks.
67. The best audits uncover those who made mistakes and make them pay.
68. Auditing is about basic common sense and gut instinct.
69. Auditing is a specialist role best left to the experts.
70. The past is past and is best forgotten.
71. Once the risk register is complete it can be left until next year.
72. The risk register need not be incorporated into the performance management system.
73. The risk register should be kept confidential.
74. Recording risks puts people off.
75. Auditing is about looking into things and not following a formal process.
76. It takes a really special person to undertake an audit.
77. Internal reviews are essentially about getting more work from fewer people.
78. Internal reviews tend to lead to action plans that are not really important.

(Continued)

Please mark your score for each of the following questions	1 2 3 4

79. Auditing enhances stress.
80. Auditing means keeping people at a distance.
81. TIA is seen as a fad that will go away soon.
82. Initial audits are by definition unreliable.
83. TIA is really about ticking the 'review' box for the auditors.
84. TIAs should be led by the line manager.
85. Hold TIA workshops at least once a month.
86. An investigation that does not result in dismissal is a waste of time.
87. The investigators should alter the terms of reference as they see fit.
88. Fraud should be covered up if it embarrasses the organization.
89. Noncompliance is about incompetent staff.
90. Successful risk management is pretty easy to implement.
91. We need to avoid all risks.
92. Empowerment is about performance not responsibility.
93. Initial audits mean creating extra work for no more money.
94. Risk management should be left to the specialists.
95. If people know that initial audits will be reported they will panic.
96. All initial audit reports should contain detailed findings and give the full story.
97. Negative findings should be left out of the initial audit report.
98. The risk register should be kept confidential.
99. If auditors do not check our systems, why should we bother to do these checks?
100. Operational problems should always be referred to top management for resolution.

Index